D0205268

CLARENDON LIBRARY OF LOGIC AND PHILOSOPHY

General Editor: L. Jonathan Cohen, The Queen's College, Oxford

SENSORY QUALITIES

The Clarendon Library of Logic and Philosophy brings together books, by new as well as by established authors, that combine originality of theme with rigour of statement. Its aim is to encourage new research of a professional standard into problems that are of current or perennial interest.

General Editor: L. Jonathan Cohen, The Queen's College, Oxford.

Also published in this series

Sensory Qualities

AUSTEN CLARK

CLARENDON PRESS · OXFORD
1993

Oxford University Press, Walton Street, Oxford OX2 6DP

Oxford New York Toronto
Delhi Bombay Calcutta Madras Karachi
Kuala Lumpur Singapore Hong Kong Tokyo
Nairobi Dar es Salaam Cape Town
Melbourne Auckland Madrid

and associated companies in
Berlin Ibadan

Oxford is a trade mark of Oxford University Press

Published in the United States
by Oxford University Press Inc., New York

British Library Cataloguing in Publication Data
Data available

Library of Congress Cataloging in Publication Data
Clark, Austen.
Sensory qualities / Austen Clark.
p. cm.—(Clarendon library of logic and philosophy)
Includes bibliographical references.
1. Senses and sensation. 2. Perception. 3. Philosophy of mind.
4. Psychology—Philosophy. I. Title. II. Series.
BD214.C53 1993 152.1—dc20 92–27327
ISBN 0–19–824001–5 (alk. paper)

Typeset by Austen Clark

Printed in Great Britain
on acid-free paper by
Bookcraft (Bath) Ltd., Midsomer Norton, Avon

To Brian Farrell

Preface

In this book I analyse the character and defend the integrity of psychophysiological explanations of sensory qualities. Many philosophers doubt that one can provide any genuine explanations of how things look, feel, or seem to a perceiving subject. To invoke one popular formulation, facts of that sort seem to be essentially subjective, so that they can be understood only in their own terms. Any attempt to analyse or explain qualitative facts in non-qualitative terms seems doomed. According to this conception, no existing discipline—and no currently imaginable discipline—could explain the qualitative character of conscious experience.

We could perhaps resign ourselves to a pensive scepticism about qualia, but only if we could somehow ignore the discomfiting agitation produced by the experimental disciplines. Psychology and psychophysiology provide what at least seem to be genuine explanations of some qualitative facts—of how things look, feel, or seem to someone. Although some of the empirical premisses in such explanations are undoubtedly incorrect, and large gaps remain, the explanations contain no obvious logical flaws, and in principle seem capable of explaining what they are intended to explain. In particular, colour science seems to be *the* success story of scientific psychology thus far—and the scope of its explanations seems to expand monthly, without resistance. Are all its explanations bogus? They seem sometimes to account for the fact that a particular stimulus *looks red* to a particular subject in a particular situation. Are there some hidden errors in such explanations that vitiate them? Is the *explanandum* something other than a qualitative fact? These and other questions immediately arise when one confronts qualia scepticism with some real examples from current psychophysiology.

The goal is to explain qualitative facts in terms that do not presuppose other qualitative facts. I argue that this can be done. A solution is possible, and one can see its outline in psychophysics, sensory neurophysiology, and psychometrics.

I describe an explanatory strategy used in those disciplines to explain qualititive facts. I do not argue that current explanations are complete, or even true, but merely that the approach has no conceptual flaws, and can answer the various a priori objections. In short, it could succeed. That finding would suffice to defeat the sceptic, or at least to postpone the onset of melancholia. More importantly, it suggests an analysis of qualia using the terms of the experimental disciplines. I sketch how that account might eventually reduce to neurophysiology.

This project differs somewhat in intent from the recent spate of books on colour perception (Hilbert 1987, Westphal 1987, Hardin 1988, Landesman 1989). While those recent books are largely concerned with variants of the question, What kind of property (if any) is colour? and with different answers to that question—objectivism, subjectivism, colour scepticism, anthropocentric realism, and so on—I am concerned with the slightly different question, Can we provide genuine explanations for any of the facts about how things look, feel, or seem to a perceiving subject? I do not directly address the issue of what sort of property if any can be identified with *red*, but instead ask: Can we explain why a particular stimulus in a particular situation to a particular subject *looks red*? I think we can, and endeavour to show how. Certainly the account I develop has various implications about the project of attempting to identify and characterize what sort of properties colours might be; but that project is not my project here.

I began research on these topics while holding a post-doctoral fellowship at the L. L. Thurstone Psychometric Lab at the University of North Carolina, Chapel Hill. That fellowship was supported by NIMH Grant NH 01-23F-S1288, and I would like to thank Lyle Jones, Mark Appelbaum, Tom Wallsten, and Marcy Lansman for their help during that year. I would like to thank the University of Tulsa, which provided a research fellowship in the summer of 1984 and a sabbatical in 1989. I am grateful to the National Endowment for the Humanities, which provided a research fellowship in 1986 under Summer Fellowship Program grant NH-86-P31-1454.

Many people have given me comments, criticisms, and advice on preliminary versions of the ideas presented here. I would like to thank my departmental chair, Paul Brown, who did much to create an environment in which research could be done, as well as the other members of my department, particularly Christopher Hernandez, Leigh Kelley, and Richard Lind, who commented on parts of the argument. Leonard Zusne of the Psychology Department gave me helpful comments on the manuscript and assistance with the psychological literature. I am especially grateful to Bill Lycan, who provided encouragement and advice at the beginning of the project and suggestions and criticisms on the first draft. My most voluminous and helpful critic was Larry Hardin, with whom I corresponded intensively while this book was taking shape. He pointed out numerous errors of fact and interpretation in preliminary versions, as well as weaknesses in parts of the argument. I would like to thank an anonymous referee at Oxford University Press, whose careful commentary saved me from other errors. Those that remain are my own.

Some of the problems I consider have a long lineage, but most are of more contemporary origin. I focus particularly on problems deriving from Rudolf Carnap and Nelson Goodman's early constructionist efforts; from J. J. C. Smart's now classic articles on the identity theory, and the literature it engendered; and from the contemporary philosophical debate on materialism and sensations, including particularly the writings of Ned Block, Paul and Patricia Churchland, Larry Hardin, Bill Lycan, Sydney Shoemaker, and Hilary Putnam. My debt to the writings of all of these authors will be obvious. Finally, I would like to acknowledge and thank my supervisor at Oxford, Brian Farrell. Years ago, he chided us to try—at least briefly—to adopt the point of view of experimental psychologists and neurophysiologists when thinking about conscious 'experience' (Farrell, 1950); to look at the problem in their terms, not ours. The advice is still good, and this book represents a lengthy effort in that direction.

A.C.
Tulsa, Oklahoma
August 1991

Contents

List of Figures

1
Introduction

1.1 Sensory Qualities

A whiff of lilacs presents a particular sweet odour. The warmth of the rising sun yields certain tactile sensations. Bees' honey has a specific taste. The qualities that characterize the smell of the lilacs, sensation of the sun, or taste of the honey are all what I will call *sensory* qualities.

Broadly speaking, such qualities characterize what it is like to sense or perceive things. One perceives the blooms, sun, and honey in a particular way; sensory qualities characterize the way such things appear.

There are various names for the qualities in question. Our problem concerns the nature of *qualia*, of the *qualitative character* of some mental states (Block 1978; Shoemaker 1975a). These qualities characterize how the world seems from a particular point of view, so they are also labelled *subjective* qualities (Nagel 1986), *phenomenal* properties, and *phenomenological* properties. Other authors have named them *raw feels* (Feigl 1967) and *sensuous* qualities (Perkins 1983).

Some mental states have a 'qualitative' character, while others do not. The state of seeming to smell lilacs has such a character: an olfactory experience with a different qualitative character would be a different olfactory experience. In contrast, the mental state of thinking about lilacs has no particular qualitative character: while it may be associated with other mental states that have some qualitative character, one can continue thinking about lilacs even as the qualitative character of the experience changes. No distinctive *quale* is essential to the thinking.

Sensation and perception have as necessary conditions the occurrence of various internal states of the subject. The subject senses or perceives objects in virtue of having those states, and would not sense or perceive those objects if those states were not present. Call such states 'sensory' states. They have a specific character, and it is in part because they have the character they do that one perceives just what one does. Let us define the 'qualitative' character of such states as those qualities that determine exactly how the world appears. Intuitively, if later the subject has an experience with exactly the same qualitative character, then it will seem to the subject that he or she is perceiving exactly the same objects. *Sensory qualities* are those qualities of sensory states that account for this appearance.

An ambiguity is introduced by the fact that one can smell blooms that, as it happens, are lilacs, even while having an olfactory experience whose character is that of smelling a lemon. So 'lilacs odour' has what we might call a 'transparent' and an 'opaque' rendering. Opaquely, a 'lilacs odour' is an olfactory experience with a particular qualitative character. The presence of lilacs may fail to elicit an experience of that type, and an experience of that type may be elicited by things other than lilacs. If one construes 'lilacs odour' transparently, however, then any time one has an olfactory experience caused by lilacs, no matter what its particular qualitative character, one has (transparently) an experience of smelling lilacs.

Qualitative character is opaque. Qualia are defined by what it seems one is perceiving, not by what caused the episode. If Monday one smells lilacs in bloom, and Tuesday one has an olfactory experience with just the same qualitative character, then Tuesday it will seem that one smells the same lilacs encountered Monday. This can happen even if on Tuesday there are no lilacs in the vicinity.

Sometimes things are not as they appear. For example, a red car may look blue when viewed under a sodium-arc street light. If visual sensory qualities characterize how things look, they should characterize the similarities between seeing a blue car and seeing a car that merely looks blue. We have no need to distinguish, among all the colour appearances an object may present during its career, some one, 'real' colour. The characterization of sensory qualities does not require that distinction. What goes on when one perceives a car that is blue resembles what goes on when one perceives a (red) car that, as we say, merely looks blue. Sensory qualities should characterize those similarities.

This book will be concerned exclusively with the qualitative character of the mental states involved in the various sensory processes. There may be other mental states with qualitative character: dreams, mental imagery, some moods, some introspective states, and perhaps others. The argument to be developed does not apply directly to any of them, although at the end it may suggest an approach to the study of their qualitative character.

1.2 Some Classic Formulations

One flawed characterization of sensory qualities identifies them as those qualities of which one is aware when one senses something. Unfortunately, 'qualities of which one is aware' can be read in several senses. When one perceives the heat of the coffee in the coffee mug there is a perfectly straightforward sense in which the quality of which one is aware is the mean kinetic energy of the molecules of the mug. One simply reads 'that of which one is aware' as referring to whatever property is causally responsible for the sensory episode. This reading does not characterize the qualitative content of the perception in the sense we need, since 'mean kinetic energy of molecules' does not characterize the way in which the coffee mug appears. The heat of the coffee mug does not present itself as mean kinetic energy of molecules.

Sensory qualities characterize what it is like to perceive or to sense things. We want to include the various modalities of bodily sensation; pain is the paradigm *raw feel*. But one might argue that the various modalities of bodily sensation are not perceptual modalities. Illusions in the body senses are oddly restricted. A sensation that feels like pain *is* pain. Call a modality in which this distinction collapses a 'sensory' modality. Qualities characterizing appearances in such a modality are also sensory qualities.

Although 'sensation' proper is a term confined to bodily sensation, often one extends its use to describe appearances in all perceptual modalities. Whenever any creature perceives something, there is some internal state of the creature in virtue of which it perceives that thing. One can label that state the creature's 'sensation of' or 'sense impression of' or 'experience of' the perceived thing. So, for example, the internal state in virtue of which I now see the red rug and without which I would not see the red rug is (by stipulation) my visual sensation 'of' the rug. Sensory qualities are the qualities of sensation, construed in this broad way.

One might say that sensory qualities are just the properties of sensations; but, apart from the problem just mentioned, there is a second problem with that formulation. Not all properties of sensations are qualitative properties. If sensations are brain states, for example, a sensation will have many properties that are not qualitative properties. If the specific qualitative character of the process of sensing something derives from patterns of electrical activity across membranes, the fact that it is sodium ions that carry the electric charge (and not hydrogen ions) is presumably not a qualitative feature of the process. The experience of having the sensation will be identified with processes occurring in cells with a particular mass and chemical composition. Any such physical details that are unrelated to the way the sensation feels are non-qualitative properties of the sensation.

For similar reasons, it will not do for a sense-data theorist to identify the qualitative character of experience with the properties of sense data. Only if all the properties of sense data were qualitative properties could one make this identification. If sense data (or sensings, for that matter) can be identified with brain states, then they will have many non-qualitative properties.

The characterization of sensory qualities should not be interpreted to endorse a sense-data theory. It does not imply that appearances are mental objects that have various qualities. If something looks blue, it presents a characteristic appearance; but the locution does not commit us to the existence of something (an appearance) that *is* blue. Various analyses of apparent qualities avoid that implication. Some deny that one ascribes *any* quality to anything when one judges that something looks blue (see Lycan 1987, p. 88; Armstrong 1984, pp. 171, 174). Sense-data accounts invariably propose that there is some mental object with a certain property in both situations. Adverbial analyses and topic-neutral accounts both deny this inference.

At this stage we leave it an open question how those qualities common to veridical perception and mere appearance are to be analysed. Perhaps they are properties of mental objects, and perhaps (as on a traditional view) those properties are intro-spectible. Possibly the qualities common to veridical perception and mere appearance are to be analysed some other way. Perhaps an adverbial analysis is most appropriate, or a topic-neutral analysis, in which there is no quality attributed to anything when one says the car looks blue.

The qualitative and subjective character of some mental states is sometimes called the 'phenomenal' or 'phenomenological' character of experience. These latter terms are sometimes used as technical epistemological terms, in which, for example, 'phenomenal' properties are those about which one cannot be mistaken. Such epistemological uses are not coextensive with descriptions of the qualitative character of experience. One might stipulate that 'phenomenal' properties are just those properties of one's experience concerning which one can gain absolute certainty, but then such properties form a much narrower class than the qualitative properties. Perhaps there are characteristics of the ways in which things appear concerning which one cannot be certain.

Only if 'phenomenal' means merely 'characterizing the appearances of things' can one identify sensory qualities with phenomenal ones. Sensory qualities are just those needed to describe the character of one's experience of the world. They are also aptly known as 'subjective' qualities, characterizing the 'subjective character' of sensory states.

1.3 The Problems with Sensory Qualities

Why are sensory qualities so troublesome? One problem is that they have yet to be assigned a fixed place within the understanding of the world provided by physical science, and many have argued that such qualities may find no place at all in such an understanding. Materialist theories of mind face particular difficulties in accounting for the properties of sensation. Finally, there are some grounds for thinking that the conundrums concerning sensory qualities are not confined to any particular ontology or methodological framework, that such qualities resist *any* sort of reduction, and that they can only be understood on their own terms. These three problems will be considered in turn.

1.3.1 *Secondary Qualities*

The world as described by natural science has no obvious place for colours, tastes, or smells. Problems with sensory qualities have been philosophically and scientifically troublesome since ancient times, and in a modern form at least since Galileo in 1623 identified some sensory qualities as characterizing nothing real in the objects themselves:

> that external bodies, to excite in us these tastes, these odours, and these sounds, demanded other than size, figure, number, and slow or rapid motion, I do not believe; and I judge that, if the ears, the tongue, and the nostrils were taken away, the figure, the numbers, and the motions would indeed remain, but not the odours nor the tastes nor the sounds, which, without the living animal, I do not believe are anything else than names, just as tickling is precisely nothing but a name if the armpit and the nasal membrane be removed . . . (translation from Burtt 1954, p. 88).

The qualities of size, figure (or shape), number, and motion are for Galileo the only real properties of objects. All other qualities revealed in sense perception—colours, tastes, odours, sounds, and so on—exist solely in the sensitive body, and do not qualify anything in the objects themselves. They are the effects of the primary qualities of things on the senses. Without the living animal sensing such things, these 'secondary' qualities (to use the term introduced by Locke) would not exist. For that reason they are subjective properties (see Burtt 1954, p. 84).

Much of modern philosophy has devolved from this fateful distinction. While it was undoubtedly helpful to the physical sciences to make the mind into a sort of dustbin into which one could sweep the troublesome sensory qualities, this stratagem created difficulties for later attempts to arrive at some scientific understanding of the mind. In particular, the strategy cannot be reapplied when one goes on to explain sensation and perception. If physics cannot explain secondary qualities, then it seems that any science that can explain secondary qualities must appeal to explanatory principles distinct from those of physics. Thus are born various dualisms.

At the very least, it becomes difficult to see how to explain the mental states underlying perception using the same ontology and methodology so successfully applied to physical things. That secondary qualities are qualities inhering in the mind and not in physical things seems to imply that the mind cannot consist merely of physical things. The problem of reconciling materialism with the phenomenal qualities of sense impressions in this way dates from the very beginnings of natural science and modern philosophy. Hobbes was perhaps the first of many materialist philosophers to attempt to explain how the qualities of sense impressions (which he sometimes called 'phantasms') could be understood in terms of the motions of particles within the human organism (see Hobbes 1651, bk. 1, ch. 1). In his view phantasms were the results of motions caused by objects impinging on sensory nerves and rebounding internally. Unfortunately, this proposal did not answer the question of why some motions have a 'phantastic' or qualitative character, while other motions do not.

1.3.2 Contemporary Materialism

Contemporary materialists are still wrestling with this issue, which in many ways seems just as intractable as it did in Hobbes's time. Although we now know much more about how the nervous system works, it still seems impossible to explain the qualitative character of sensory states. An apparently unbridgeable explanatory gap yawns open between the qualities presented by sense and any possible physical explanation (see Levine 1983).

The problem might be described as follows. For the materialist, mental states are identical with physical states of the brain. Neurones have an intricate system for maintaining small voltage differences—of about 70 millivolts—across their cell membranes. Differing concentrations of various ions on the two sides of the membrane generate this small difference in electric potential. Changes in the potential across the membrane can alter its permeability to sodium ions, sending a wave of sodium ions flowing through the membrane. The wave sweeps from one end of the cell to the other. This 'depolarization' affects specialized structures at the end of the neurone, which in turn alter the probability of depolarizations of adjoining cells.

A system of neurones has enormously complex patterns of electrochemical activity. Voltage differences across the membranes of its neurones are a function of the electrical activity of thousands of other neurones, each of which in turn reflects activity in thousands of its neighbours. Now the materialists propose to identify sensory processes with some of these events, and the obvious question is, How could any of *that* ever add up to a *sensation*? Suppose one is seeing a red car under a sodium-arc street light, so that it looks blue. The visual experience of the car is to be identified with particular brain processes. How could any pattern of ion concentrations across membranes constitute the experience of the car looking blue to me now? The character of the experience seems utterly incommensurate with any such physical state. This quandary is not generated by the mistake of thinking that the visual experience is itself blue, while brain states are not blue. Rather, there is some aspect of the process of sensing the car in virtue of which the car looks blue to me now. It seems fantastic (or, in Hobbes's words, 'phantastic') to suppose that this aspect could be reduced to some distribution of differences in ion concentrations across cell membranes.

Furthermore, the materialist proposes that some patterns of physical activity suffice to give some states of the person a qualitative character, while other patterns lack any such qualitative character. How could any physical differences make that difference? How could the difference between an itch and a tickle be explained by citing differences in ion concentrations among excitable cells? It seems preposterous to suppose these questions could be answered.

Now undoubtedly our understanding of the physical functioning of the nervous system will improve significantly in future years, and possibly many of our current beliefs about its operation will be overturned. This prospect seems to make no difference at all—in principle, no difference at all—to the philosophical problem. No matter what we learn about the physical function of the nervous system, it seems that the same question can be raised. What is the connection between all those goings-on and the experience of something looking blue? How could any differences between such goings-on yield the difference between seeing something blue and seeing something red? It seems there is not and could not be any rationale for assigning qualitative content to any physical processes, no matter what they are or how they are understood. Hobbes, after all, thought that information transmission in the nervous system occurred mechanically—as if in a colossal pinball machine. The fact that we now know such transmission occurs electrochemically seems not to have advanced at all our ability to explain why sensations have the qualities that they do.

1.3.3 *Explaining, Analysing, Reducing*

The fundamental challenge is to explain qualia in non-qualitative terms. The task seems impossible. It seems that qualia cannot be reduced to or analysed by any theory that contains only non-qualitative terms. If no non-qualitative explanation of qualia is possible, then any 'reducing theory' containing only non-qualitative terms will fail to explain the facts of sensory experience. For similar reasons, any analysis of such facts in non-qualitative terms also must fail. Qualia are indigestible, and resist assimilation into any framework attempting an analysis or reduction.

Both the 'absent qualia' and the 'inverted qualia' objections are variants of this view (see Block 1978, 1980*a* and Shoemaker 1975*a*, 1982). Consider the objections as construction games. At the beginning of the game one can take whatever conceptual 'building blocks' one wants from several bins: physical states to serve as 'inputs' and 'outputs'; internal states, defined by causal connections to inputs, outputs, and other internal states; and any physical mechanism desired, to instantiate that 'functional' model. The 'absent qualia' objection is that, no matter what creature one constructs from such a basis, one can coherently suppose that none of its internal states have any qualitative character at all. The 'inverted qualia' objection is that one could construct *two* creatures from such a basis in identical fashion yet assign different ('inverted') qualitative contents to their corresponding internal states.   Both objections give the psychophysiologist some conceptual building blocks, and argue that from that basis one cannot explain qualia: those resources are inadequate to capturing qualitative facts.

If one admits the possibility of absent qualia or inverted qualia, then it seems that psychophysiological explanations of sensory qualities are in principle impossible. The possibility of inversion seems to show that the qualitative character of a psychological state is independent of all the relations that it bears to other psychological states, stimuli, and behaviour.   But psychophysiological explanations of perception can only characterize relations between stimuli, psychological states, and behaviour. No such considerations can ever explain the particular qualitative content possessed by the items so discriminated. So psychology cannot explain qualia.   The discipline lacks the conceptual resources. As Ned Block says in 'Troubles with Functionalism',

> psychophysics touches only the *functional* aspect of sensation, not its qualitative character. . . . Indeed, on the basis of the kind of conceptual apparatus now available in psychology, I do not see how psychology in anything like its present incarnation could explain qualia. We cannot now conceive how psychology *could* explain qualia . . . (Block 1980*c*, p. 289)

Block goes on to suggest that qualia may not be in the domain of psychology (Block 1980*c*, pp. 288, 289). If the facts to be explained are qualitative and the reducing theory contains no qualitative terms, then it seems that reduction is impossible. The qualitative character of consciousness cannot be explained by psychologists or neurophysiologists; it is *in principle* beyond their grasp.

Nagel's arguments (1979*b*, 1986) are also variants of anti-reductionist claims. Nagel argues that facts concerning what it is like to be a subject experiencing something—he cites the example of a bat using echo location—appear to 'embody a particular point of view' and seem to be inaccessible except from that point of view (Nagel 1979*b*, p. 171). No 'objective' characterization can capture facts of this sort, since the 'real nature' of experience cannot be described by leaving behind the creature's point of view, but only by retaining it, and (if possible) by adopting that point of view (p. 172). This is possible only for someone sufficiently similar to the creature in question. So we cannot expect to be able to describe bat phenomenology with any current methods (p. 177). That task requires a new discipline: one of 'objective phenomenology'. No current discipline can do the job.

Problems with qualia infect any analysis of mental terms. Nagel's argument would apply to explaining qualia from any non-qualitative basis, whether physical or not. Embracing dualism will not bridge the chasm. For a (substance) dualist, mental states are not states of the brain, but of some non-physical substance. The problem still arises that characterizing states of that substance does not seem to give us any purchase at all on what it is like to be the affiliated creature. Behaviourists and functionalists seem to fall into the same hole: none of the facts adduced in their accounts seem at all relevant to the character of sensory qualities—to the problem of what it is like to be a conscious creature experiencing things.

Instead, according to Nagel, what we need is an objective

characterization of the mental in its own right, one that would enable a creature incapable of having a particular experience to comprehend what it would be like to have that experience. Nagel notes that such an 'objective phenomenology' would describe 'structural features of perception' (1979b, p. 179). The discipline should provide a conception of subjective phenomena that is not limited to our own versions of subjective phenomena. It should enable us 'to think of ourselves from outside—but in mental, not physical terms' (Nagel 1986, p. 17). To do this, we would need to be able to conceive of our own point of view as a particular instance of something that can be described more generally. Our own subjective experience could then be seen as an instance of 'certain general features of subject experience—subjective universals' (1986, p. 21). According to Nagel, until such methods are developed, the status of physicalism

is similar to that which the hypothesis that matter is energy would have had if uttered by a pre-Socratic philosopher. We do not have the beginning of a conception of how it might be true. (Nagel 1979b, p. 177)

Like Block, Nagel suggests that the difficulty is not merely empirical, but conceptual. 'Subjective facts' cannot be explained by any existing discipline, and we cannot even imagine the concepts used by a discipline that could explain them.

1.4 Scope of this Book

The only obvious problem with the preceding arguments is that the conclusion seems to be false. Visual science provides a large collection of what at least appear to be genuine explanations of the qualitative character of some sensory states. In this book I will defend the view that some of these explanations are, at least in principle, good ones. I will argue that psychophysiology can in principle succeed in explaining qualia, in the following sense: the purported explanations have an appropriate structure; they can be defended against all the extant philosophical objections; and if the essential premises of the explanations were true, then we would have genuine explanations for some qualitative facts. I am not claiming that we can establish now that all the essential premises are true, or that at this moment we possess genuine explanations for qualitative facts, but merely that something like this *would* work if the premises *were* true.

It is disconcerting to find plausible philosophical arguments contradicting what seems an obvious fact. Either there is some error in the philosophical arguments, or the apparently successful explanations provided by contemporary visual science are bogus. The qualia objections can be viewed as sceptical attacks on those purported explanations. If the philosophical worries over qualia were correct, it would follow that not one of those purported explanations is successful: they must in principle all fail. So qualia worries can be rephrased as sceptical attacks on the legitimacy and success of the purported scientific explanations.

Such a formulation provides a strategy and outline for the argument of the entire book. I will describe and analyse the structure of current psychophysiological explanations of perceptual effects, then subject those explanations to an intensive bombardment of philosophical objection. Sifting through the rubble, we will assess how much damage has been done and how much is irreparable. I hope to show that there is a robust and powerful underlying structure to those explanations that emerges unscathed. It is solid, it endures. Some qualia *can* in principle be explained: the purported explanations provided by psycho-physiology have a defensible structure.

Undoubtedly, these pages will fail to answer all the philosophical objections to the project that might be raised. A secondary purpose of the book is to focus attention for a while on the way psychologists look at the problem, and to demonstrate the power and attractiveness of their approach. The disciplines involved are psychophysics, neurophysiology, psychometrics, and the experimental psychology of perception. I hope to clarify the scope and limits of a particular explanatory strategy employed by practitioners of those disciplines.

The philosophical problem is that no explanation of sensory qualities in non-qualitative terms seems possible. The gap from physical states of the nervous system to sensory qualities seems unbridgeable. The philosophical problem can be resolved by showing at least one way in which the gap can be bridged: one way in which one can understand the nature of sensory qualities and their place in the physical world. The point of this book is to describe one possible solution: the one current in psychophysics.

2

Explaining Looks

2.1 Perceptual Effects

In 1824 the French chemist M. E. Chevreul travelled to the Gobelin tapestry works to respond to complaints of the weavers that some of the dyes were inferior, and rapidly faded or changed in hue after a tapestry was completed. Chevreul determined that some of the complaints were well founded, and embarked on some of the early chemical investigations on the stability of colourant pigments. Other complaints though seemed to have no basis in chemistry. Particularly persistent were complaints that black threads lost vigour or altered hue when woven with blues and violets. Chevreul eventually demonstrated that such shifts in hue were not caused by any change in the threads, but were a perceptual effect arising within the weaver. He provided some of the earliest experimental demonstrations of what are now called *colour contrast* effects: a grey surrounded by blue will look somewhat yellowish, simply because of its contrast with the surround. Chevreul also investigated what are now called *edge enhancement* effects, and published (in 1839) a figure similar to Fig. 2.1 (see Ratliff 1965). Each strip in the figure is in fact a uniform grey, although it looks lighter on one side and darker on the other.

Since its birth in Chevreul's day, the experimental psychology of perception has uncovered many such effects. Many of them have proper names, such as 'Mach bands', the 'Hermann grid', the 'Purkinje effect', the 'McCullough after-effect', and so on. These names denote various experimentally replicable stimulus configurations that for most observers generate some sort of illusory perceptual appearance. For example, 'Mach bands', studied by Ernst Mach in the 1860s, are illusory bands of brightness or darkness that sometimes appear when regions of

differing luminance are connected by a gradual transition from
one luminance to the other. They are related to the effect seen in
Chevreul's array; both involve heightened contrast at luminance
edges. The 'Hermann grid' is a grid of squares laid out like city
blocks (see Fig. 2.2). Most observers will notice what appear to
be small grey spots in the (unfixated) intersections of the white
strips. These spots seem to move about as one shifts one's gaze,
being least apparent at the visual focus and most apparent at the
periphery. A grey spot that seems to fill an intersection vanishes
on direct inspection, but with the shift in gaze previously
unoccupied intersections acquire shadowy visitors.

Fig. 2.1. Chevreul's array

Note: Each of the strips above is a uniform grey, as can be verified by blocking off its
neighbours with two pieces of paper. Nevertheless, each strip looks as if it has a light
band on its right side and a darker band on its left. This effect gives the array a
'scalloped' or 'fluted' appearance. The variation in lightness is particularly noticeable
when the figure is held at arm's length.

Many of these perceptual phenomema have no proper names,
but are identified as effects of specific experimental procedures.
For example, colour adaptation effects are produced by somehow
flooding vision with a particular hue—using tinted glasses,
coloured illuminants, or simply by staring for a period at a highly

saturated colour patch. The 'effect' in question is a shift in the apparent hue of things examined immediately after the flooding stops.

FIG. 2.2. The Hermann grid

Note: Grey spots appear at the intersections of the white strips.
Source: From Schiffman, H. R. (1982, p. 266). *Sensation and Perception: An Integrated Approach*. 2nd edition. Copyright © 1982 by John Wiley & Sons. Reprinted by permission of John Wiley & Sons, Inc.

These perceptual effects provide a fertile experimental domain for the various theories of visual perception; each effect requires some explanation, and as a group they pose a daunting challenge to any pretender to a unified theory. What unites all these various perceptual 'effects' is that in each there is some quality that the stimulus configuration will appear to have, even though it lacks that quality. At arm's length the edges in Chevreul's array appear to stand up off the page and cast shadows rightwards. Each strip looks concave or 'scalloped', but it is not. The

Hermann grid appears to have dark circles in some of its interstices, but it does not. To most observers the stimulus configuration will present an illusory perceptual appearance.

How does one know, in each case, that the stimulus configuration lacks a quality that it appears to have? One simply carries out some further experimentally replicable procedure after which one can see that the configuration lacks that quality. For example, one can block all but one strip in Chevreul's array, and see that the strip is in fact a uniform grey. No intersection in the Hermann grid retains its illusory circle when fixated directly. Colour contrast effects vanish when one simply covers the surround. Some illusions are so powerful that more arduous methods are required; one may need to measure the lines in a Müller–Lyer illusion to convince oneself that in fact they are of the same length. Nevertheless, in each case one can somehow show that the given stimulus configuration is not as it appears.

Each of our experimentally replicable perceptual effects produces a sense impression with a particular illusory qualitative content. Sensory qualities characterize the appearances of things, and in particular characterize what is common between perceiving something that has a given quality and perceiving something that merely appears to have that quality. In brief, then, each of these perceptual 'effects' involves *qualia*.

Do psychologists succeed (at least sometimes) in explaining how things look, or do they not? If the philosophical objections concerning sensory qualities were cogent, then psychology ought not to be able to explain any qualia, and in particular it ought not to be able to explain any of the noted perceptual 'effects'. To assess this claim I shall analyse the logic of such explanations and consider the import of various qualia-based objections. I hope to show that some of these explanations are in principle successful, and that all the objections can be answered. The empirical premisses may be (and at some level of detail probably are) false, but the logic of the explanations is flawless. A vindication of that logic would suffice to show that there is no *conceptual* bar to explaining qualitative content.

2.2 Some Examples of Explanations

A distinctive pattern of explanation for perceptual effects recurs throughout psychophysics, psychophysiology, and experimental psychology. The strategy underlying this explanation is best revealed by examples. I will consider three: edge enhancement effects, the Hermann grid, and colour adaptation effects.

2.2.1 *Edge Enhancement Effects*

Mach bands are illusory bands of light or dark that occur near the ends of transition zones between regions of differing luminance. One can see the effect in Chevreul's array (Fig. 2.1). Each strip appears to have a darker band towards the edge where it adjoins its lighter neighbour, and a lighter band towards the edge where it adjoins its darker neighbour.

How do psychologists explain this phenomenon? Very roughly, and leaving aside many details, the story goes like this. The initial stages of visual processing occur directly inside the retina, shown in Fig. 2.3. Visual receptors line the retinal wall, so that light proceeds through the various neural layers before reaching the receptors at the top of the diagram. The story starts with the absorption of photons by receptors. Receptors themselves do not generate action potentials; instead, absorption of photons alters the electric potential at the receptor synapses with bipolar (and horizontal) cells. The response of the receptor is roughly logarithmic to the intensity of light, so equal increments in receptor response correspond roughly to equal *multiples* in light intensity.

Investigators have discovered some—but not all—of the functional relations among the cells in the synaptic layers of the retina. The first action potentials occur in the amacrine and ganglion cells (Boynton 1979, p. 90). Synapses between cells can be either excitatory or inhibitory. A potential at an excitatory synapse will increase the probability that the recipient will fire, while one at an inhibitory synapse will decrease the probability. Retinal processing ends at the ganglion cells; the axons of the ganglion cells form the fibres of the optic nerve, which proceeds inward to the central nervous system. There are far fewer ganglion cells than receptors; hence activity in a ganglion cell cannot be derived from a single receptor, but must sum the activities of a number of them. This 'summation' will include excitatory and inhibitory effects.

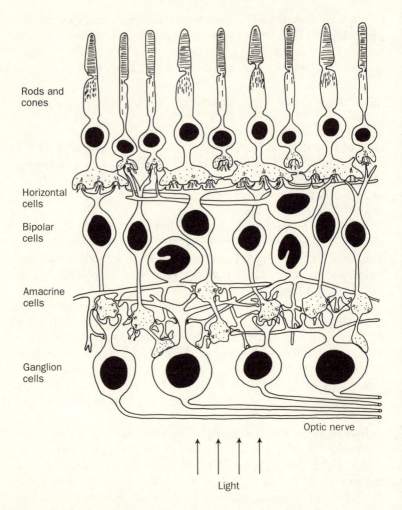

Rods and
cones

Horizontal
cells

Bipolar
cells

Amacrine
cells

Ganglion
cells

Optic nerve

Light

FIG. 2.3. Anatomy of the retina

Notes: Rods and cones are at the top; the lens of the eye is towards the bottom. Light travels through all the neural elements pictured here before reaching the receptors. Bipolars receive stimulation from receptors, with some lateral influences from the horizontal cells. Similarly, ganglion cells receive stimulation from the bipolars, with some lateral influences from the amacrine cells. Axons of the ganglion cells (at the bottom) form the optic nerve leaving the eye. Lateral inhibitory effects are found in many places in those two main circuits.

Source: From Hurvich (1981, p. 124). Reprinted by permission of Sinauer Associates, Inc.

One can clarify the inhibitory and excitatory relations within the retinal synaptic layers by impaling a single ganglion cell with a microelectrode, presenting controlled stimuli to the retina, and measuring the response of the cell. Figure 2.4 shows some results.

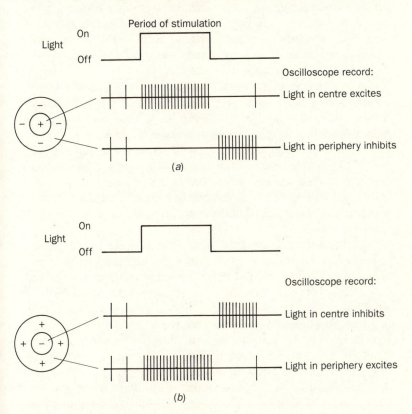

FIG. 2.4. Ganglion cell receptive fields

Notes: Two different ganglion cell receptive fields are pictured. Part (*a*) has an on-centre off-surround organization, and part (*b*) is off-centre on-surround. Four sample oscilloscope tracks show the spike frequency of the cell when a spot of light is turned on for the period indicated and aimed either in the centre of the field or in its antagonistic surround. In part (*a*), light shone in the on-centre of the field greatly increases spiking frequency, while if shone in the off-surround spiking is greatly inhibited. Part (*b*) shows opposite effects.

Source: From Schiffman, H. R. (1982, p. 204). *Sensation and Perception: An Integrated Approach*. 2nd edition. Copyright © 1982 by John Wiley & Sons. Reprinted by permission of John Wiley & Sons, Inc.

The *receptive field* of a given sensory neurone for a particular stimulus is that region of the receptor surface where presentation of that stimulus will affect the activity of the neurone. The effect may be either inhibitory or excitatory. Cells with an on-centre off-surround receptive field are excited when light is shone in the centre region, and inhibited when it is shone in the surround. Cells with the off-centre on-surround fields show the opposite behaviour: inhibited by a light increment falling in the centre, excited by one in the surround.

Such ganglion cells might account for edge enhancement effects. Why does each grey strip in Fig. 2.1 appear darker towards the edge where it adjoins its lighter neighbour, and lighter towards the edge where it adjoins its darker neighbour? Consider several ganglion cells arrayed across the luminance edge (Fig. 2.5). A cell aimed at the middle of a strip will have its on-centre and off-surround receptive fields stimulated at the same intensity. The response of the cell will depend on the extent to which it is naturally activated by its 'on' compared with its 'off' receptive fields.

The on-centre off-surround organization of receptive fields will cause noteworthy responses in cells near luminance edges. For example, cell (*b*) has part of its off-surround in a darker region of the array. It will therefore receive *less* inhibition than its neighbour (*a*), and so will have a higher level of activation than (*a*). As the on-centres fall into shadow, activation rapidly drops, so cells like (*b*) will have the highest activation of any in the area. Similarly, cell (*c*) has a portion of its off-surround still in the brighter part of the array, so it will be much more inhibited than its neighbour (*d*), entirely in shadow. Cells like (*c*) will have the lowest levels of activation of any near the edge, much lower than those like (*d*).

The complete array of cells will enhance or amplify luminance edges. The edge of a strip facing a brighter neighbour will look as if it has a dark band in that region where the brighter neighbour increases inhibition in the on-centre off-surround cells. Similarly, an edge facing a darker strip will look as if it has a bright band due to the lower inhibition. These alternating excitatory and inhibitory amplifications give the array of grey strips its 'scalloped' look. Cell (*b*) fires at the same rate that cell (*a*) would have if presented with a brighter strip. Cell (*b*) responds as (*a*) would

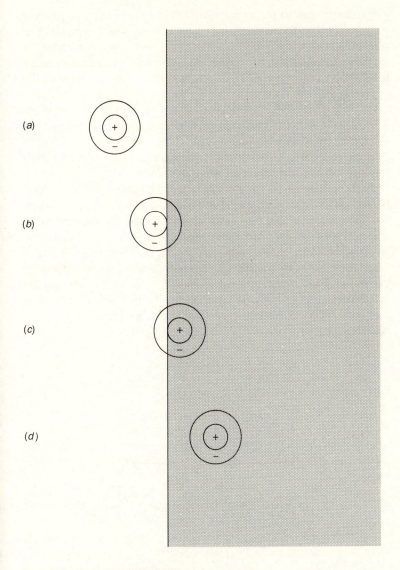

FIG. 2.5. Receptive fields near an edge
Note: Four on-centre off-surround cells are shown near a luminance edge.

respond if some activation were added. The visual system registers no difference between the left side of the edge and a bright strip, and so the subject finds that side of each edge to be indiscriminable from a brighter area. Now the bright strip in question *looks* bright, and the left side of the edge is indiscriminable from it. Hence the left side of the edge looks bright too.

2.2.2 *The Hermann Grid*

The same principles can explain why grey circles appear in the intersections of the Hermann grid. The underlying brute fact is that an on-centre off-surround ganglion cell will be increasingly inhibited as the surround receives more stimulation.

Now consider how ganglion cells will respond when stimulated by various portions of the Hermann grid (Fig. 2.6). We show receptive fields of two on-centre off-surround cells, superimposed on portions of the Hermann grid from which they receive stimulation. One cell is aimed at an intersection; the other at a white strip between two blocks. Both receive the same amount of excitation from their on-centre fields. The cell aimed at the intersection has a greater portion of its off-surround stimulated by the white strips. Consequently, it will be more inhibited than the cell above it.

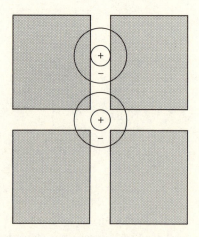

FIG. 2.6. An explanation of the Hermann grid

Note: The cell aimed at the intersection of the white strips is more inhibited than the cell above it.

Why then does a grey spot appear at the intersection? Cells aimed at an intersection respond just as the others would if some activation were subtracted—if, for example, they were not stimulated so energetically in their on-centres. That reduction yields the same level of activity as would be caused by a stimulus that was not so bright—as, for example, by a slightly greyish spot in the on-centre portion of the field. Since the receptors are active at the rate they would be when stimulated by a grey spot, the intersection of the grid is encoded the same as a grey area. The subject finds the intersection to be indiscriminable from a grey area—which *looks* grey. Hence the intersection appears to be filled with a grey spot.

Of course, this account is elliptical in various ways. For example, why should one see a grey spot only in the on-centre portion of the receptive field of cells centred on an intersection, instead of across the entire field? Why do the grey spots disappear when one looks directly at the intersection? And why do we get these effects when roughly half the ganglion cells are *off*-centre *on*-surround?

A slight elaboration can answer all three questions. First, the receptive fields of neighbouring ganglion cells overlap. The overall perception of brightness of a given region is presumably a function of the outputs of many such cells. When these are summed, the darkest portion of the 'streets' will be found at the intersections, but apparent brightness will drop off smoothly. This also explains why the borders of the grey spots are indistinct.

The grey spots vanish on direct inspection because of some anatomical peculiarities of the retina. The Hermann grid effect depends on a close fit between the size of the 'intersections' and the width of the receptive fields of ganglion cells. For example, if the visual angle of the off-surround is equal to or less than that of a 'street', cells aimed at streets will be inhibited as much as cells aimed at intersections, and the contrast effect will not occur. Receptive fields of ganglion cells at the fovea—the part of the retina that receives stimulation from whatever one fixates—are much smaller than those towards the periphery. So, unless it occupies a very small visual angle, one does not see grey spots at a fixated intersection. The grey spots move closer to one's fixation point as the intersections shrink. One can use the Hermann grid to plot the angular size of intersection required to make a grey spot appear at various angles away from the fixated point. Such plots correspond with direct physiological measurements of receptive field widths at different points in the retina (Frisby 1980, p. 138).

Off-centre on-surround cells would show precisely the opposite effects from those described: cells aimed at an intersection would show greater activation than those aimed at a street. Such cells contribute to edge enhancement, but with an opposite 'sign'. Other things being equal, we perceive more luminous regions as brighter, not darker, so in generating a perception of brightness presumably the sign difference is somewhere eliminated. The actual brightness perceived in a given region seems to correlate instead with activation levels of on-centre off-surround cells at the edges of the region.[1]

2.2.3 *Colour Adaptation*

As a final example, consider colour adaptation effects. These can be demonstrated in various ways. Skiers who remove yellow ski goggles after a morning of skiing may notice that the snow looks quite blue for a few moments. If you stare at green letters on a computer monitor for a while and then try to read something printed in white on a black background, you may notice that the letters all look pink. The simplest demonstration is to close one eye and stare through the other at a brightly illuminated colour patch (of almost any colour) for thirty seconds to a minute. Then blink left and right eyes successively, and notice how the colour of the object seems to shift. The colour will look much brighter through the eye you kept closed, but the complement of the colour will look brighter through the eye that was open.

How can these effects be explained? There are three types of colour-sensitive retinal receptors, which differ in the specific wavelengths to which each is optimally sensitive. These receptors will respond to light of different wavelengths, but their response is likely to be weaker; and they tend to be named in honour of their

---

[1] The perception of brightness in a given region (and brightness contrast effects) cannot be fully explained in terms of the mechanisms of *edge* enhancement described here. Edge enhancement effects disappear if the stimulus is presented dichoptically, while brightness contrast effects do not (see Uttal 1973, p. 451). Furthermore, brightness contrast effects disappear if the edges in question are perceived to be at different depths (Gilchrist 1977). Depth perception presumably depends on mechanisms outside the retina.

optimal stimulators. So we have L (long-wavelength), M (middle-wavelength), and S (short-wavelength) receptors. A second relevant fact is that, if a receptor system is presented with a strong stimulus, the response of the system gradually decreases over time—a process known as 'adaptation'. This may be due in part to bleaching of the photopigment in the receptor, but also there must be neural interactions that decrease the response of the system to constant stimuli. Finally, some retinal ganglion cells combine activity from the different receptors in such a way that they function in a 'spectrally opponent' fashion. They are excited by presentation of a given colour and inhibited by presentation of its complement. A $+L -M$ cell, for example, is stimulated by activity in the long-wavelength (L) receptors, and inhibited by activity in the middle-wavelength (M) receptors. Such cells tend to respond to long-wavelength stimuli with activity above their baseline, and to middle-wavelength stimuli with activity below their baseline. For example, some cells are excited maximally by monochromatic red light (with a long wavelength) and inhibited by green. There are three such spectrally opponent channels: red–green, yellow–blue, and white–black.

These facts can explain colour adaptation effects. Suppose you stare at a red book through your left eye, keeping your right eye closed. Why does the red book thereafter look brighter through the right eye, while a green book will look brighter through the left eye? Closing the right eye spares it from any adaptation effects. Its long-wavelength receptors (which are maximally sensitive to the wavelengths probably reflected from the book) avoid adaptation. The left eye becomes adapted, however. The effect will be most pronounced in receptors maximally stimulated by long wavelengths, towards the red end of the spectrum. Such cells will lose response faster than the other sorts, and so a given stimulus will excite a lower response in the red–green chromatic channel. One rarely notices this adaptation as it occurs; it is apparent only when one blinks and examines the same book successively through the two eyes. Compared with cells in the right eye, cells in the (adapted) left eye will respond at the rate they would to a stimulus from which some long wavelengths had been subtracted—that is, to something that would look to be a dimmer red. So the book will look brighter to the unadapted right eye.

Selective adaptation has the opposite effect on the perception of complementary colours. Suppose one examines a green book with a red-adapted eye. In the adapted eye, long-wavelength receptors will produce a lowered output to the red–green channel. The overall level of activation in this channel will therefore be depressed compared with the unadapted eye. Red things will look less red, but green things will look greener.

The strategy of explanation is the same as in the preceding examples. The book looks less red because it is encoded (in the channels serving the left eye) in just the same way that a book which *is* less red would be encoded by the right eye. A green thing affects the left eye the same way a more saturated green affects the right eye.

2.3 A Schema for Explanation

We seem to have three different explanations of why in some particular situation something appears to have a quality it lacks. All three explanations rely on showing how, in that particular situation, the object has the same effect on the visual system as something that one perceives to have the given quality.

Does demonstrating such an identity of effects suffice to explain why something appears a certain way? Four apparently fatal objections to this explanation spring to mind. First, the explanation seems to leap from the claim that stimuli have identical effects on retinal ganglion cells to the claim that they are indiscriminable. How can that implausible inference be defended? Second, even if one can demonstrate indiscrim- inability, how does that show anything about the qualitative content of either member of the pair? Third, the explanation seems to presume a correlation between the output of retinal ganglion cells and the quality of visual sensations, and this presumption seems more questionable than the phenomenon it is invoked to explain. Are we committed to the bizarre claim that retinal ganglion cells instantiate sensations of brightness? Finally, the key to the explanation is to show an identity of effects between the first stimulus configuration and a second one that 'really' has the quality and is perceived to have that quality. But this reference to a second 'paradigm' stimulus that is veridically perceived to have a certain quality seems to doom the explanation either to circularity or to vacuity. For we fail to explain why that second stimulus is *perceived* to have the quality it does, and so fail to explain the perceptual quality. On the other hand, if we eliminate any reference to such a paradigm, then we cannot explain why the original stimulus looks the way it does.

I will show how all four of these objections can be answered. Unfortunately the argument is a lengthy one, involving a complicated pattern of inference involving discriminability, encoding, information, and 'looks'. The remainder of this chapter will be devoted to the first objection; subsequent chapters will deal with the remaining ones. The argument will be complete only at the end of Chapter 6.

To get things started, it will be helpful to schematize. I will lay out in some detail the structure of the explanation of edge enhancement effects. This same schema will fit the explanations of the other perceptual phenomena that were described, as well as those of many other 'effects' that have not been mentioned. Our explanandum is that, under viewing conditions *C*, to some specific subject *S* the left side of each grey strip appears to be darker than the right side—the strip looks 'scalloped'. How can this be explained? The answer proceeds in four steps:

1. Show that the uniform grey strip positioned within the array has an identical effect on some stage of the visual system as a strip that is lighter on one side, darker on the other. (I will call the latter a 'scalloped' strip.)
2. Show that those identical effects at that stage of processing ensure that the uniform strip within the array is indiscriminable from a scalloped strip. (One can also show that it is indiscriminable from the same class of other stimuli as is the scalloped strip.)
3. Show that such a mutual indiscriminability from the same class of stimuli demonstrates that the strip within the array *looks* the same as a scalloped strip.
4. Conclude that, since one can perceive the scalloped strip to be scalloped, and the strip within the array looks the same as the scalloped strip, the strip within the array looks scalloped.

This example provides one instance of a general explanatory strategy, which can be schematized as follows. Suppose we are trying to explain why, under specific experimentally replicable conditions *C*, some stimulus configuration *x* to most observers looks P. 'P' is some quality of the appearance of x. We pick some y that is P and that most observers perceive to be P. The explanation then proceeds as follows.

1. *Identity of effects*. Show that x and y have identical effects on (some stage of) the visual system. The identity of effects needs not be complete, but may be only partial. One can restrict oneself to some particular cells C within the visual system and some particular properties Q, and show that both x and y cause Q in cells C. This partial identity of effects is sufficient only if it suffices to establish the following point.

2. *Indiscriminability*. Show that, if x and y have identical effects Q on cells C, then x will be indiscriminable from y. One also must demonstrate what will be called *global* indiscriminability: that for any stimulus z, x is indiscriminable from z if and only if y is as well. Stimulus x must be indiscriminable from just the same class of stimuli as is y.

3. *Qualitative identity*. Show that global indiscriminability ensures qualitative identity. If x is indiscriminable from y and from the same set of stimuli as is y, then x presents the same sensory qualities as y. The qualitative content of sense impressions of x will be the same as those of sense impressions of y.

4. Conclude that, since y looks as if it is P, and x looks the same as y, therefore x also looks as if it is P.

Most explanations of perceptual effects are elliptical, and typically the first step is the only one completed in detail. Nevertheless, the others are critical to the enterprise of explaining sensory qualities.

Already one can see how this strategy might answer the third objection lodged above. The point of that objection was that we seem to be investing retinal ganglion cells with astounding powers to influence the phenomenal properties of perceptual appearance. The schema shows we need not assume that retinal ganglion cells themselves instantiate sensations of brightness. So far the explanation says nothing directly about 'sensations' or the 'properties' of sensations. Instead, we focus on the conditions under which two stimuli will or will not match. The *relation* of qualitative identity is the initial target; and we hope later to show how that relation will allow us to define the qualities so related. But that comes much later. For now we need to understand what is meant by 'identity of effects'.

2.4 Identity of Effects

The first step in our explanation of why the strip looks scalloped can be laid out as follows:

(P_1) Many retinal ganglion cells have a receptive field with an on-centre off-surround organization. Receptive fields of such ganglion cells blanket the entire retina.

From a description of such cells one can derive:

(C_1) Ganglion cells whose off-surrounds overlap the brighter side of an edge will have a lower output than those whose off-surrounds do not. Ganglion cells whose off-surrounds overlap the darker side of the edge will have a higher output than those whose off-surrounds do not.

We add as further premisses:

(P_2) The retinal ganglion cells form the optic nerve. All visual information depends on outputs from retinal ganglion cells.

(P_3) *S* is presented with an array of grey strips of increasing darkness.

Hence:

(C_2) Ganglion cells stimulated by a given strip of the array fire exactly as they would to a strip that is darker on its left side and lighter on its right—that is, to a scalloped strip.

In effect, we can show that the output from the eye for each grey strip in the array would match the output for a scalloped strip. The 'identity of effect' is partial: we show only that those stimuli have identical effects on the firing rates of specific cells. We must later establish that all subsequent visual processing causally depends on the states of those cells. Only then can we show that such a partial identity of effects ensures that the visual system encodes the two stimuli identically.

There are several reasons to be dissatisfied with this method of demonstrating identity of effects. For one, it seems *ad hoc*, and there is no clear or workable way to extend it to deal with systems of millions of neurones. One would like to build some generalizable experimental laws describing classes of stimuli that have identical effects. Reasoning about a few neurones at a time seems unlikely to yield such a theory.

A simple formulation goes far in meeting these desiderata: *wavelength mixture space*. This system can predict and explain chromatic matches. Philosophers have in the past attempted to identify distinct colours with distinct wavelengths of light. Such attempts must fail, since infinitely many distinct combinations of wavelengths yield stimuli that match a given colour. It is important to understand why so many combinations match. Surprisingly, one can predict *which* combinations of wavelengths will match a given colour patch, and it is important to understand how such prediction is possible. A simple model of early visual processing can provide a unified explanation of colour mixing and matching. It also can explain adaptation effects and some aspects of abnormal and defective colour vision. My description draws heavily on Cornsweet (1970), the classic source.

Figure 2.7 shows why transducer signals are equivocal. It shows the absorption spectrum for rhodopsin, the visual pigment

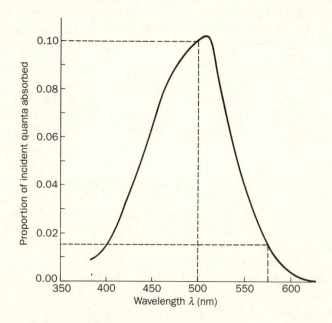

Fig. 2.7. The absorption spectrum for rhodopsin

Note: The pigment absorbs quanta at some wavelengths more readily than at others. The horizontal scale gives the wavelength of the stimulus in nanometres (nm) and the vertical scale gives the proportion of quanta absorbed.

Source: From Cornsweet (1970, p. 157). Reprinted by permission of Harcourt Brace Jovanovich, Inc.

contained in rods. The curve shows the proportions of photons absorbed by the receptor at different wavelengths. The optimal stimulator for rhodopsin is light with a wavelength of about 500 nanometres (nm). The pigment absorbs 10 per cent of quanta at that wavelength. The proportion falls for quanta with higher or lower wavelengths.

The curve illustrates the difficulty in discriminating wavelengths. Photons produce their effects on receptors by isomerizing molecules of the photopigment in the receptor. (An *isomerization* is a change in the configuration of a molecule.) Such isomerizations probably affect the ion permeability of the receptor membrane, and thereby alter the electric potential across the membrane. Under optimal conditions, a single isomerization can yield a detectable signal from a receptor (Boynton 1979, p. 90). But the change in molecular configuration is the same no matter what the wavelength of the photon that caused it. Once a quantum is absorbed, its wavelength information is for ever lost. The equivalence of isomerizations caused by quanta of differing wavelengths has become known as the *principle of univariance* (Boynton 1979, p. 110).

If two stimuli of differing wavelengths isomerize the same number of photopigment molecules in a receptor, the receptor will have the same response to both. Unfortunately there are many such pairs. For example, photons at 450 nm and at 550 nm both have approximately a 5 per cent chance of absorption. Approximately the same number of absorptions will occur in response to light of 450 nm as of 550 nm, so whatever effects are produced by one can be produced as well by the other. The receptor cannot discriminate between those wavelengths.

Outputs from this cell are ambiguous in a further way. The response of the cell depends on the number of quanta absorbed. The latter number is a product of two factors: the probability of absorption of a given wavelength, and the number of incident photons at that wavelength. For example, for the receptor given in Fig. 2.7, 10 per cent of photons at 500 nm cause isomerizations, compared with about 1.5 per cent of those at 575 nm (see Table 2.1). To match the effect of 1000 quanta at the 500 nm wavelength, one simply needs to increase the intensity of the stimulus at 575 nm, to make up for the lower rate of absorption. The second row of the table shows that 6667 quanta at 575 nm will have an identical effect on the receptor as does the 500 nm stimulus. If the 500 nm stimulus doubles in intensity (as in the third row of the table), one simply increases the intensity of the 575 nm stimulus by the same factor. The receptor will confound intensity and wavelength.

TABLE 2.1. Effects of stimuli on a rhodopsin receptor

Wavelength (nm)	Quanta incident	Per cent absorbed	Quanta absorbed
500	1000	10.0	100
575	6667	1.5	100
500	2000	10.0	200
575	13334	1.5	200

Note: The receptor will respond identically to the stimuli listed on the first and second rows, and to those on the third and fourth rows.
Source: Cornsweet (1970, p. 157).

The problem is quite general. An absorption spectrum similar to Fig. 2.7 can be drawn for any transducer. Any such cell has some optimal stimulus, but stimuli differing slightly from the optimum are merely less likely to cause a response. A transducer cannot be considered as a simple 'detector' of the physical magnitudes that cause its response, simply because it equivocates across such magnitudes.

How then do we ever manage to perceive differences among wavelengths? Different wavelengths must somehow cause distinguishably different effects. A receptor on its own cannot produce such effects, and adding more receptors with the same absorption spectrum will not help. The evolutionary solution is elegant: populate the critical surfaces with transducers having different absorption spectra, and compare their results.

Figure 2.8 illustrates the principle. It plots hypothetical absorption spectra for two different photopigments. (They are absorption spectra for hypothetical middle- and long-wavelength photopigments, here labelled 'M' and 'L'.) The M system has an optimal sensitivity at 550 nm, and will respond roughly equally to wavelengths equidistant from that optimum. For example, it absorbs approximately 10 per cent of photons at 600 nm, and 10 per cent of those at 500. Equal numbers of photons at those two wavelengths will produce approximately the same number of isomerizations. How then can one discriminate 600 nm light from 500 nm light? While the two produce equal effects on the M system, their effects on L differ dramatically. As the figure illustrates, only about 3 per cent of photons at 500 nm cause isomerizations in the L system, while at 600 nm about 19 per cent do. In the L system we will find vastly more isomerization occurring in response to the second stimulus. If one combines outputs from both systems, different wavelengths have differentiable effects.

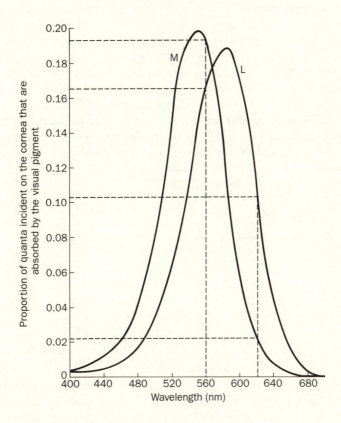

FIG. 2.8. Two distinct absorption spectra

Note: The M (medium-wavelength) system is optimally sensitive at about 550 nm, and the L (long-wavelength) system at 590 nm. Pairs of stimuli that M cannot distinguish will have drastically different effects on L.

Source: From Cornsweet (1970, p. 176). Reprinted by permission of Harcourt Brace Jovanovich, Inc.

A given wavelength typically yields a unique ratio between the outputs of the two systems. This can be seen from Fig. 2.8. It is important to think here in terms of ratios, not differences. If we employed the difference between the number of isomerizations in the M system and in the L system, we would again confuse differing wavelengths with differing intensities.

Table 2.2 provides an example. The first two rows show how 1000 quanta at two different wavelengths would affect the M and L systems. The differences in the number of isomerizations in the two systems would suffice to distinguish those two stimuli. Unfortunately, that strategy will not differentiate all pairs of different wavelengths. In the third row of the table, we increase the intensity of the 560 nm stimulus roughly fourfold. The brighter light now produces the same difference in the number of isomerizations in M and L as does the 520 nm stimulus. If we were sensitive to the differing numbers of isomerizations occurring in our retinas, we would therefore find the stimuli of the second and third rows to be indiscriminable. In fact, the first is seen as green and the second as a much brighter yellowish green: they differ in both hue and intensity. The ratios of isomerizations distinguish the two stimuli, not the differences.

TABLE 2.2.   Ratios *v.* differences

Wavelength (nm)	Quanta incident	Absorbed by M	Absorbed by L	Differ- ence	Ratio
560	1000	192 (19.2%)	165 (16.5%)	27	1.16:1
520	1000	165 (16.5%)	62 (6.2%)	103	2.66:1
560	3814	732 (19.2%)	629 (16.5%)	103	1.16:1

We have seen that it is possible to encode wavelength differences (and to distinguish them from changes in intensity) using differences in the ratios of activation of cones with two distinct absorption spectra. Normal human beings have *three* distinct absorption spectra for their different cones. Figure 2.8 resembles the absorption spectra for a 'dichromat', who is lacking one of the normal receptor systems—in this case, the short-wavelength system. As predicted theoretically, however, even dichromats can distinguish between different wavelengths; they simply cannot make as many distinctions as can a trichromat. For example, our particular observer could distinguish reds from greens, but would find yellows to be indiscriminable from blues.

Various colour-matching tasks can reveal the differences between dichromats and normals. Suppose we have a device that can present two distinct mixtures of wavelengths to an observer. Each mix might be presented as half the field visible through an eyepiece. In one half of the field we have a test stimulus. The experimenter controls its wavelength mixture. In the other half the mix consists of a few 'reference' wavelengths whose relative intensities can be adjusted by the observer. The observer attempts to match the test stimulus by adjusting the relative intensities of the reference wavelengths. Dichromats can match any test stimulus by adjusting relative intensities among just two reference wavelengths.[2] Trichromats require three.

How can this fact be explained? Figure 2.9 yields some clues.

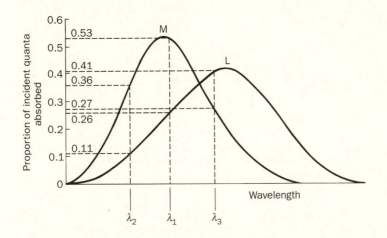

Fig. 2.9. Matching adjustments for a dichromat

Note: M and L are the middle- and long-wavelength systems of a dichromat. One stimulus is λ_1 alone, while the other is a mix of λ_2 and λ_3. By adjusting the intensities of λ_2 and λ_3, it is possible to match λ_1.

Source: From Cornsweet (1970, p. 165).

[2] The reference wavelengths must be carefully chosen. It is not true that one can match any test stimulus by adjusting the relative intensity of any two reference wavelengths.

It shows absorption spectra for systems M and L, and the effects of three wavelengths on those systems. The first stimulus consists only of λ_1, while the second stimulus is a mixture of λ_2 and λ_3. The observer is allowed to adjust the relative intensity of λ_2 and λ_3 in the second stimulus, and can produce a match between that mixture and λ_1. The proportions of quanta of a given wavelength absorbed by a given system are constant, but by varying the intensity of the light one can change the total number of absorptions. For example, the M system absorbs 36 per cent of the quanta of λ_2 and 27 per cent of the quanta of λ_3 (see Table 2.3). So stimulus λ_2 has more of an effect on the M system, while λ_3 has more of an effect on the L system. By adjusting the relative intensities of those two wavelengths, therefore, one can adjust the relative activation of both systems. In effect, we solve two simultaneous equations in two unknowns,[3] and, provided our

TABLE 2.3. Matching adjustments for a dichromat

Wave-length	Quanta incident	Per cent absorbed by M	Quanta absorbed by M	Per cent absorbed by L	Quanta absorbed by L
λ_1	1000	53.0	530	26.0	260
λ_2	1250	36.0	450	11.0	137
+			+		+
λ_3	300	26.6	80	41.0	123
Total			530		260

Note: The intensities of λ_2 and λ_3 can be adjusted to produce the same number of absorptions in both the L and the M systems as does λ_1.
Source: Cornsweet (1970, p. 165).

[3] The numbers of quanta for the two wavelengths to be combined provide the unknowns. The total number of isomerizations produced by the test stimulus in one of the systems (M or L respectively) provides the right-hand term for each equation. The left side of each equation, containing the unknowns, is the sum of isomerizations produced in the given system by the two combined wavelengths. With curves as shown in Fig. 2.9, one can find a solution whenever the wavelength of the test stimulus falls between those of the reference wavelengths. To avoid negative solutions, one reference wavelength must have a higher M : L ratio than the test stimulus, and the other must have a lower one. If the test stimulus falls outside the 'gamut' of the two reference stimuli, to get a match one must mix some quantity of one of the reference wavelengths with the test stimulus. This corresponds algebraically to a negative term on the reference side of the equation.

reference wavelengths allow us to avoid negative solutions, a physical match can be produced. As seen in the bottom row of the table, when we sum the effects of λ_2 and λ_3 on M and L, we get the same physical effect on the two systems as produced by λ_1 alone.

The principles of mixing and matching wavelength combinations are much more easily understood when put in the form of Fig. 2.10. This is the *wavelength mixture space* for the dichromat whose transducer absorption curves were displayed in Fig. 2.8.

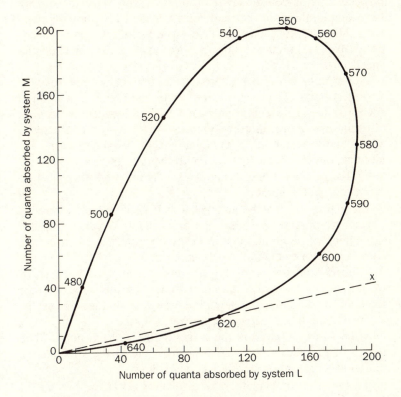

FIG. 2.10. Dichromatic wavelength mixture space

Note: Axes give the number of absorptions in systems M and L. The curved line is the *spectral locus*, showing the effects on M and L of 1000 quanta of monochromatic light at various wavelengths (labelled in nanometres). Point x marks the effects of 2000 quanta of monochromatic light of 620 nm.

Source: From Cornsweet (1970, p. 176). Reprinted by permission of Harcourt Brace Jovanovich, Inc.

A wavelength mixture space has as axes the number of absorptions of quanta in the two systems. The curved line is a *spectral locus*, showing the number of absorptions in the M and L systems for spectral wavelengths ranging from 400 to 680 nm. Its construction is straightforward; we take each wavelength in turn, find the absorption rates for that wavelength for the M and L systems, multiply those rates by some fixed number of photons (here 1000), and finally use the two resulting numbers—absorptions of photons in the M and L systems respectively—as coordinates to plot the given wavelength. So, for example, the point labelled '620' will yield 100 absorptions in L and about 21 in M. We get a closed curve for our locus because both absorption curves fall to zero at the extremes of the spectrum.

A wavelength mixture space is the first of several sorts of perceptual 'space' to be considered in this monograph. A point in such a space represents a particular effect on receptor systems; differing points are differing effects. Wavelength mixture space allows one to predict which combinations of wavelengths will have identical effects on receptors. The remainder of this section will detail the principles underlying this prediction, and some of their extensions and limitations.

Predicting a match among wavelength combinations in wavelength mixture space is a matter of adding *vectors*. Consider the effect of doubling the intensity of some monochromatic stimulus, as for example the 620 nm point in Fig. 2.10. Since the wavelength composition of the stimulus is unchanged, the ratio of M absorptions to L absorptions must remain the same. Hence the point representing the new stimulus will lie on the same vector as the 620 nm point, but will be further from the origin. In fact, it must lie twice as far from the origin as the 620 nm point. The length of the vector represents the intensity of the stimulus; its direction represents wavelength composition.

To find the total number of absorptions occurring in the M system in response to a combination of wavelengths, one simply sums the absorptions produced by each component. The same technique works for the L system (see Fig. 2.11). Point *C*, our test stimulus, represents a monochromatic stimulus of 1576 photons at 560 nm incident at the retina. (The locus represents stimuli of 1000 photons incident at the retina, and the test stimulus is outside the locus, since it is more intense.) As shown at the bottom, this stimulus can be matched by mixing λ_a (2100 photons at 515 nm) with λ_b (1166 photons at 615 nm). Using the absorption rates from before, the match can be predicted algebraically as shown in Table 2.4. Vector addition represents this match much more easily, and is equivalent to the algebraic formulation.

Clearly, point C can be reached by indefinitely many vector sums, each corresponding to some combination of wavelengths. It follows that the test stimulus can be matched by indefinitely many different combinations of wavelengths. The existence of such *metamers* refutes the idea that a given colour can be identified with light of a particular wavelength. Because each of those combinations can be shown to be equivalent to the test stimulus, one can 'reduce' even very complicated combinations of wavelengths—those needing a full spectrum to depict—to a single equivalent vector.

TABLE 2.4. Algebraic predictions of a match

Wave-length (nm)	Quanta incident (count)	Per cent absorbed by M	Quanta absorbed by M	Per cent absorbed by L	Quanta absorbed by L
560	1576	19.7	310	16.5	260
515 +	2100	13.1	275 +	5.7	120 +
615	1166	3.0	35	12.0	140
Total			310		260

Note: The combination of wavelengths in the second and third rows will match the stimulus in the first row, producing the same number of absorptions in both the L and the M systems.

Some examples of different combinations of wavelengths that match one another are shown in Fig. 2.12. Although these combinations differ physically, they can be shown to have equivalent effects on receptor systems, using the principles outlined here.

Adjusting the relative intensities of just two reference wavelengths such as λ_a and λ_b can yield a match for any wavelength between them. This principle explains why a dichromat (with only two distinct cone systems operative) can match most colours by adjusting only two reference wavelengths. The same principles underlie the reproduction of colours in printing and on film. One can reduce complicated spectra to a single equivalent vector. By adjusting relative intensities of two or three colours—vectors within mixture space—one can match any colour within the volume defined by those vectors. It is therefore possible to reproduce naturally occurring colours with just a few inks or colour filters (see Cornsweet 1970, pp. 182–7).

Finally, some laws of colour mixing fall out immediately. Let the equality sign stand for matching, and all the rules of algebra emerge in the new domain. The resulting laws are known as *Grassman's laws* (Boynton 1979, p. 112; Kaufman 1974, p. 162). For example, mixing matched pairs yields a (new) matching pair. Algebraically, if $A = B$ and $C = D$, then $A + C = B + D$. If we have a match ($A = B + C$), then doubling the intensity of each component yields a new match ($2A = 2B + 2C$). If two combinations of wavelengths match one another ($A + B = C + D$), then adding the same stimulus to both will yield a new match ($A + B + E = C + D + E$). All these laws can be explained in terms of wavelength mixture space: they are all instances of vector addition or multiplication. Indeed, once we represent the effect of a given stimulus by the numbers of isomerizations produced in each receptor system, Grassman's laws are no longer merely analogies to algebraic laws. One can interpret addition as vector addition, and equality as vector equality. Each point in a (dichromatic) wavelength mixture space is a sum of vectors $k_1M + k_2L$, where M and L are vectors representing the two receptor systems, and k_1 and k_2 are weights.

The same principles apply to the normal three-dimensional wavelength mixture space as to the dichromat's two-dimensional space. We simply add a third system, S, which is most sensitive to much shorter wavelengths than are M or L. The addition of a

---

Fig. 2.11. Vector addition in wavelength mixture space

Note: Point *C* is a stimulus of 1576 photons with a wavelength of 560 nm. The top panel shows how *C* can be matched by combining light of 515 and 615 nm; the vector lengths give the required intensities. The lower panel shows how *C* can be matched by a mixture of lights of three different wavelengths.

Source: Derived from Cornsweet (1970, p. 181). Reprinted by permission of Harcourt Brace Jovanovich, Inc.

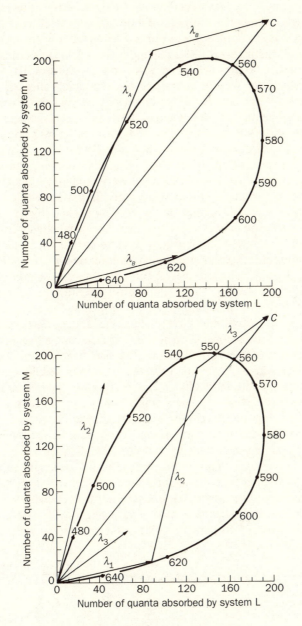

FIG. 2.11. Vector addition in wavelength mixture space

third system gives wavelength mixture space three dimensions; our vectors acquire a third coordinate. The projection in the S dimension is small, however, given the relative insensitivity of that system. Combinations of wavelengths can again be analysed as vector sums, and they will match any stimulus represented by that sum. The rules for colour mixing and matching all carry over unchanged. One can see why a person with normal vision must be allowed to adjust the intensity of *three* independent reference wavelengths to match all colours. Any two vectors will only allow matches on the plane defined by those vectors.[4]

Wavelength mixture space can in principle provide quantified predictions of which combinations of wavelengths will match one another. In practice there are some limitations. For one, predictions generalize only under conditions like those in the laboratory. Stimuli must occupy a small visual angle (usually around 2°). Larger stimuli have other effects that upset matches, and additional explanatory principles are needed (see Evans 1974). The task must be carried out with a neutral surround and with the observer in a state of neutral adaptation. Coloured surrounds have induction effects and simultaneous colour contrast effects that can alter matches (Hurvich 1981, p. 295). Finally, predictions for colour mixing and matching all rely on the precise form of the absorption spectra for receptors, and these differ slightly from individual to individual. In principle, one can take those additional effects into account, and generalize predictions of what matches what; the point is simply that wavelength mixture space on its own does not suffice.

Still, we should here flag a remarkable scientific achievement: if we know the absorption spectra for receptors of a particular individual, we can quantify that individual's wavelength mixture space and predict exactly which combinations of wavelengths that individual will find to match under laboratory conditions. In principle, one can determine exactly how much of one stimulus to mix with a second to match a third—and do this for matches of any complexity.

Wavelength mixture space also can help to explain the phenomena of colour adaptation mentioned above. The effect of

---

[4] This explains why reference wavelengths must be chosen so that no possible adjustment in intensities of two of them will match the third. If the third can be matched in that way, it lies on the same plane as the other two reference wavelengths.

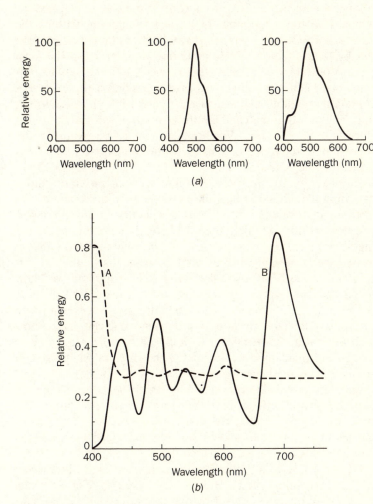

FIG. 2.12. Metameric matches

(*a*) For a particular observer, each of the three wavelength distributions shown will produce a sensation of a *unique* green—one that is not at all yellowish and not at all bluish.

Source: From Hurvich (1981, p. 78). Reprinted with permission of Sinauer Associates.

(*b*) Two spectra, *A* and *B*, that will match for a particular observer.

Source: From Wyszecki and Stiles (1967, p. 351). *Color Science*. Copyright © 1967 by John Wiley & Sons. Reprinted by permission of John Wiley & Sons, Inc.

prolonged activation of a given cone system is to depress its sensitivity to further stimulation. Such stimulation flattens the entire absorption spectrum, as if one had multiplied absorption rates by some fraction. Such multiplication is precisely the form of the Von Kries coefficient law, named after the nineteenth-century German physiologist who first considered the effects of adaptation on colour matches (see Hurvich 1981, ch. 15). Within limits, any pair that matched before adaptation will match after it (Hurvich 1981, p. 207). Furthermore, if one can estimate the proportionate reduction of sensitivity due to adaptation, one can predict the hue shift that results.

Consider, for example, the eye-blink demonstration of colour adaptation mentioned in Section 2.2.3. Adaptation of one eye to a red stimulus causes reds to look less saturated and greens to look more saturated than in the other eye. In adapting to red, the long-wave receptor system is most dramatically affected (since it absorbs the largest number of photons from that stimulus), but the other two systems also adapt somewhat. Suppose we knew the coefficients expressing the loss in sensitivity for all three systems in the adapted eye. The loss flattens wavelength mixture space in a predictable fashion. For example, one can predict how much less saturated a red patch would have to be when viewed through the unadapted eye to match the original patch as seen through the adapted eye.

Some individual differences among trichromats are similar to colour adaptation effects, resembling an overall reduction in the sensitivity of one or another of the cone systems. The colour matches made by such 'anomalous' observers can be predicted quantitatively (see Hurvich 1981, ch. 16).

A given hue is, to a first approximation, associated with a given ratio of absorptions in the three cone systems. For example, across a wide range of intensities, one sees yellow hues if one's M, L, and S systems are active at a ratio of about $98:40:1$. This ratio defines a straight line proceeding from the origin, and along that line in wavelength mixture space one finds the yellows. At higher intensities there is some deviation from the rule, but hues are approximately constant across changes in intensity.[5]

---

[5] Receptor output is not exactly logarithmic with respect to intensity. Instead, the best fitting equation (derived from the molecular dynamics of bleaching and regeneration of the photopigment) is that activation is proportionate to $k_i I/(I + k_j)$,

How can we explain sensitivity to equivalent ratios among the various receptor systems? While synaptic inhibition can be considered a sort of subtraction, division is a bit beyond the capabilities of a single neurone. But a combination of processes can yield a ratio. Recall that receptor activity is roughly proportionate to the logarithm of stimulus intensity. Equal increments in receptor activity derive from equal multiples of intensity, not equal sums. Subtraction of logarithms is equivalent to division. To explain neural sensitivity to ratios of intensities, we need merely to recall that, initially, neural outputs are roughly proportional to the logarithm of intensity. By subtracting one such output from another—following that first stage with a second in which there are inhibitory connections between systems—we obtain division. There is considerable evidence that early vision works just this way (see Cornsweet 1970, p. 246).

2.5 Discrimination and Information

Suppose one shows that two stimuli have identical effects on particular cells in a sensory system. The second step of the explanation is to show that such identity of effects ensures that the two stimuli are indiscriminable. To do this, we must first define 'indiscriminable', consider its experimental determination, then ask what sorts of inferences one can make from discrimination data. The ultimate goal is to define the relation of qualitative identity in terms of indiscriminability, and this achievement will rest on a complicated pattern of inference involving discriminability, encoding, information, and sensory appearances.

2.5.1 Indiscriminability

A given thing can be encountered on multiple occasions, and during them can present distinct appearances. Different presentations of a given thing are distinguished temporally; each occurs but once. The notion of a *stimulus* is allied to (but not quite the same as) that of a presentation of a thing. First, stimuli require some causal impact on one or another sensory

where I is the intensity and the k are constants. The deviation between this function and a logarithmic function can explain the curvatures in the colour loci in wavelength mixture space (Cornsweet 1970, pp. 254–6).

transducer.[6] If on a given occasion an object did not affect any of the sensory systems of a subject, then no presentation of the thing occurred, and consequently no stimulus was to be had. Furthermore, 'thing' in this context is applied quite broadly; it is not restricted to medium-sized dry goods, but can include any physical phenomenon one likes—the luminous flux from an instrument, a diffraction grating, virtual image, or whatever. With these provisos, our initial understanding of a *stimulus* is: a presentation of some thing to a subject that affects some sensory transducer of the subject.

One must distinguish the *proximal* stimulus—whatever events occur at sensory transducers because of the presentation of the thing—from the *distal* stimulus, or 'thing' (broadly construed) that caused those events. A second distinction concerns the counting criteria for stimuli. Can one encounter the same stimulus twice? Sometimes a 'stimulus' is a single datable occasion, counted in the same way as presentations; and sometimes it is applied to an entire class or type of occasion. If one can present the 'same' stimulus twice, one is using the latter notion. Physics often provides the individuating criteria for distinct classes of presentations. For example, one might specify a stimulus to be electromagnetic radiation of a certain wavelength and intensity, atmospheric compression waves of a particular frequency and pressure, gases with various chemical components at differing concentrations, and so on. Then to present the 'same' 450 nm light stimulus to a subject means to present another instance of that *class* of presentation.[7] Sometimes type criteria for

[6] Sometimes an even more restrictive criterion is employed: the presentation must have effects to which the organism can make a discriminative response. Many effects that things have on transducers would fail this test. The more restrictive criterion is difficult to apply, since, to establish whether an organism can make a discriminative response to a given effect, one needs to make multiple trials; and how can one be sure those effects are constant over trials? No harm is done by broadening the definition and allowing *any* effect on transducers to suffice.

[7] Note that one cannot control the wavelength of every photon in the packet, and so a second presentation of the 'same' 450 nm stimulus will differ somewhat from the first in its wavelength composition. Even in purely physical parameters, 'same stimulus' is defined statistically. Furthermore, conditions in the cornea, lens, and vitreous humour of the eye change, altering the numbers of quanta reaching the retina on different occasions. Receptor conditions vary over time in an unknown fashion. Finally, the absorption of photons by receptors is ultimately a quantal phenomenon. In theory we would like a stimulus to be a class of nomically similar transducer events; in practice one can only get a statistical approximation of that goal.

presentations are not explicitly physical, but rest on presupposed criteria of identity for whatever 'thing' provides the distal stimulus. For example, one might treat a standard colour chip in the *Munsell Book of Colour* as a stimulus; the various presentations of that patch are treated as a single class because they are all presentations of the 'same' thing. The latter notion is scientifically the least useful. Ideally, our stimulus classes would be classes of transducer events that share some nomically significant similarity, and there is no guarantee that differing presentations of a given thing will produce such a class. To treat a stimulus as the class of presentations of one 'thing' also presupposes an ability to identify and individuate those 'things' coherently. Some have denied the coherence of our purported identity criteria for 'things'.

If we could understand the relation of qualitative identity, we could understand sensory qualities. Our goal is to explicate that relation in terms of some equivalence relation such as 'match' or 'appear the same'. The best candidate is the technical relation 'indiscriminable', holding for subject S between classes of stimuli x and y when S cannot discriminate between x and y.

Indiscriminability is a failure to discriminate. The term does not mean 'matches' or 'looks the same'. The fact that a person avers, after casual or even scrupulous inspection, that x and y 'look the same' does not suffice to justify application of the term. The subject may insist the two stimuli look the same even if, in some context, that subject could somehow discriminate—pick up some difference—between them. 'Match' is closer in meaning, but fails to imply that the subject is utterly unable to differentiate between stimuli in classes x and y.

Indiscriminability relates classes of stimuli. The criteria used to identify a class of stimuli are deliberately left unspecified. In psychophysics one typically uses physical terms—wavelength spectra combined with careful specification of ambient lighting, subject adaptation, and so on. But one can be much cruder, and identify classes of stimuli by their distal cause. Classes x and y might be specified simply as presentations of two distinct objects (probably under specified conditions C). Then the two objects are indiscriminable under conditions C for a subject S if S cannot discriminate between the classes of presentations of the two objects.

How does one assess indiscriminability? One method uses a forced-choice task. Label one stimulus the 'target', and present target and non-target simultaneously, randomly altering the placement of target from left to right. Ask the subject to identify the target each time. If, over sufficient trials, the subject identifies the target no better than randomly, then the two stimuli are indiscriminable for the subject. If the subject can pick the target at a better than chance level, then he or she can discriminate the two stimuli. Some information about their differences must somehow be accessible to the subject. That he or she loudly insists they look the same does not preclude this possibility. To say that the subject cannot discriminate between the two patches means that discrimination between them is at the chance level, so that no difference between the patches can be identified.

While indiscriminability applies only to classes of stimuli, matching can apply to particular occasions. This logical feature helps differentiate the two relations. On a particular occasion one might be presented with two objects. Scrutiny of their appearances on that occasion will establish whether they match. But no single choice suffices to show that a subject can *discriminate* between two stimuli. A single miss does not show that the subject cannot tell the two things apart. To discriminate is to demonstrate a statistically reliable identification over trials. Indiscriminability is revealed only by a random distribution of responses.

Why do we need a statistical definition? Consider some everyday examples of matching judgements over repeated trials. One might try to match various paint mixtures, or to match a sample of a previously painted surface with samples of new paints. At the optometrist's one may need to judge which of two lens prescriptions gives one better vision. At an audio store one might attempt to detect differences between various pairs of speakers.

All these tasks become more difficult as the differences between presentations decrease. Oddly enough, confidence in one's judgement diminishes as the stimuli get closer to matching. We find increasing variability in the matching judgements. For example, if you have no access to the labels of the paint chips, sometimes you will judge one to be brighter than the other, sometimes not. As the optometrist narrows the search for an optimal prescription, he or she will begin repeating trials with various pairs. Eventually the differences between lenses shrink to the point that your preferences for one lens over the other seem to become increasingly random. Sometimes one lens will be judged best, but equally often the other will. If matching judgements show such variability, how can one pick the matching paint, the sharper lens, or the better speaker? One must employ statistical inference, even in one's own case. If over a series the distribution of hits is random, the two items are indiscriminable. This finding is consistent with a long series of loud, confident judgements, provided the verdicts vary. Our customer, patient, or subject may even be a partisan of the incorrigibility of the mental. Indiscriminability is demonstrated not by a particular judgement that two things match, but by a random distribution.

Discriminability and matching can be dissociated in a second way. Often subjects can identify the target class at a greater than chance level even though on most occasions they avow that both 'look the same' or 'match'. Statistically reliable identification is possible even if on each particular trial the subject claims to be merely guessing.[8] To such a subject it may seem that the two presentations are identical, and that the choice of a target is purely a guess; yet those 'guesses' track the target in a statistically reliable way. Identification at a greater than chance level shows that the subject can discriminate between them.

The number of trials needed to assess discriminability is readily computed. Once one stipulates the size of the difference required for a distribution to be considered 'significantly' different from a random one, and the degree of confidence one would like to have in the verdict, the question is statistical. Can one confidently reject the hypothesis that the choices do not differ significantly from a random distribution? Using standard equations, one can compute the probability of correctly accepting the hypothesis that the stimuli are indiscriminable, given a distribution that is actually random. The sample size will determine the confidence one can have in the verdict. Indiscriminability is indiscriminability-at-a-confidence-level, and is inherently statistical in conception. Given stipulated significance and confidence levels, the size of sample required can be calculated.

[8] See Marcel (1983a, 1983b). Marcel reports that subjects in these experiments tend to think the task is ludicrous, and get rather annoyed at the experimenter for asking them to identify invisible stimuli.

Discriminability is a purely physical notion. The term can immediately be admitted into physicalist vocabulary. Its import is just that a particular statistical relation obtains among classes of stimulus events and choices.

Some philosophers are apt to scoff at the use of 'discriminable' (or 'match') as the central predicate of a theory of sensory qualities. 'Such a predicate merely provides a characterization of *behaviour*', they are likely to say. 'It has no logical relation to the character of internal states involved in perception. I can imagine a machine that makes just the discriminations I do, but whose internal states have no qualitative character at all. So discriminability does not license any inferences concerning the character of inner perceptual states.'

Whatever the outcome of this thought experiment, here a narrow ruling on its logic suffices for our current purposes. One cannot infer from this experiment that no inferences are possible from discrimination data to sensory qualities. Discrimination data license powerful inferences concerning those inner states. I will show that there is a connection between discriminability and the qualitative character of sense impressions, although it proceeds indirectly, and relies on some inferences derived from information theory.

2.5.2 *An Information-Theoretic View*

To apply any of the terms of information theory, one must first specify the relevant *ensembles*. An ensemble is just a class of events. An event *per se* carries no information: one must group events into ensembles and describe the relations between ensembles. Showing that one event causes another does not license the inference that the cause is 'encoded' or 'registered' by the effect (see Dretske 1981, pp. 33–5). Instead, one must specify the range of potential alternatives: the class or ensemble of effects other than the one that occurred, and the class or ensemble of other causes of the given effect. To ascribe information content to any event, one must group events into classes, organize those classes of events into ensembles, and finally specify the various cause–effect paths between them.

The fundamental idea of the mathematical theory of information is to treat information as that which reduces uncertainty, and to measure reduction of uncertainty by the probability of the given event. In any ensemble the probability of an event determines the 'amount' of information it carries. It bears an inverse relation to the probability of the event.[9] Highly probable events are not particularly surprising when they occur and they do not much reduce one's uncertainty over which event would occur, and so they have low information content. Improbable events have high information content.

What does it mean to say that one event 'encodes' or 'registers' the occurrence of another event? One must first specify an input ensemble and an output ensemble. For a channel to exist between the two ensembles, occurrence of events in one must reduce one's uncertainty concerning events in the other. Reduction of uncertainty will again be measured in terms of probabilities, although here we are dealing with contingent probabilities: the probabilities of particular 'output' events y_j given that 'input' events x_i occurred.

If information transmits perfectly, each class of inputs is associated with just one class of outputs. All the conditional probabilities $p(y|x)$ (the probabilities of y, given x) are either zero or one (see Dretske 1981, pp. 12–26). The information contained in the output ensemble is exactly that of the input ensemble, and any event will reduce uncertainty about both ensembles to just the same degree. We can then say without reservation that a particular output event encodes the particular input event with which its contingent probability is one.

Perfect transmission provides the paradigm for talk of codes. Most transmission is sadly imperfect. 'Noise' exists in the channel if any of the contingent probabilities departs from zero or one. In a noisy channel, occurrence of a given output does not eliminate the uncertainty concerning which input event occurred. One sort of input is still the most likely, but since the contingent probability is not unity, other possibilities arise.

With perfect transmission, the amount of information flowing across the channel is equal to the amount in either ensemble. Suppose the input ensemble consists of stimuli, and the output ensemble consists of neural events. Adding noise makes the neural events ambiguous. The uncertainty added is a function of

---

[9] If the probability of the event is p, the amount of information associated with its occurrence is the logarithm (to the base 2) of $1/p$. Logarithms are used for their handy mathematical properties.

the extent to which the various conditional probabilities depart from zero or one.[10]

For a channel to exist, the two ensembles must be linked by both causal and informational relations. Causal connections alone do not suffice. Consider stimuli as an input ensemble and neural events as output. One might find that occurrence of a particular neural event in no way reduces uncertainty concerning the input ensemble. For stimuli x and neural event y, the conditional probabilities $p(x|y)$ may render y so equivocal as to be useless. To justify the 'encoding' or 'registering' idiom, we must exclude this possibility. We can talk meaningfully of neural events 'encoding' stimuli only if the conditional probabilities linking neural events to stimuli depart markedly from a random distribution.

2.5.3 Discriminability and Information

Consider discrimination as a problem in information transmission. This perspective will enable us to complete the explanation of why stimuli that have identical effects on retinal ganglion cells are indiscriminable.

Consider stimuli x_i and x_j the input ensemble, and choice behaviours ('target left' v. 'target right') the output. Now if x_i and x_j are discriminable, then the distribution of choices differs in a statistically significant way from a random distribution. One finds a higher contingent probability that the target is on the left, given the choice 'target left', than that it is on the right. That contingent probability is also higher than the a priori or unconditional probability that the target is on the left.[11] Hence the choice behaviour signals the input, and a channel exists between event ensembles. The system retains information concerning the difference between x_i and x_j and manifests that retention in its behaviour.

It is, alas, easy to lose information. Suppose at some stage y the effects of a stimulus x_i are identical with those of another stimulus x_j. Events at that stage could then no longer signal any

---

[10] One sums for all x and all y the factor $p(x) \cdot p(y|x) \cdot \log(1/p(y|x))$. The loss due to noise also can be expressed in terms of the conditional probabilities $p(x|y)$ (see Pierce 1961, pp. 150–5).

[11] If the choice distribution is not random, then there is a statistically significant relation between target presentation and choice; consequently, non-zero contingent probabilities must link events in the two ensembles.

difference between x_i and x_j. In effect, the output events for x_i and for x_j collapse into one class, and the conditional probabilities $p(x_i|y)$ and $p(x_j|y)$ become equal. Subsequent neural events can never reliably regain the information lost (see Cornsweet 1970, p. 180). This eventuality does not imply that a guess will always fail. Suppose that an announcement is to be made of the first-place and second-place winners. Our microphone always garbles proper names, however, and they always come out sounding like 'Bob'. One might still succeed sometimes in naming the winner. Over the long run, however, one's success would be no better than guessing.

To discriminate, one must retain information about differences. If one can complete an identification task at a better than chance level, then information (in the technical sense of the word) concerning the differences between stimulus events is somehow available.[12] If information concerning the differences between stimulus events is available to the subject, then at no stage can the differences between their effects disappear. So we get:

(P₁) If stimulus events x_i and x_j can be discriminated, then at no stage of visual processing do effects of x_i and x_j share all properties.

To show that identical effects on retinal ganglion cells ensure indiscriminability, all that remains is to show that those effects form a 'stage' of visual processing. Talk of 'stages' and 'processing' should not be invested with cognitivist assumptions; if one likes, the terms can be translated into the spare idiom of ensembles and conditional probabilities. One needs to show that states of the cells form an intermediary ensemble in an informational cascade.

Suppose we are dealing with states Q of cells C. The simplest way to show that they form an ensemble is to establish some principle of the form:

(P₂) All subsequent visual information is causally dependent on states Q of cells C.

This is easy to show for retinal ganglion cells. Those cells *form* the optic nerve. Nothing that happens in the retina will affect

---

[12] If identification proceeds at a better than chance level, then some members of the output ensemble must have strong conditional probability relations with some input events. We would have an informational link between the two ensembles; see Dretske (1981, pp. 23–6); Sayre (1976, pp. 26–30).

subsequent developments unless it affects the ganglion cells. They form an informational choke-point, a funnel through which all visual information must flow. Although those cells form a very early stage of the visual system, a confusion there is permanent.

Perhaps the need to establish something like (P₂) accounts for the fact that so many perceptual effects are explained by citing features found very early in sensory processing. As one advances from the periphery, it becomes more difficult to establish anything like (P₂) for the candidates under consideration. Oddly enough, the closer we can stay to the retina, the more confident we can feel about explanations of perceptual effects. (P₂) also helps to clarify what sort of partial identity of effects is sufficient. We might for example be concerned only with hue discriminations, or only with the ability to distinguish sweet from sour tastes. In such cases the stimulus classes forming the input ensemble and the behaviours forming the output ensemble will be restricted accordingly. States Q in cells C form a 'stage' of processing if they satisfy (P₂) for those ensembles.

This completes the first and second stages of explaining why edge enhancement effects appear in Chevreul's array. We first saw how a uniform strip in the array and a 'scalloped' strip have identical effects on retinal ganglion cells, and then how such an identity of effects ensures that the two are indiscriminable. We have also completed an answer to the first main objection lodged in Section 2.3 against explaining looks: that the relation between retinal ganglion cells and indiscriminability is inexplicable. The account just presented provides at least one way in which it *could* be explained.

3

Matching and Qualitative Identity

A successful explanation of why two stimuli are indiscriminable seems to say nothing about how either of them *looks*. The third stage in our explanatory schema (Section 2.3) is to show how indiscriminability ensures identity of qualitative contents, and a few minutes of philosophical reflection seem to prove a priori that the project is impossible. It seems easy to imagine a robot that has all our discriminative responses but no qualia, so it seems impossible to capture qualitative content by appealing to facts about discriminations. Even if the initial steps in an explanation of sensory qualities were successful, we seem here to run into an insurmountable roadblock.

This chapter will show how the roadblock can be avoided. It is true that a particular qualitative content—such as the smell of lilacs—cannot be defined directly in terms of particular discriminations. It does not follow that there is no relation between the concepts. Progress can be made if one forgoes a direct assault on particular qualitative contents, and instead concentrates on the relation that obtains between two sensory episodes when they are qualitatively identical. I will detail the connections between matching, indiscriminability, and qualitative content, and show how the relation of qualitative identity can be derived from indiscriminability. This leaves other philosophical objections on the road ahead, but at least it will complete the third stage of our explanation of 'looks'.

3.1 Qualitative Identity

It seems easy and natural to rank sensory experiences by their qualitative similarities. The odour of lilacs is like that of a rose, but relatively unlike that of garlic, ammonia, or petroleum. The limit of this resemblance is an exact *qualitative identity*, which holds just in case two sensory states share all qualitative characteristics. The qualitative content of experiencing one would then be the same as the qualitative content of experiencing the other.

Qualitative identity is connected to discriminability. To explicate the connection, it will help to revert to *matching*. Recall that matching obtains between single presentations, while indiscriminability relates classes of presentations. Is qualitative identity nothing more than matching?

One bar to identifying the relations is that they have distinct domains. Things (or better: stimuli) match, but only the internal sensory states caused by such stimulation are or are not qualitatively identical. The problem is readily solved: one can propose simply that

(1)   Two sensory states are qualitatively identical if and only if the stimuli that cause them match.

This gives a necessary and sufficient condition for qualitative identity in terms of matching. The necessary condition for qualitative identity is unobjectionable:

(N)   If two sensory states are qualitatively identical, then the two stimuli that cause them match.

If two stimuli fail to match, they do not look (or feel, or seem) the same to the subject, and so do not present identical qualia to that subject. To accept (1), then, we need merely to establish the converse of (N):

(S)   If two stimuli match, then the sensory state caused by one is qualitatively identical with the sensory state caused by the other.

Unfortunately, as shown by Goodman (1977), principle (S) must be rejected. One reason is technical. Qualitative identity is presumably a transitive relation, so that if x is qualitatively identical with y, and y is qualitatively identical with z, then x must be qualitatively identical with z. However, as many forebears recognized (Hume 1739, bk. I, pt. I, s. I; Russell 1914, p. 141), and Goodman (1977, p. 196) emphasized, matching is non-transitive. One can find stimuli x, y, and z where x matches y, y matches z, yet x fails to match z.

Colour gradations provide classic examples. A swath of hues

can appear to be continuous, in the sense that any two points sufficiently close to one another will match. Yet points more widely separated do not match. In Hume's words, "tis possible, by the continual gradation of shades, to run a colour insensibly into what is most remote from it' (1739, bk. I, pt. I, s. I). The 'insensible gradation' is that neighbours match. So the matching of x and y, and of y and z, fails to establish the matching of x and z. Non-transitivity is not confined to colour perception: it is found in any sensory modality in which some non-zero differences elude detection.

Two differences below threshold may sum to one above threshold. If qualitative identity is transitive, but matching is non-transitive, then the first relation cannot be identical with the second. Matching will not provide a sufficient condition for qualitative identity, and principle (S) must be revised.

In such demonstrations one must ensure that x, y, and z each name just one presentation, since otherwise one fails to show that matching is non-transitive. If one presents the pairs of colour patches successively (x with y, then y with z, and finally x with z), then those variables range over things (or perhaps distal stimuli), not presentations. The x that can be presented twice is a colour *patch*; a presentation makes an appearance only once. To test matching, presentations must be simultaneous.

With this proviso, it becomes more difficult to demonstrate the non-transitivity of matching. It is difficult, for example, to judge whether three visual items match without fixating them successively. Even if one could make the comparisons of x to y and y to z fixating each item only once, the final comparison (of x to z) calls for a second glimpse. But a second glimpse is impossible if x is a singular, datable presentation. Further difficulties arise from the variability in matching judgements. Suppose Sally is trying to match a chip of her house paint with samples in a store. She finds first that her chip matches some x from one vendor, then that it matches some y from another, and finally that x does not match y. We might claim that her chip could not have matched x, since her chip matches something (y) that x does not. Several authors have cited such phenomena to argue that matching colours cannot be treated as non-identical (see Peacocke 1981, p. 134; Travis 1985, p. 356). Frank Jackson has argued on similar grounds that it is *logically impossible* to present simultaneously a trio of colours A, B, C such that one is 'unable to tell' A from B and B from C although one 'can tell' A from C (Jackson 1977a, p. 114).

Perhaps the colour of a single presentation is indeterminate simply because one cannot precisely ascertain its colour without making a multitude of matching judgements, and one cannot make a multitude of matching judgements concerning the same presentation. These difficulties provide ample reason to move to the relation of indiscriminability. After all, the stimulus *class* is naturally more salient to us than the ephemeral presentation. One would naturally say that, when Sally matches her paint chip against one vendor's sample, and then later against the other, she has compared the same thing to two samples. To capture this sense, our variables must range over classes of presentations.

Non-transitivity is a feature of indiscriminability just as it is of matching. For the former it can be established in a non-problematic way. For example, we can find colour chips x and y that an observer cannot tell apart with any better success than would be had by guessing. We may find the same for chips y and z, but not for the pair x and z. It is implausible to argue that the latter finding shows that x and y must be discriminable. Our hapless subject simply cannot manage to discriminate the two.

Non-transitivity demonstrates that some indiscriminable stimuli nevertheless have distinct effects, and that those effects can make a difference. If indiscriminability ensured an identity of effects, then chips x and y would have identical effects within the visual system, as would chips x and z. One would conclude that x and z should be indiscriminable. Since they *can* be discriminated, indiscriminability does not guarantee identity of effects. Two presentations can have distinct qualitative contents although the distal stimuli are indiscriminable.

How is indiscriminability connected to qualitative identity? Principle (N) emerges unscathed:

(N) If two sensory states are qualitatively identical, then the stimuli that cause them are indiscriminable.

Its converse is:

(S) If two distal stimuli are indiscriminable, then the sensory state caused by one is qualitatively identical with the sensory state caused by the other.

This again fails, for the same reasons it failed for matching. The indiscriminability of two stimuli does not suffice to show that they present the observer with identical qualia (see Goodman 1977, p. 196). Principle (S) must be revised. Peacocke (1981, p. 134) suggested one revision. If we find a third stimulus indiscriminable from exactly one member of a pair of stimuli, we can conclude that the members of that pair are qualitatively distinct. We employ a principle of the following form:

(N_2) If the sensory state caused by one distal stimulus is qualitatively identical with the sensory state caused by another, then there is no third distal stimulus indiscriminable from one of those stimuli but not the other.

Qualitative identity guarantees that two sensory states do not have any qualitative differences, even ones that might be found below whatever threshold would make the two stimuli discriminable.

A candidate for a sufficient condition is the converse of (N_2):

(S_2) If there is no distal stimulus that is indiscriminable from exactly one member of a pair of distal stimuli, then the sensory state caused by one member of the pair is qualitatively identical with the sensory state caused by the other.

One must demonstrate what I called *global* indiscriminability (in Section 2.3; see Jackson 1977a, p. 114, and Linsky 1984, p. 366). Not only are the two distal stimuli indiscriminable from one another, but no discrimination task suffices to distinguish them: no result from any sort of matching or discrimination task holds for one but not the other. (S_2) states that global indiscriminability suffices for qualitative identity.

Principle (S_2) resembles Goodman's definition for identity of qualia in *The Structure of Appearance* (1977); they differ only because the primitive terms do. 'Quale' and 'qualia' are for Goodman qualities, not concreta; the atoms in his system are colours, times, visual-field places, and other non-visual qualia (1977, p. 139). For Goodman a quale is a repeatable and recognizable element in various presentations (p. 97). In a system which uses presentations as atoms, his 'matching qualia' would need to be reconstrued to refer to something like indiscriminable classes of presentations. With these various transmutations in mind, Goodman's discussion is entirely acceptable:

> Although two qualia q and r exactly match, there may be a third quale s that matches one but not the other. Thus matching qualia are not always identical. Now this is somewhat paradoxical; for since qualia are phenomenal individuals we can hardly say that apparently identical qualia can be objectively distinct. Offhand, it seems that color qualia, for example, that look the same must be the same. Yet if we say that q is identical with r because the two match, then we shall have to say that q does and does not match s. Must we then deny after all that the appearance of identity is a sufficient condition for the identity of appearances, and try to explain how a difference between phenomena can be nonphenomenal? Actually, the fact that some matching qualia are distinct can be accounted for without going beyond appearance; we need only recognize that two qualia are identical *if and only if they match all the same qualia.* Although distinct qualia must indeed be phenomenally distinct, to say they are phenomenally distinct is to say not that they fail to match but that there is some quale that is matched by one but not by the other. (Goodman 1977, p. 196)

This strategy is not unique to Goodman. Russell adopted it as well in his *Inquiry into Meaning and Truth* (1940, ch. 6).

Why does global indiscriminability suffice for qualitative identity? Goodman suggests one reason in the passage quoted above. If global indiscriminability does not suffice for qualitative identity, then some further condition must be added to (S_2). What could it be? (S_2) already contains all the information one could extract from all possible matches among items. To require some further test for qualitative identity seems, in Goodman's words, to 'try to explain how a difference between phenomena can be nonphenomenal' (1977, p. 196). Such a test would make distinctions between sensory qualities rest on non-qualitative facts. To make such distinctions, one may need to refer to some large portion of the corpus of matching judgements, but the entire corpus should exhaust all the distinctions possible. Suppose that even after employing judgements drawn from the entire corpus of matching data, one cannot defeat the claim that two items are qualitatively identical. It is hard to believe that there is some further court to which one could appeal. It is especially difficult to believe that there could remain some *qualitative* difference between the items.

Consider the position of someone who denies that global indiscriminability suffices for qualitative identity. Call the objector Ned. Ned admits that he cannot discriminate one item from another, but insists that one of them presents a quale distinct from that of the other. He simply knows, directly, that the two differ qualitatively, although his behaviour over multiple trials does not support the claim that he can discriminate the two.

Suppose the two items are wines, and Ned claims that their tastes are qualitatively distinct although indiscriminable. According to Ned one of them has a superior bouquet. Now if the two are indiscriminable, then Ned's identification of which of the wines has a superior bouquet varies from trial to trial, and the distribution of his choices is statistically indistinguishable from a random distribution. One might think that this finding would immediately defeat Ned's claim that the two are qualitatively distinct. It would certainly deflate his pretensions to be a wine-taster. Someone who claims to know the difference between beeches and elms ought to be able to identify which is which, and a random distribution of identifications would be taken to defeat the claim that the person knows any such thing.

Ned might respond that, even though the sequence of trials shows a random distribution of identifications, during each trial just one of the wines clearly and distinctly presents that particular bouquet. He simply invokes the *ad hoc* hypothesis that over the sequence of trials that quale shifts its affiliation from wine to wine in a random fashion, accounting for his seemingly random identifications. There is no immediate disproof of this hypothesis. It merely complicates any possible account of sensory qualities. We would give up the principle that, unless there is some relevant change in circumstances, the same distal stimulus presented twice will present the same qualia twice. We also would give up the principle that citing such changes in circumstances (sensory adaptation, say) can sometimes explain why the sensory qualia change. Ned might respond that a complex theory is needed to account for the facts of sensory awareness.

A second line of response to the objection is more compelling. To establish qualitative identity we must demonstrate not merely pairwise indiscriminability, but global indiscriminability. In our example this would imply that no third wine is discriminable from just one of the two. If the two are globally indiscriminable, then the contents of a third glass—no matter what they are—will be discriminable from one if and only if they are discriminable from the other.

Ned asserts that although the two wines are globally

indiscriminable they present distinct qualia. Suppose he picks one of the wines as having a superior bouquet. Fill the third glass with that same wine. There is no coherent description of the result. First, take the counterintuitive possibility that the contents of the third glass will somehow be discriminable from its source—the 'superior' member of the original pair. By global indiscriminability the wine in the third glass must be discriminable from the other, 'inferior' member of the pair. But since the members of the pair were indiscriminable from one another, we get the result that the 'inferior' wine both is and is not discriminable from the 'superior' one.

The other more intuitive possibility is that Ned finds the contents of the third glass to be indiscriminable from (and qualitatively identical with) its source—that is, to the 'superior' member of the original pair. By global indiscriminability, the contents of the third glass must then be indiscriminable from the 'inferior' wine as well. We get the result that the taste of the wine in the third glass is qualitatively identical with *some* wines with which it is indiscriminable (e.g. its source) but not with others. Since the original two were indiscriminable, Ned cannot reliably identify with which one the third is qualitatively identical and with which it is not. In short, the taste of the wine in the third glass is claimed to be qualitatively distinct from one but not both of the wines with which it is indiscriminable, even though no one can reliably distinguish those two wines from one another. As Goodman charged, such a claim indeed elevates differences between sensory qualities into some non-qualitative—and unnamed—realm. Far from being intuitively obvious, this stance is less credible than the definition it is designed to attack, and provides no good reason for discarding the definition of qualitative identity provided by global indiscriminability.

3.2 Methodological Solipsism

The claim that qualitative identity of sensory states can be defined in terms of global indiscriminability of stimuli derives support from a version of methodological solipsism.[1] Suppose you wish to

---

[1] I mean it in the sense given in Carnap's *Logische Aufbau der Welt* (see Carnap 1967, s. 64). Jerry Fodor (1980) has a different version of methodological solipsism, although the notions share some family resemblances.

catalogue your sensory qualities. The method will be *solipsistic* if you make no presumption that others experience the same qualities and if you disallow any methodological rule that would require such an assumption. Furthermore, the method will be similar to Carnap's in that

we do not make a distinction between experiences which subsequent constructions allow us to differentiate into perceptions, hallucinations, dreams, etc. . . . . At the beginning of the system, the experiences must simply be taken as they occur. (Carnap 1967, p. 101)

The only resources allowed are those available to a psychophysically sophisticated introspective subject. How might one proceed?

Let us suppose that our psychophysically sophisticated solipsist has access to laboratory instruments that enable her to generate and replicate classes of stimuli. One would hope to find instruments that at a given setting reliably produce instances of indiscriminable stimuli. Changing the settings sufficiently would generate a discriminable stimulus. Since a complicated packet of different wavelengths can be matched by a single three-element vector in wavelength mixture space, for example, our solipsist might use a colorimeter with three adjustments for the reference wavelengths. Furthermore, at least some of these instruments can produce stimuli that match those found outside the lab. We might find that, for any paint chip viewed under appropriate conditions, there is some setting of the instrument that produces a stimulus indiscriminable from the chip.

We can in principle construct such instruments for any sensory modality in which we understand what constitutes the relevant identity of effects on transducers and in which we can replicate those effects. Colour-matching and non-chromatic intensity arrays have earlier served as examples; similar feats are possible in audition, and some replication of indiscriminable classes of stimuli has been achieved in taste and smell. Such instruments make it far easier to continue the introspective investigation into sensory qualities, since with them our solipsist can transcend the fleeting and irreplicable qualities of experiences outside the lab, and systematically explore the relations between qualities of now replicable stimuli.

Our solipsist will savour many sorts of differences between those stimuli that fail to match. Presumably each difference shows at least one sensory quality presented in one episode but not the other. To cope with all these differences, one requires an enormous number of matching judgements, in all different modalities. All the resemblances and similarities within and between modalities can be explored. Our solipsist finds that identical instrument settings lead to some variation in her matching judgements, and so, being psychophysically sophisticated, she moves to a statistically based notion of indiscriminability.

One cannot directly define a particular sensory quality—such as the apparent colour of a rose—in terms of matching judgements. Although some instrument setting could (at least in principle) yield a stimulus indiscriminable from the colour of the rose, the quality of that colour cannot be defined by those settings. Those instrument settings identify a class of stimuli that have identical effects on transducers. Although such an identification is related to the qualitative character of the sensory state caused by the stimulus, it does not define or describe that qualitative character. Our solipsist must first frame a definition for qualitative identity, and then use the latter definition to define particular qualities.

How would our solipsist frame identity criteria for the sensory qualities of her experience? They could be framed in terms of discriminability. If two switch settings produce stimuli that she could discriminate, then there is some difference in the sensory qualities of the engendered experiences, and so those experiences are not qualitatively identical. This is principle (N). Those stimuli will not *seem* the same to her; what it is like to be a solipsist experiencing one of them differs from what it is like to be a solipsist experiencing the other. We can know they differ, even if we do not know the qualitative character of either one.

Furthermore, suppose our solipsist discovers two switch settings that produce stimuli that are pairwise indiscriminable and are either both discriminable or both indiscriminable from all other stimuli. Then there is no qualitative evidence that would prevent her from concluding that the two switch settings yield experiences without any difference in their sensory qualities, or in short that the experiences are qualitatively identical. This is principle (S). So it seems that, no matter what it is like to be our solipsist, we would know that what it is like to be our solipsist sensing stimuli produced at one setting is just the same as what it is like to be our solipsist sensing stimuli produced at the other. No difference between the two ever shows up in any matching task.

Take your own putatively private qualia: if two stimuli do not match, then the experience of one is not qualitatively identical with the experience of the other; and if the sensory experiences of two stimuli are qualitatively identical, then there is no third stimulus that matches one but not the other. What sense of similarity could overrule these principles? One never has the same qualitative content crossing discrimination lines, or different contents indiscriminable from all the same points.

So far we have merely said what it is for two experiences to have the same qualitative character; we have said nothing about what that character is. Nevertheless, the foray into methodological solipsism has reinforced the idea of defining qualitative identity in terms of indiscriminability. This methodological perspective will continue to prove useful through the end of the next chapter, and I will continue to assume that the goal is to describe the qualitative character of a single subject's experiences. Only in Chapter 6 will the first intersubjective comparisons be made.

3.3 Cascading into the Brain

We have now answered the second major objection lodged in Section 2.3 against our explanation of 'looks'—namely, that there is no connection between indiscriminability and qualitative identity. Suppose we show that the grey strip within Chevreul's array and a scalloped strip have identical effects on retinal ganglion cells, and that all visual information is causally dependent on states of those cells. Since both strips have identical effects on that early stage of visual processing, no third stimulus could be indiscriminable from one but not the other, and so the two are globally indiscriminable. According to the argument in the previous two sections, the sensory state caused by one is therefore qualitatively identical with the sensory state caused by the other. So the sensory state caused by the solid grey strip within Chevreul's array is qualitatively identical with the sensory state caused by the scalloped strip.

A short step lands us at the conclusion of our explanation. The scalloped strip in question *is* scalloped, and it *looks* scalloped. Since the sensory state caused by the grey strip is qualitatively identical with that of the scalloped strip, the grey strip also will look scalloped. QED.

This denouement is likely to seem perfunctory, incomplete, and unsatisfying. In effect, we have 'explained' why something seems to have a particular quality by showing how the sensory state it causes is qualitatively identical with the sensory state caused by something that is perceived to have that quality. We fail to describe what that qualitative character is. We also seem to be explaining the qualitative character of sensory states without defining exactly what 'sensory states' are. Instead, we mention only states of retinal ganglion cells.

This latter problem reiterates the third objection raised in Section 2.3: that the explanation seems to commit us to the (absurd) view that cells in the retina instantiate sensations of brightness. A fuller response to that objection can now be given. One demonstrates identity of effects at the retinal ganglion level because states of those cells form one ensemble in the channel between stimuli and behaviour. Demonstrating identity of effects at any such ensemble will suffice to demonstrate indiscriminability. One is not committed thereby to the claim that sensations *are* those states. Presumably it takes more than four synapses to engender experiences; they will be found much later in the cascade.

The objection does raise the legitimate question of how one might locate sensory states within this cascade. Where are the states that have qualitative character, if not in the retinal ganglion cells? If we wish to explain the qualitative character of sensory states, it seems we must identify the sensory states, and specify which of their properties are qualitative properties. Both tasks are difficult, since no current models make it their ambition to describe the qualitative content of sensory experience. What sort of psychological model could capture qualia? In contrast to some philosophers mentioned in Chapter 1, I believe that something useful can be said in response to this question, and that one can describe some global features of the landscape within which qualia are likely to be located. I will start by listing several characteristics of qualia, without presuming that they are definitive. Only after the characterization is much fuller will I consider whether anything that satisfies it is a sensory quality.

3.3.1 *Encoding*

Our stratagem is to follow the cascade of information ensembles beyond the retina into the brain. The channel between stimuli and response in a perceptual discrimination task is a real channel, not a correlational fluke. Discriminations are enduring and reflect the law-like behaviour of the subject's sensory systems. States and processes in the system can therefore be identified as elements of intermediary informational ensembles.

Events in ensembles are grouped into types that are mutually exclusive and jointly exhaustive. The member events have many properties other than those that lead to the grouping, but those other properties do not contribute to the job of transmitting information. In Morse code, for instance, the property that groups events into ensemble types is the duration of the signal; the voltages (or the size of the light, the colour of the light, the frequency of the sound, and so on) are irrelevant. The properties that sort events into the various types in an ensemble will be called *indicator properties*. They are the ones that carry the news.

As mentioned above (Section 2.5.2), the first step in pursuing information is to identify the relevant input and output ensembles. Different choices of ensembles give very different results for entropy, equivocation, information transmission, and so on. The same applies to indicator properties. Here, different choices of ensembles yield different pictures of which properties of internal states of the system bear information, and of how much information they bear. Consider the sequences of voltage changes along a telegraph line. If one groups the sequences into Morse code for various letters of English, each sequence reduces equivocation over a possible ensemble of 26 letters, 10 digits, and various punctuation marks. The amount of information transmitted then gives a measure of the redundancy of English. If one groups the sequences into an ensemble of proper names—the winners of the latest election, for example, given the list of candidates—one will have a very different reduction in uncertainty. The amount of information transmitted depends on the choice of ensembles (see Dretske 1981, pp. 61–2).

To 'follow the cascade' into the brain, one must do two things.

First, one must identify ensembles and show that knowing what happens in one reduces uncertainty about events in the other. Second, one must show that the reduction of uncertainty is law-like and not merely coincidental. (On this latter requirement see Dretske 1981, pp. 74–7.) Sensory systems satisfy both requirements. Events in retinal rods, for example, are related to later events in retinal bipolar cells by generalizable functions, and thence to events in retinal ganglion cells. At each stage there is some function, determined by the biophysics of the cells, mapping earlier events to subsequent ones.

I shall call the function mapping stimulus events to properties of subsequent internal states an *encoding* function. The term carries no anatomical connotations. We do not require the function always to be subserved by the same biological structures.

3.3.2 *Sensory States as an Ensemble*

Sensory states and their qualitative properties will presumably be located somewhere along the channel between stimulus and discriminative response. Differences in sensations allow one to discriminate things. Qualia are properties of sensory states, and if you ask 'which properties?' the immediate answer is that they are properties that enable you to discern differences in stimuli. They convey news about contrasts encountered at the periphery. That is one function that sensory qualia serve. To locate qualia we need to identify states that can do that job—that make it possible for you to detect differences among the things you encounter.

The idea that some but not all properties of a signal bear information can help to explain one odd feature of sensory qualities. Materialists hope to identify sensory qualities with some physical properties of internal states. For example, things sometimes look green to a subject in virtue of the subject having sensory states with a particular qualitative character. Those states may ultimately be identified with some pattern of spiking frequencies in specific pathways. But characterizing the state as a pattern of spiking frequencies in specific pathways does not characterize the qualitative character of the state. Its qualitative character is that *things look green*, not that specific spiking frequencies occur. How can this be explained? I suggest that it reflects the fact that qualia are indicator properties for ensembles defined in a particular way. The qualitative 'content' of the given state is that this thing looks like leaves and grass (i.e. other green things), not that it is spiking frequency x rather than y. Just as in the Morse code example, the informational properties assigned to the sequence of voltages over the wire change dramatically when one redefines the relevant ensemble. No feature of those voltages intrinsically conveys information concerning the recent elections. Similarly, there need be nothing intrinsic to the physical properties underlying sensation that identifies some of them as qualitative properties. They are qualitative properties because they carry information about ensembles of discriminated stimuli.

3.3.3 *Indiscriminability and Encoding*

If at some stage the indicator properties of encodings of two stimuli are identical, then the two stimuli will be indiscriminable: the system will lose its grip on their distinctness. It follows that, if two stimuli are discriminable, the indicator properties of the effects of one must at all stages differ from those of the other. This is an information-theoretic version of principle (P_1) of Section 2.5.3.

Indiscriminability is non-transitive. Even if two stimuli are pairwise indiscriminable, their effects may have distinct indicator properties at every stage of the channel. Indiscriminability is not co-extensive with identity of properties of encodings at some stage of processing. The presence of identical encodings is a sufficient condition for indiscriminability, but not a necessary condition. At best, pairwise indiscriminability shows something of the following form:

(P_3) If two stimuli cannot be discriminated from one another, then effects of the two stimuli within the visual system share all properties whose absence would make the stimuli discriminable.

Inability to discriminate does not imply that processing proceeds identically, but merely that the differences between the effects are less than those required to make the pair discriminable. The stimuli may still be *globally* discriminable; the two may be encoded differently. The difference may be too slight to allow one to discriminate one stimulus from the other, but it may be sufficient to allow one to discriminate some third stimulus from exactly one member of the pair.

3.3.4 *Which Properties are Discriminated?*

We are left with the problem of defining the *sufficient* conditions
for discriminability. Such a definition is very hard to provide. It
will not do to claim that every difference in the effects of two
discriminable stimuli will ensure their discriminability. Many
characteristics of those effects are not relevant to the
discriminability of the stimuli that cause them, play no role in the
information transmission involved in discriminations, and are not
indicator properties. Similarly, as argued earlier (Section 1.2),
many properties of sensations are not qualitative properties.

Many differences between differing stimuli will not be
discriminated differences, and so will have no bearing on whether
the stimuli match. Asking 'Which of the differences between
sensations are sufficient to ensure the discriminability of the
stimuli that cause those sensations?' is hence related to the
question, 'Which of the differences between stimuli are
discriminable differences?' Only those differences between
stimuli that lead to differences among the qualitative properties of
sensation will be discriminable ones. In effect, we need some way
to pick out which properties of a stimulus are discriminated
properties.

3.3.5 *The Differentiator*

The answer to the last query cannot be a priori. Which properties
are discriminated depends on what does the discriminating. To
discriminate is to compare. At some stage of processing there
must be a 'discriminal process'[2] or 'differentiator' that has the job
of comparing encodings. I will use the label 'differentiator' for
whatever parts of the system carry out this job. Some differences
between encodings are sufficient to distinguish the respective
stimuli; others are not. Properties of encodings that are
sometimes sufficient to reject a match and assure discriminability
of the respective stimuli will be called *differentiative* properties.
They are the ones that determine the issue: the critical ones on
which an 'aye' or 'nay' depends. I will also call them differentiative 'attributes' or 'features' of encodings. They are the ones
that can make a difference to discriminations.

---

[2] The term derives from Thurstone (1927). See also Torgerson (1958, pp. 156–8).
It should not be taken to imply a single, fixed, central location, or to imply the other
properties of what Dennett (1991) rightly castigates as the 'Cartesian Theatre'.

Consider a matching task. Stimuli S_1 and S_2 both set off a train of internal events. Some attributes of those events bear information, and some do not. Somewhere along the channel a match/no-match decision is reached. The discriminal process compares some attributes and not others. If the differentiator were a homunculus, the differentiative properties would be the features of signals received from the outside world that he examines before issuing a verdict in a discrimination task. A match is rejected if the differentiator finds a sufficient difference among the differentiative features of the codes; otherwise the match is accepted. What counts as a 'sufficient' difference can vary from occasion to occasion. In different circumstances the criterion for a match can be set at different levels; but in principle one can ascertain what that criterion is.[3]

In a particular modality, the differentiator might be sensitive to (say) three differentiative attributes. If encodings of two stimuli differ sufficiently in any one of those three attributes, the stimuli are discriminable; otherwise not. Clearly, such pairwise discriminability does not guarantee *global* indiscriminability for the two stimuli. Some third stimulus might be encoded so that it differs significantly from just one member of the pair, showing that the first two are not qualitatively identical.

Examples of differentiative properties are the hue, saturation, and brightness of colours; the pitch and intensity of tones; and the sweetness and saltiness of tastes. Sensory states can differ in each such attribute independently of the others. A differentiative property is a respect in which encodings can differ that renders the stimuli discriminable. Two colour patches matched in hue and saturation may differ in brightness, and that difference will ensure their discriminability. Brightness is a respect in virtue of which colour patches are (sometimes) discriminable. It is therefore one dimension of the assessment made by the differentiator. 'Same colour' applied to colour patches is co-extensive with 'same hue, same saturation, *and* same brightness'; a difference in any one of these three features suffices to defeat a

---

[3] One can use signal detection theory to derive what is called a 'receiver operating characteristic' (ROC) curve. The criterion I have in mind is d'—the separation (in standard deviations) of the two distributions that best fits the observed false positive and false negative rate (see Welford 1968, ch. 1; Hardin 1988, ch. 3). There is no fixed homunculus, but, at best, multiple series of evanescent homunculus-stages, whose locations, job descriptions and tastes may change from moment to moment.

match. This identity holds only for colour patches presented in a laboratory under controlled viewing conditions to observers in a neutral state of adaptation. If we allow luminance variations, depth cues, and temporal effects, additional dimensions of discriminability are introduced.

It is best to think of the differentiative features of encodings as *gamuts* or *ranges of variation*. Terms such as 'hue', 'saturation', and 'brightness' are ambiguous: sometimes one uses them to name a particular instance of the feature in question, and sometimes to name the gamut of different instances. Consider two colour patches matched in saturation and brightness but differing in hue. In the first sense we might say the two patches have two hues. In the second sense we might say the two patches differ in just one property, namely their hue. If we say simply that the two 'differ in hue', we treat 'hue' as a range of variation that has diverse instances. A differentiative feature of encodings is best construed in that manner: it is a range of variation over multiple instances.

Each sensory modality has some finite number of distinct ranges of variation among encodings that can make a difference to discriminations. We can discover their number. Suppose we have some tentative list of the different 'dimensions' along which encodings in that modality vary. Our list is incomplete if two things can appear the same in all those respects, yet present differing appearances (and so be discriminable). In that case we must add an additional dimension along which encodings can differ. If we add some aspect to the list that does not vary independently of all the others, then our list of the differentiative attributes in that modality is redundant. The list is correct if it is neither redundant nor incomplete.

For example, our sensations of surface colour must have at least three distinct differentiative attributes because patches matched in hue and saturation can differ in brightness, patches matched in saturation and brightness can differ in hue, and so on. (Note that here we treat a differentiative attribute as a range of variation, since there are many different hues, but we treat the entire range as just one differentiative attribute.) To show that hue, saturation, and brightness are the only qualitative dimensions of surface colour, we must show that any two colour patches that match in all three are globally indiscriminable.

If a difference between encodings is sufficiently salient to engage the differentiator, then the information that transducer events are distinct is retained, and the stimuli can be discriminated. Two transducer events are indiscriminable if and only if their respective internal encodings share all properties whose absence would make the events discriminable. To say that two codes are identical in all respects to which the differentiator is sensitive is to say something stronger, namely that the stimuli engendering each are indiscriminable from the same *class* of stimuli.

The differentiative attributes of encodings are those that, if fully shared by two encodings, ensure that their respective stimuli are globally indiscriminable. If two encodings diverge in some differentiative attribute, their respective stimuli are globally discriminable: some stimulus will be discriminable from one stimulus but not the other. Let us suppose that u is an encoding of some stimulus x, and v is one of y. Attribute P is a differentiative attribute of u just in case there is a v such that a difference between u and v in P is by itself sufficient to ensure the discriminability of the stimuli u and v encode. One way to capture the force of P being by itself sufficient to ensure discriminability is to show that u and v match in all properties Q other than P that can assure discriminability among any stimuli. So P is a differentiative attribute of u if and only if there are stimuli x, y, and encoding v such that:

1.   encodings u and v differ in P;
2.   that failure is sufficient to make their respective stimuli discriminable; and
3.   that mismatch alone suffices to make those stimuli discriminable, since u and v match in all other properties Q that would suffice for the discriminability of their respective stimuli.

Using 'P is differentiative' to abbreviate those three conditions, our minimal theory of discrimination is as follows:

1.   If x and y are pairwise indiscriminable, then their encodings match in all differentiative attributes that if not matched would suffice to make x and y discriminable.
2.   If their encodings match in all differentiative attributes (not merely those that would make x and y discriminable, but all of them), then x and y are globally indiscriminable.

Neither condition is a logical truth, since both relate properties of encodings to the discriminability of stimuli. But the first is a truism, while the second is not. If two stimuli match, then nothing happened that would have prevented that match. But condition 2 is no truism. The absence of a guarantee of discriminability does not guarantee indiscriminability.

The analysis is thoroughly circular unless one can somehow identify the differentiative attributes. We need a means of identifying such attributes that does not rely on their being sufficient for discrimination. Surprisingly enough, such a means can be found, and will be described in the next chapter.

3.3.6 *A Home for Qualia*

If sensory qualia are to be located and identified within any psychological theory, it will be a theory of discrimination. Such theories have some analogue of internal *discriminanda*—states that encode stimulus classes and whose features determine the outcome of discrimination tasks. To explain why some events are sensed as being similar and others are not, one postulates internal machinery that classifies transducer events. Its encoding functions throw away information concerning some physical differences of stimuli while retaining others. Differences between codes are at some stage assessed, and a match is either accepted or rejected. The attributes of codes to which that assessment is sensitive are the 'differentiative' attributes. I suggest they are also *sensory qualia*.

Qualia are properties that enable one to discern similarities and differences among stimuli. They engage discriminations. Items identically encoded yield qualitatively identical presentations, and differences at that stage occasion differences in qualia. Qualia play the same role in explanations of visual discrimination as do differentiative attributes. Principles relating sameness and difference of qualia to discriminations are precisely the ones applying as well to differentiative attributes.

First, suppose that u presents the same qualitative content as v, so that u and v are qualitatively identical. Then the stimulus encoded by u will be globally indiscriminable from the stimulus encoded by v, and so u and v share their differentiative attributes. Suppose, conversely, that u and v do not present the same qualitative content. Then either the stimuli that cause them are pairwise discriminable, or there is some stimulus discriminable from one but not the other. In either case, u and v then have distinct differentiative attributes. In short, identity of differentiative attributes mirrors Goodman's definition of identity of qualia (1977, p. 196), and yields the notion of qualitative identity developed above.

4
Quality Space

4.1 Identifying Differentiative Properties

Efforts thus far have yielded an ability in principle to predict which classes of stimuli a given subject will find to be indiscriminable, and hence which pairs of stimuli the subject will find to be qualitatively identical. Of course, there are various practical limitations on this ability. For one, we cannot make such predictions for all varieties of stimuli, but only for particular, limited domains. In predicting matches among chromatic stimuli, for example, we might be limited to those occupying a 2° foveal angle and presented under rigidly controlled laboratory conditions.   Furthermore, such predictions may require such precise and inaccessible information on a given individual that they are difficult or impossible to complete. For example, to predict the exact colour matches an individual will make, one needs the spectral absorption curves for the three kinds of colour-sensitive receptors in that individual's retina. While one can approximate those curves using other techniques, direct measurement of them is extremely difficult.

In spite of the contrariety of nature, proceeds from this approach have been impressive. At least in some stimulus domains, we can predict which pairs of stimuli a given subject will find to present qualitatively identical sensory experiences. Colorimetry is the measurement and prediction of colour stimuli that match, and it has had noteworthy success. We can measure many of the factors that bear on the discriminability of stimulus domains, and construct mathematical models that predict matching with a fair degree of success. Much of the progress in the empirical study of perception since the mid-nineteenth century could be detailed under this rubric. While qualia may still prove elusive, *qualitative identity* is increasingly within our grasp.

Does knowledge of qualitative identity tell us anything about qualia? To explain perceptual effects, we show how a stimulus presents the same qualitative content as some paradigm object, and conclude that, since the paradigm appears to have a particular quality, the given stimulus appears to have that quality as well. The complaint is that such an approach does not explain why the given stimulus presents the particular quality that it does: it merely explains why the given stimulus presents the same quality as the paradigm. It does not explain the phenomenal properties of the given stimulus in terms of non-phenomenal properties. If we simply assume that the paradigm appears to have that quality, the explanation is vacuous, since that assumption employs precisely the sort of qualitative character-ization we would like to explain. We must explain why the paradigm presents the appearance that it does.

If we wish to elucidate the nature of the qualitative contents associated with sense impressions, we must propose an analysis of the different ways in which one experience can be qualitatively similar to or dissimilar from another. But thus far our resources are limited to a list of those pairs of stimuli a subject finds to match or not match. Presumably there are many different ways in which sensations can serve to distinguish things. These different 'respects' are the differentiative properties. They jointly deter-mine the outcome of discriminations; a significant difference in just one is sufficient to reject a match.

The problem remains of how to *identify* the differentiative attributes in a given domain. While it is a truism to say that there are characteristic properties to which the mechanisms of discrimination are sensitive, it is not trivial to identify those properties. The 'differentiator' is not sensitive to some properties because they are differentiative properties: instead, some properties are differentiative properties simply because the mechanisms of discrimination are sensitive to them.

We need some way to identify the attributes to which the differentiator is sensitive. Our data comprise classes of presenta-tions at the input end and discriminative responses at the output end. In intermediary ensembles there are encodings with many properties. Among them are the differentiative properties: the ones on the basis of which the match/no-match judgement is made. Yet all we have available is a long 'pair list' of those

presentations that the subject judged to match or not.[1] How can
we identify the grounds on which the judgements were made?

A deliciously dangerous way to put the problem is as follows.
Suppose some instance of the differentiator really were a little
man in your head—a homunculus—whose job is to render a
decision in a particular discrimination task. When he receives a
job order, he pays attention to *some* features of the codes he
receives from the outside world, but not to others. How could we
determine which features he uses to carry out his job?

We do not need to *define* differentiative properties in terms of
pair lists.   Such definitions would require a thoroughgoing
behaviourism about such qualities. We must though have the
wherewithal to *identify* such properties. We must be able to do
this to avoid circularity in the analysis given in Chapter 3. To
show two stimuli discriminable, it suffices to show that encodings
of those stimuli fail to share some differentiative property.
Differentiative properties were then identified as those properties
sometimes alone sufficient for discriminability.   To avoid
circularity, we need to provide some independent characterization
of   those   properties   that   determine   the   outcome   of
discriminations—the 'differentiative' properties of sensory
encodings.

The final reason why we need some means of identifying those
features to which discriminations are sensitive dates back to a
classic article by J. J. C. Smart (1959). Smart defended an early
version of the view that sensations are identical with states of the
brain. Critics objected that ordinary talk of sensations seems to
ascribe to them properties that are not properties of states of the
brain. For example, 'yellow orange' might be the colour of one's
after-image, but is certainly not the colour of a brain state. To
avoid positing phenomenal properties, Smart proposed to analyse
'I have a yellow orange after-image' as 'Something is going on in
me which is like what goes on when I see an orange.' Critics
charged that this analysis was insufficiently specific (Cornman
1962). It is true that the victim of an after-image has something
going on which is like what goes on when seeing an orange. The
problem is that seeing an orange is also like what goes on when
seeing a basketball (i.e. something round). How can one specify

---

[1] 'Pair list' is Carnap's term (see his 1967, s. 12). For a psychometrician, a pair
list is a *raw data set*.

that one means similarity with respect to colour and not with respect to shape? It seems that the only way to do this is to specify the phenomenal property with respect to which similarity is to be judged; and so one fails to avoid positing phenomenal properties.

The physicalist has traditionally attempted to define sensory qualities in terms of similarities. Critics object that any attempt to define sensory qualities in terms of similarities between internal processes is circular, requiring the use of sensory qualities to specify the different ways in which such processes are similar or dissimilar. A major task of this chapter is to show how a definition of sensory qualities can avoid such circularity; how, that is, one can specify the way in which two experiences might be like one another without presupposing the notion of sensory qualities.

4.2   Order from Indiscriminability

Surprisingly enough, these various desiderata can be satisfied. Techniques exist that can isolate the number of differentiative features found in a given modality and identify those features in terms of matching data. These techniques have all been developed since the first publication of Nelson Goodman's *Structure of Appearance* (in 1951), and all share the same basic analytical strategy developed in the latter part of that book. The key idea is to use *matching* to construct an *order*.[2] The various differentiative features are dimensions of that order. A *space* is just a multidimensional order, and so for each sensory modality we will have a distinct *quality space*. A phenomenal property is a *location* within such a space.

So much for preview. The argument to establish all these claims will occupy the remainder of this chapter, parts of Chapter 5, and Chapter 6.

An order consists of a set and a relation that orders that set. The relation must have special properties if it is to order the set, and relations with different properties generate different sorts of orders. Suppose the relation is *R*, so *Rab* means '*a* stands in relation *R* to *b*'. Perhaps the fundamental property required to generate an order is that the relation be transitive, so that if *Rab*

2 There are also some direct influences from Goodman to particular psychometric theorists; see, for example, Coombs' *Theory of Data* (1964).

and *Rbc* then *Rac*. The simplest sort of order is a linear series, requiring in addition only that the relation is irreflexive (no element bears *R* to itself) and connected (between any two members either *R* or the converse of *R* holds). The 'less-than' relation orders the natural numbers in a linear series. A slightly more complicated relation gives a *partial order*. In such an order the relation is again transitive; it is also reflexive (every element bears *R* to itself), and anti-symmetric (between any two distinct elements, *R* and the converse of *R* cannot both hold). The natural numbers form a partial order under the relation 'less-than-or-equal-to'. If the relation is also connected, it yields a *simple order*.

How do we generate order from indiscriminability (or in Goodman's (1972*a*) phrase, 'order from indifference')? Indiscriminability does not itself serve to generate an order, since it is non-transitive. Indiscriminability is analogous to a relation 'is not significantly different from' defined over distributions of rational numbers, where the numeric difference needed for a significant difference is statistically defined. Such a relation does not order the rationals: we need something like 'is greater than'.

We need to define a new relation that can order the stimuli. There are various ways to do this, but all of them use the partial and total *overlaps* between classes whose members are indiscriminable from each other. For example, in an analogy to Carnap's (1967) system, a *similarity circle* might be defined as a class of (distal) stimuli each of which is indiscriminable from all the others. Since indiscriminability is non-transitive, similarity circles will overlap. One might find stimuli *x* and *y* in one similarity circle, *y* and *z* in another, but *x* and *z* in distinct ones. So two similarity circles both contain *y*. One can then define qualities as classes not divided by any similarity circle, in which case *x* and *y* will not be members of the same quality. The chain of overlapping similarity circles will, in favourable conditions,[3] order the qualities.

An element overlapped by two similarity circles lies between them. 'Between' is ideal for generating a simple order. As Russell (1903, p. 210) puts it, 'To say that *y* is between *x* and *z* is equivalent to saying that there is some transitive asymmetrical relation which relates both *x* and *y*, and *y* and *z*.' If betwixtness

---

[3] Goodman (1977, ch. 5) has an acute analysis of the 'favourable' conditions required for Carnap's system to succeed.

can be defined, a relation that generates a simple order can be defined. We need a relation like 'less than or equal to' among the integers. The analogous notion among stimuli is to find a connected path of overlapping similarity circles from one to the other. Stimuli x and y stand in this relation if and only if x and y either are indiscriminable (hence in the same similarity circle) or are connected by a chain of similarity circles, every element of which is indiscriminable from its neighbour.

Roughly speaking, two similarity circles that are 'near' one another will overlap more than two circles that are far apart. More precisely, two similarity circles A and B are closer to one another than are A and C if the overlap between A and B is contained within the overlap of A and C.

Goodman's system (1977) starts from a different basis (his atoms are qualities and not concreta), employs different primitives ('match' instead of 'recollection of similarity'), and uses a different logical apparatus (a nominalistic calculus of individuals instead of set theory). Nevertheless, the strategy of construction is similar. To ascertain the order among qualities that match, one uses the overlap of those sums of individuals that match each. Goodman calls the sum of atoms that match x the *manor* of x. The overlap of manors determines the order of atoms. Suppose, for example, we have the following pair lists, showing for each individual the list of individuals it matches:

a:	a	b		
b:	a	b	c	
c:		b	c	d	
d:			c	d	e
e:				d	e

Intuitively, these five atoms are ordered in a linear array, just as they are listed. That intuition is vindicated by the overlapping of their manors. Individual c is between b and d, for example, because c matches both b and d, but b and d do not match one another.

Goodman showed how these pre-systematic intuitions can be developed into a complete theory for the ordering of linear arrays, using pair lists like the one above. That pair list is a 'regular' array, in which each atom matches the same number of others. The theory is not limited to regular arrays, but can cope with pair lists in which 'matching spans' are variable. It does not rely on the (faulty) principles that the distances between any two matching qualia are the same (Goodman 1977, p. 212), or that the distance from any quale to the first non-matching quale is a constant (p. 226).[4] Instead, the only principle Goodman employs to generate order from matching is

> no span between two non-matching qualia is enclosed in a span between two matching qualia; or more simply, that every quale between two matching qualia matches both. (Goodman 1977, p. 213)

Only if one desires a uniform distance measurement does one need the stronger principle that 'the span between any two matching qualia is less than the span between any two non-matching qualia' (Goodman 1977, p. 213).

Order emerges from overlapping as follows. Goodman first shows how to define 'y is between x and z' so that it works for central cases as well as odd ones such as atoms near the endpoints, irregular arrays, and even some nonlinear arrays. The resulting definition is complex: y is *between* x and z if and only if all three match one another, the sum of the atoms that match x or z but not both is greater than the sum of the atoms that match x or y but not both, and the sum of the atoms that match x or z but not both is greater than the sum of the atoms that match y or z but not both (Goodman 1977, p. 219). Again, the overlapping of manors defines betwixtness.

From betwixtness it is a short step to besideness. Individual y is beside x if y is between x and z and no w is between x and y. Once besideness is available, an order of one sort or another can always be constructed. Goodman remarks that besideness is an ordering relation (1972a, p. 424), but he does not provide details of how a series or partial order is constructed. Either is easy. For example, a transitive and irreflexive relation can be constructed from besideness: the relation 'has a non-looping path to'. This obtains between x and y if some power of besideness obtains between x and y (i.e. x beside y, or x beside z beside y, or x beside u beside v beside y, etc.) and none of the elements in that chain

---

[4] As Goodman notes, the latter derives from the hoary fallacy that a just noticeable difference represents some constant distance between qualities. Goodman shows that in some cases the relation of just noticeable difference is not even symmetric. The 'equality of just noticeable differences' has long since been replaced in psychometric circles by an 'equality of equally often noticed differences', but, as noted below, there are problems with the latter formulation also.

occur more than once.[5]   The non-looping path relation is irreflexive and transitive. If it is connected (as it must be if any two atoms are related by some power of besideness), then it puts the atoms in a *linear series*.[6]

For a partial ordering, we need a reflexive and anti-symmetric predicate. This too is easy to define, given besideness. One can define a segment as a pair of atoms beside one another (as they are represented in a graph). Some set of paths contains any given segment. Set inclusion among these sets of paths gives a partial ordering for the segments. The set of all paths containing a segment X is a subset of the set of all paths containing a segment X, so the relation is reflexive. If the set of all paths containing a segment X is a subset of the set of all paths containing a segment Y, and conversely, then $X = Y$, so the relation is anti-symmetric. Set inclusion is of course transitive, so we have a partial ordering. If some chain of besideness relations connects any two atoms, then each segment has some path to every segment. Set inclusion among the sets of paths will be a connected relation, yielding a simple order.

Once an order is constructed, the relative similarities among its elements will correspond to their relative 'distances' in the order. Atoms that are relatively similar will be relatively close to one another. One should not confuse this notion of *similarity* between atoms with the notion of *discriminability*. Similarity corresponds to distances within the order, and although discriminability is the foundation on which the order is constructed, the notions are distinct. For one thing, not all pairs of indiscriminable atoms are equally similar. In Goodman's terms, matching qualia may have varying numbers of distinct qualia between them. The number of besideness segments to get from one quale to a matching quale may vary at different parts of the order. Furthermore, pairs of discriminable atoms vary widely in their relative similarity. Many pairs might be equally discriminable but not equally dissimilar (see Goodman 1972*a*, p. 425). Finally, treating discriminability as

---

[5] The constructions for linear series (and partial ordering in the next paragraph) are mine, not Goodman's. Goodman nominalistically eschews the use of powers of a relation and of set inclusion, although nominalistic versions of both devices are available.

[6] Besideness will be connected if no proper subset of the atoms is such that each member matches only other members. In such a case the members will be isolated from the other atoms. If there is no such subset then all are connected.

a direct measure of similarity generates anomalies, a point recognized in contemporary psychometrics:

> Two equally discriminable stimulus pairs, where discriminability is taken as measured by a probability of correct detection of a difference, are not necessarily equally similar, and both the discriminability and similarity measures can be reliably and consistently different from each other. More precisely, in theoretical psychology, discriminability is a probability of not-confusing, whereas similarity is a number whose use need not follow the same axioms as a probability measure . . . (Gregson 1975, p. 9)

Goodman anticipated these points (1972*a*, p. 425).

One aspect of the distinction between discriminability and similarity creates some difficulties. Since discriminability is a statistical notion, it is modelled mathematically as if it were a continuous function. There is no absolute threshold above which items are always discriminable and below which they are never discriminable; instead, we find varying proportions of correct choices, and varying probabilities that the given distribution is non-random. Goodman's constructions apply only to finite sets, but in the domain of a continuous function no element is 'beside' another. (The field of such functions is always *dense*: between two elements there is always some distinct third element.)

Can constructions like Goodman's be applied if one thinks of qualities not as fixed points on a graph, but as statistical distributions? Goodman's solution to the variability of matching judgements is to stipulate some fixed proportion of choices as a criterion for matching:

> If the same stimuli are presented more than once under the same conditions, with some positive and some negative matching-responses, some arbitrary rule is adopted that counts qualities as matching if they are judged to match a stated percentage (say 51 percent) of the time. (Goodman 1972*a*, p. 425)

While this suffices to convert a distribution into a match/no-match dichotomy, it is worrisome that any amendment to one's 'arbitrary rule' can change the eventual order among the qualities. A construction that can directly cope with continuous functions might be preferable (though not of course to a nominalist!).

4.3 Multidimensional Orders

Still more information lies buried within the pair list. Not only can one determine which atoms lie between which by comparing the overlap of the sets that match each, but one can also determine whether just one differentiative feature suffices to generate the order, or, if more are required, how many are needed. This number emerges as the *dimensionality* of the order implicit in the pair list. That one can ascertain dimensionality from such meagre data is, at least initially, difficult to believe, and to show that the thing is possible I will work through some simple examples.

The previous example of a pair list yields a simple linear ordering:

a:	a	b			
b:	a	b	c		
c:		b	c	d	
d:			c	d	e
e:				d	e

Each manor of an atom includes its neighbours, and only includes atoms within the manors of those neighbours. If we abide by the rule that no non-matching pair is enclosed within a matching span, we are forced to a unique ordering, namely:

a   b   c   d   e

Now suppose our pair list is as follows:

a:	a	b				
b:	a	b	c			
c:		b	c	d	f	h
d:			c	d	e	
e:				d	e	
f:		c		f	g	
g:				f	g	
h:		c		h	i	
i:				h	i	

Items *a–e* are linearly ordered as before, but where does *f* belong? A moment's reflection will show that it cannot be placed anywhere within that linear order. Item *f* does not match *d*, and so it cannot be placed between *c* and *d*, since non-matching pairs (*f–d*) cannot be placed between a matching span (*c–d*). Nor can *f* be placed beyond *d* (that is, between *d* and *e*), since *d* and *e* match, while *d* and *f* do not. For similar reasons, *f* cannot fit between *b* and *c*, since it fails to match *b*; and it cannot go beyond *b*. In short, *f* cannot be placed within the linear order of the first five elements. The mere structure of the pair list forces us into a two-dimensional order, as follows:

$$
\begin{array}{ccccc}
 & & g & & \\
 & & f & & \\
a & b & c & d & e \\
 & & h & & \\
 & & i & &
\end{array}
$$

Not only does the overlapping of manors determine which atoms are between which, but it can also determine the dimensionality of the order. One is pushed into an additional dimension by the impossibility of fitting an atom into the order thus far developed.

The impetus to add a dimension can arise at any stage of the construction. We start by taking whatever atoms have a progression of overlapping manors, and generate a linear array. Some remaining elements presumably match some atoms in our linear array, as otherwise we would have at least two disjoint sets. We demonstrate that the element is not *co-linear* with the given array by showing that it matches just one atom in the line, but fails to match any atoms in the line that match that one. The fact that item *f* matches *c* but fails to match any of the items in the line that match *c* pushes *f* out of the linear array.

We can show a given atom is not co-planar with others using the same rule: show that it matches one atom in the plane, but fails to match any of the atoms in the plane that match that one. For example, suppose our pair list is as follows:

a:	*a*	*b*						
b:	*a*	*b*	*c*					
c:		*b*	*c*	*d*	*f*	*h*	*j*	*l*
d:			*c*	*d*	*e*			
e:				*d*	*e*			
f:			*c*		*f*	*g*		
g:					*f*	*g*		
h:			*c*			*h*	*i*	
i:						*h*	*i*	
j:			*c*				*j*	*k*
k:							*j*	*k*
l:			*c*				*l*	*m*
m:							*l*	*m*

We can show the new elements *j–m* are not co-planar with *a–i*. Again, *j* matches *c*, and it cannot be co-linear with *a* through *e*, since any such placement would create a non-matching pair within a matching span. For the same reason, it cannot lie between c and f or between c and h. It is ejected from both linear orders, and so lies in a new linear order, which (with provisos mentioned below) requires a third dimension. It is extruded from the plane; our order is at least three-dimensional.[7] This can be represented as follows:

```
            g       k
            f   j
    a   b   c   d   e
        l   h
    m       i
```

Here the m–l–c–j–k line should be thought of as orthogonal to the other two and extending off the plane of the page. Technically, the pair list as given does not prove that j is not co-planar with the nine points a–i, since it could lie on a diagonal on the same plane. Nevertheless, one can see in principle how the structure of a pair list could force one to a three-dimensional order. For example, if each of the four neighbours of c match one another—f and d, d and h, and so on—but j matches none of them, then j cannot lie in the same plane. We are forced into a new dimension by the need to avoid placing non-matching pairs between a pair that match.

A two-dimensional structure is revealed by matches that would be impossible if the structure were only one-dimensional. A three-dimensional structure is revealed by matches that would be impossible if the structure were two-dimensional. The definition of dimensionality is recursive. The pair list is at least $(n + 1)$-dimensional if there are matches inconsistent with its being n-dimensional. It has the dimension number M if it is no more than M-dimensional.

We see how a pair list can generate an order of similarities, a dimensional structure for that order, and a place for each element in the pair list. Some pair lists have a structure that yields this information. Thus far, it is unclear whether this information can be had from *all* pair lists; only one example has been provided in which the inferences succeed. There are different conditions within a pair list that can justify the same inferences.

---

[7] In this context 'line' and 'plane' should not be taken to refer to the familiar geometric entities, but as synonyms for one- and two-dimensional orders. These orders lack many of the properties associated with geometric lines and planes.

I will present one such set of conditions. Its rationale is that stimuli whose encodings share all differentiative properties should be indiscriminable. We attempt to construct an order, following the rule that no discriminable pair can be placed between an indiscriminable pair. A failure in constructing a one-dimensional order can arise as follows. Let *Ixy* mean '*x* is indiscriminable from *y*'. Suppose we have three stimuli such that *Ixy*, *Iyz*, and ~*Ixz*. Stimuli *x* and *z* are discriminable, and *y* is 'between' them. If encodings of these stimuli had but one differentiative property, then any stimulus *u* indiscriminable from both *x* and *z* would also be indiscriminable from *y*. (If *u* is 'between' *x* and *z*, then it must be indiscriminable from that point *y* which is indiscriminable from both. Otherwise its placement would violate our rule.) But with two dimensions, there could be some *u* indiscriminable from both *x* and *z* and discriminable from *y*. Intuitively, *u* does not lie on the line between *x* and *z* (as it must if the encodings had only one differentiative property), but somewhere else on the two-dimensional plane.

This pattern recurs in higher dimensions. We define a structure of points and a new point *u* that is indiscriminable from some of them. If the structure is only *n*-dimensional, then *u* must be indiscriminable from other specified points in the structure. If *u* can be discriminated from those others, then the structure cannot be *n*-dimensional but must be at least $(n + 1)$-dimensional. Dimensionality is a product of the structure of betwixtness relations, and is here applied to finite orders. We are forced into additional dimensions by the need to avoid placing any discriminable pair between an indiscriminable one.

Two-dimensionality is demonstrated by the failure of some point to be co-linear with others. Co-linearity fails if two stimuli are discriminable though both are indiscriminable from the same pair of points. Three-dimensionality will be demonstrated by a failure of some point to be co-planar with others. Suppose *w*, *x*, *y*, and *z* make up a 'square', as follows. Each is indiscriminable from two of the other points (the adjacent 'corners'), but not from the third (the far corner). Suppose there is a point *u* that is 'within' the square: it is indiscriminable from two non-adjacent corners. Then, if *u* is co-planar with the other points, it should be indiscriminable from the two remaining corners. If it can be discriminated from one of the remaining corners, then it cannot be co-planar with the square, and we must add a third dimension to the order. That is,

$$Iwx \ \& \ Iwy \ \& \ {\sim}Ixy \ \& \ Izx \ \& \ Izy \ \& \ {\sim}Izw$$

and

$$(\exists u)(Iux \ \& \ Iuy \ \& \ {\sim}Iuw \ \& \ {\sim}Iuz)$$

so that u cannot be within the square.

We can next construct a three-dimensional cube, and show the structure to be four-dimensional if there is some point matching diagonal corners that is discriminable from all other corners. Each corner is indiscriminable from adjacent corners and discriminable from all non-adjacent corners. Each edge represents an indiscriminable pair. Suppose a point is indiscriminable from two far corners of the cube. If the structure is three-dimensional, such a point must be 'within' the cube, and so it must be indiscriminable from at least one of the remaining corners. If not, the structure is at least four-dimensional, and encodings have at least four differentiative properties.

These definitions generalize easily. We show discriminations to be $(n + 1)$-dimensional by showing that the pair list could not be n-dimensional. Failure in n dimensions is demonstrated by finding an n-dimensional structure (line, plane, cube, and so on) and a point that is not co-n-dimensional. The latter is demonstrated by finding a point contained 'within' the n-dimensional structure (i.e. indiscriminable from its far corners) yet failing to match any other corners. Since a point cannot both be within the structure and fail to match some other corner, the discriminations cannot be only n-dimensional.

4.4 Relative Similarity as a Basis

I have described two ways in which one can discover the dimensionality of the order underlying discriminations. Goodman provides a third approach in *The Structure of Appearance*, based on the idea of constructing lines, polygons, polyhedra, and so on. For example, if one finds each point to be an element of exactly two linear cells, the structure must be two-dimensional. If one finds each linear cell is an edge of exactly two polyhedra, the structure is three-dimensional. These conditions are (again) sufficient to demonstrate dimensionality, but not necessary. As Goodman notes, it is possible to conceive of a two-dimensional order constituted by two linear orders that intersect in just one point, or a three-dimensional order constituted by two polygons that share just one edge.

There may be other sets of sufficient conditions; the ones given are in no way exhaustive. We would like to have some generalizable method for establishing the dimensional structure underlying a pair list, and it is not clear how the examples in the previous section will yield such a method. One cannot easily generalize definitions suited for *linear* arrays. In Goodman's system, besideness is defined by betwixtness, and betwixtness is initially defined for linear arrays. Goodman's definition does not always succeed for two-dimensional arrays. For example, consider the two-dimensional pair list given above:

$$
\begin{array}{llllll}
a\text{:} & a & b \\
b\text{:} & a & b & c \\
c\text{:} & & b & c & d & & f & & h \\
d\text{:} & & & c & d & e \\
e\text{:} & & & & d & e \\
f\text{:} & & & c & & & f & g \\
g\text{:} & & & & & & f & g \\
h\text{:} & & & c & & & & & h & i \\
i\text{:} & & & & & & & & h & i \\
\end{array}
$$

corresponding to the structure:

$$
\begin{array}{ccccc}
& & g \\
& & f \\
a & b & c & d & e \\
& & h \\
& & i \\
\end{array}
$$

The definition for betwixtness here fails to show that c is between f and h. There are four atoms that match f or h but not both, but there are also four atoms that match f or c but not both (and four that match h or c but not both). Goodman's definition is acknowledged to fail in some nonlinear arrays (see Goodman 1977, pp. 236, 250).

The failure of this definition leaves the project of extracting order from overlap in a precarious position. The theory for linear arrays is satisfyingly complete: Goodman proves the adequacy of the definition of betwixtness, shows how to rectify irregular linear arrays to make 'just noticeable difference' symmetric, and cites a proof that such rectification is always possible for a linear array.

The only problem is that the definitions developed for those notions are guaranteed to succeed only when used on linear arrays. Yet to determine whether an array is linear, one must first determine which atoms are between which. If we know the given array to be linear, our path is an easy one; but if it is nonlinear, we lack even a test to show which atoms are beside which.

We want a method for deriving order that does not presuppose that we know the dimensionality of that order. Partial solutions to this problem are available, using methods known collectively as *multidimensional scaling* (MDS). With certain sorts of data, multidimensional scaling can determine the dimensionality of the underlying order and locate each atom at some place within it.

4.4.1 *Defining Relative Similarity*

For various technical reasons that will become apparent later, it is preferable to move from the dyadic predicate 'indiscriminable' to a triadic predicate for relative similarity: *x* is more similar to *y* than to *z*.

Relative similarity can be defined in terms of discriminations, but the definition is complex. One might think that one could define it simply by counting the number of besideness 'steps' between the two pairs—from *x* to *y* and from *x* to *z*. The proposal would be to define 'besideness' in terms of indiscriminability (as Goodman defines besideness in terms of matching), and then to stipulate that *x* is more similar to *y* than to *z* (*Sxyz*) if and only if the minimum number of besideness steps between *x* and *y* is less than the minimum number of steps between *x* and *z*.

One difficulty with this approach is that it assumes that there is some finite number of 'indiscriminably small' steps between two stimuli—that one element is *beside* another in the order. As mentioned above, it is difficult to reconcile this assumption with a statistical understanding of discriminability, in which absolute thresholds are replaced by continuous probability functions.[8] More serious are the various difficulties caused by the assumption that all besideness steps are of the same 'size'. In particular, one can produce linear orders that follow the proposed rule but in which *x* would be treated as more similar to *y* than to *z* even

---

[8] Recall that discriminability is always discriminability-at-some-confidence-level, and that by increasing the sample size of trials one may be able to discriminate previously 'indiscriminable' stimulus classes. In a continuous function no two elements in the range are beside one another.

though x and z are indiscriminable, while x and y are not. Goodman calls these arrays 'irregular'. In them one characteristically finds two neighbouring atoms, one of which has a larger manor than the other. For example, consider:

a:	*a*	*b*					
b:	*a*	*b*	*c*				
c:		*b*	*c*	*d*	*e*	*f*	
d:			*c*	*d*	*e*	*f*	
e:			*c*	*d*	*e*	*f*	*g*
f:			*c*	*d*	*e*	*f*	*g*	*h*
g:				*e*	*f*	*g*	*h*

Here c and f match, while a and c do not. But c and f are separated by three besideness steps, while c and a are separated by two. Our rule would count c as more similar to a than to f, even though c matches f and does not match a. This violates the intuitive principle that no non-matching span should be larger than a matching span. Note that the order is in accord with the weaker rule that no non-matching span resides within a matching span (Goodman 1977, p. 227). That weaker rule suffices to generate the linear order above. The stronger principle is needed only to derive some metric for distance.

Another characteristic of irregular arrays is that 'just noticeable difference' behaves in an objectionable way (see Goodman 1977, p. 226). Starting at a, one could notice the first difference at c (the first non-matching atom), but from c the first noticeable difference would be found at g. Just noticeable differences are here of different 'sizes'. They are also non-symmetric: if one started at g and proceeded in the opposite direction, the first noticeable difference would be found at d, not at c. Goodman shows how to eliminate these problems by 'regularizing' the order. One inserts vacant positions so that no matching pair is separated by fewer steps than those between any non-matching pair. In the example above, we would insert a vacant position somewhere between a and c. Vacant positions must be added until all non-matching spans are longer than the longest matching span; only then can distance measurements satisfy the stronger rule, and so only then can relative similarity be defined by counting besideness steps.

The weaker rule of order yields only ordinal positioning. Ordinal position is unaffected by any purely 'topological' deformation—by any stretching or distortion that does not tear the graph. To derive distances, however, one needs a *metric*: something stronger than ordinal position.

It is easiest to define 'relative similarity' by returning to the same foundations employed in defining 'discriminability'. Quine (1974) proposes an elegant formulation. Stimuli have effects on sensory transducers, and they can be ranked, in a purely physical way, by the similarities and differences among such effects. Quine calls this notion *receptual* similarity, and notes that

Episodes are receptually similar to the degree that the total set of sensory receptors that are triggered on one occasion approximates the set triggered on the other occasion. (Quine 1974, p. 16)

Degrees of receptual similarity can be captured using the idea of a receptual *neighbourhood*: a class of stimuli 'sufficiently' close to the given stimulus. To define 'sufficiently close' we pick some stimulus y as a 'foil'. Stimuli in the receptual neighbourhood of stimulus x are all those that are receptually more similar to x than x is to y. They are those 'closer' to x than x is to y.

Global discriminability of receptual neighbourhoods yields relative similarity. Stimulus x is more similar to y than to z if it is possible to condition some response R to all stimuli in the receptual neighbourhood of x, and to all stimuli in the receptual neighbourhood of y, but to no stimuli in the receptual neighbourhood of z (Quine 1974, pp. 17–18). That there is no receptual neighbourhood of z to which R is conditioned shows that z is outside the receptual neighbourhoods of both x and y. In effect, Quine defines relative similarity in terms of stimulus generalization. Response R demonstrates stimulus generalization between stimuli x and y, since any stimulus within the receptual neighbourhood of either will elicit R. Stimulus generalization does not extend to z, since stimuli in the receptual neighbourhood of z do not elicit R. The fact that stimulus generalization includes both x and y but not z shows that x is more similar to y than to z.

Quine's formulation distinguishes perceptual similarity from receptual similarity. Stimulus x is perceptually more similar to y than it is to z because some response is conditioned to x or y but not to z. Such conditioning is possible even if x is *receptually* more similar to z than to y. The physical effects of x on transducers may be more similar to those of z than to those of y. If a response can nevertheless be conditioned to both x and y but not to z, we have shown that x is more similar *perceptually* to y than to z.

4.4.2 *Using Relative Similarity*

Once one has in hand a workable notion of relative similarity, one can easily discover the number of dimensions needed to map a perceptual order. The definition is recursive and proceeds by setting a minimum dimensionality to the structure, and then ratcheting it upwards as needs be. Some patterns of triplets are impossible if the structure is n-dimensional, and show it to be at least $(n + 1)$-dimensional. The construction proceeds by defining when one point is co-n-dimensional with other points (co-linear, co-planar, co-three-dimensional, and so on), and then defining the dimensionality of the list as the smallest N such that all terms are co-N-dimensional.

Some simple inferences will be illustrated in this section, just to show that the feat is possible. The underlying idea has blossomed into multifarious techniques of multidimensional scaling. Those will be considered in the next section.

One can model relative similarity judgements with distances, using the single rule that, if x is more similar to y than to z, x must be closer to y than to z. It follows from this rule that, if x is more similar to y than to z, then it lies somewhere in the half-universe bounded by the midpoint of the line between y and z (see Fig. 4.1). *Sxyz* implies $xy < xz$. *Sxzy* would put x on the z side of the universe. If y is more similar to x than to z (i.e. if *Syxz*), a different inference can be drawn, for we then know that x must lie within a radius of less than yz from point y. Stimulus x would be confined within a sphere of radius less than yz. *Szxy* puts x in a sphere centred on z with radius less than yz. Finally, suppose y is more similar to z than to x. This places x *outside* the sphere centred on y of radius yz. Similarly, *Szyx* puts x outside the sphere centred on z of radius zy.

Combinations constrain the structure further. For example, if x is more similar to y than to z and y is more similar to x than to z, we can locate x to within a part of a sphere centred on y (see Fig. 4.1). *Syxz* and *Syzx* are contraries: they cannot both be true, although they may both be false. Point x cannot be both inside and outside a sphere centred on y of radius yz, though it may be located exactly on that sphere, making both claims false.

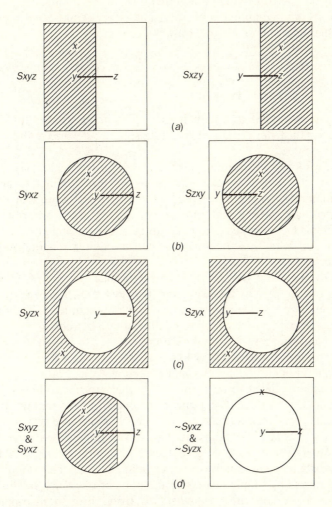

FIG. 4.1. Eight inferences from relative similarity

Note: *Sxyz* is the predicate '*x* is more similar to *y* than to *z*'. If more similar points are always placed closer together than less similar ones, then in each diagram *x* must lie somewhere within the shaded region. For example, *Syxz* places *x* somewhere in the sphere centred on *y* with radius *yz*. Part (*d*) shows how combinations of relative similarity judgements can constrain mapping even further.

Using contraries, we can express *equality* of relative distances. To show that *y* is as similar to *x* as to *z*, we show both that it is not more similar to x than to z, and that it is not more similar to z than to x. So the conjunction of $\sim Syxz$ and $\sim Syzx$ would place x and z on the same sphere centred on y. Algebraically,

$$
\begin{array}{llll}
 & \sim Syxz & \& & \sim Syzx \\
\text{hence} & \sim (yx < yz) & \& & \sim (yz < yx) \\
\text{hence} & (yx \geq yz) & \& & (yz \geq yx) \\
\text{hence} & yx = yz & &
\end{array}
$$

So y is as similar to x as it is to z. The implication is that y is equidistant from x and z: it centres a sphere on which x and z are both located.

If we know in addition that x is as similar to y as to z (i.e. that $\sim Sxyz$ & $\sim Sxzy$), we can infer that the three points form an equilateral triangle, since then $xz = yz = yx$. One can draw surprisingly strong inferences concerning the ordering of elements knowing just a little about their relative similarities. The next step is to show how to ascertain the dimensionality of that order.

Given x and u, the class of points p the same distance from x as u can be defined as the set of points p such that both $\sim Sxup$ and $\sim Sxpu$. Suppose we have some u closer to y than to x. Then u is co-linear with x and y if and only if, among all points w the same distance from x as is u, there are none closer to y than w. Since the shortest distance from y to u is a straight line, if this condition fails, u is not co-linear with x and y (see Fig. 4.2).

Similarly, given three points x, y, z that are not co-linear, u is co-planar with them if and only if, among all points that are both the same distance to x as u is and the same distance to y as u is, there are none closer to z than u is. A four-dimensional structure is found just in case u is the least distant point to v that is equidistant to three non-co-planar points x, y, z. This definition generalizes by simply increasing the number of points to which u must be equidistant. Equidistance from three non-co-planar points defines a point in three dimensions but a line in four; equidistance from four non-three-dimensional points defines a point in four space but a line in five; and so on.

It is easy to formulate many different tests for dimensionality using the triadic relation of relative similarity. It was shown above how one can demonstrate that three distinct points form the vertices of an equilateral triangle. Since such points cannot be co-linear, any such demonstration amounts to a proof that the

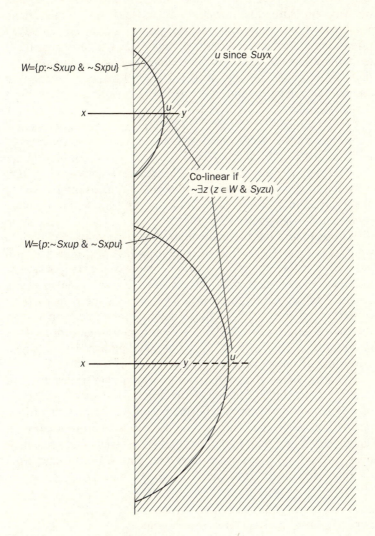

FIG. 4.2. Demonstrating co-linearity

Note: Suppose *u* is more similar to *y* than to *x*, and we want to show that it is on the line *xy*. Consider the set *W* of all points *p* such that *x* is no more similar to *u* than to *p* and no more similar to *p* than to *u*. That set defines an arc centred on *x* of radius *xu*. Point *u* is co-linear with *x* and *y* if there is no *z* in that set such that *y* is more similar to *z* than to *u*.

structure must be at least two-dimensional. All we need to find are three points such that $\sim\!Sxyz$, $\sim\!Sxzy$, $\sim\!Syxz$, and $\sim\!Syzx$, and we can be sure the structure is at least two-dimensional. Similarly, if we find four distinct points among which every threesome forms an equilateral triangle, the structure must be at least three-dimensional. In three dimensions it is impossible to find five points among which every threesome forms an equilateral triangle, and so one would need at least four dimensions.

Other findings can force one into additional dimensions. Suppose we have two distinct points x and y, and form the class of all points Z just as similar to x as to y. If our order is one-dimensional, Z must be a unit class, since there is only one midpoint to the line xy. If our order is two-dimensional, then for any given point u in that class Z, there is at most one other point v such that x is as similar to u as to v (see Fig. 4.3). With three dimensions there may be many more than two points in class Z to which x is just as similar as it is to u; in fact, the radius xu will describe a circle on what is now a plane separating x and y. Hence we can determine when a class of points has a dimensionality greater than two. This enables the constructions to iterate. For example, if the order is three-dimensional, then the class Z will itself be a plane—a two-dimensional order. If we find that the points in class Z are not all co-planar, we are forced into a fourth dimension.

In short, many different findings within the triples list can determine the dimensionality of the order. The six permutations of relative similarity each contribute constraints on the ordinal positioning of points. They can be used to define the relation of equidistance, and then to define quasi-geometrical figures such as lines, circles, and planes. Combinations can be used to ascertain the dimensionality of the order.

FIG. 4.3. Three dimensions from relative similarity

Note: Z is the set of all points p just as similar to x as to y. (*a*) If our order is one-dimensional, Z must be a unit class. (*b*) If our order is two-dimensional, then for any given point u in that class Z, there is at most one other point v such that x is as similar to u as to v. (*c*) With three dimensions there may be many more than two points in class Z to which x is just as similar as it is to u. If the order is three-dimensional, Z will itself be a plane—a two-dimensional order.

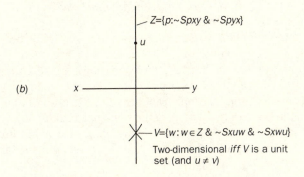

(a)

$Z=\{p: \sim Spxy \;\&\; \sim Spyx\}$

One-dimensional *iff* Z is a unit set

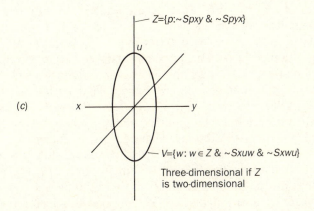

(b)

$Z=\{p: \sim Spxy \;\&\; \sim Spyx\}$

$V=\{w: w \in Z \;\&\; \sim Sxuw \;\&\; \sim Sxwu\}$

Two-dimensional *iff* V is a unit set (and $u \neq v$)

(c)

$Z=\{p: \sim Spxy \;\&\; \sim Spyx\}$

$V=\{w: w \in Z \;\&\; \sim Sxuw \;\&\; \sim Sxwu\}$

Three-dimensional if Z is two-dimensional

FIG. 4.3. Three dimensions from relative similarity

4.5 Multidimensional Scaling

While the argument in the previous two sections has shown that it is possible to infer the number of dimensions from the structure of a pair (or triples) list, the various inference routes surveyed seem haphazard and unrelated. We have nothing more than a list of different paths to a solution. We would like to replace this list with some *generalizable* method for extracting dimensionality from relative similarities, one that rests on a systematic theory and does not rely on recognition of particular patterns in the data. With some caveats and restrictions, this can often be achieved with a family of methods known as *multidimensional scaling*.

Suppose we have some stimuli $S_1, \ldots, S_n$, and for each pair of stimuli some number s_{ij} that represents the similarity between stimulus S_i and stimulus S_j. Those numbers are often called 'proximities' or 'dissimilarities'; conventionally, higher numbers represent increasing dissimilarity. We do not need metrical relations in our data. A simple ranking will suffice, so that, if S_x is more similar to S_y than to S_z, we assign a higher ranking to s_{xz} than to s_{xy}. (Stimuli S_x and S_z are less similar—more dissimilar, further apart—than are S_x and S_y.) A triples list of relative similarities provides all the data needed.

From the matrix of similarity data, multidimensional scaling constructs a spatial representation of the stimuli so that distances between points in that space correspond to the relative similarities of the stimuli. These scaling methods yield both the number of dimensions required for a space and the coordinates of each stimulus point in that space. Dimensions and coordinates can be derived even if one starts only with rankings of inter-stimulus similarities. The proximity data constrain the spatial representation: the resulting inter-point distances will be a monotonic function of their similarity. That is, for any three stimuli in the original data, if S_x is more similar to S_y than to S_z, then the distance between points S_x and S_y in the resulting space will be less than the distance between points S_x and S_z. This condition is the minimal one specified above for modelling relative similarities by distances. Finally, one can assess the 'goodness of fit' between distances in the resulting space and the original data, and estimate the extent to which increasing the number of dimensions or altering coordinates of some points changes that fit.

From a map it is easy to measure inter-point distances. Multidimensional scaling proceeds in the reverse direction: given a table of inter-point distances, construct the map. The underlying principle of multidimensional scaling is already familiar from the examples in the previous sections. Similarity data constrain the ordering of stimuli. The constraints are more or less rigid depending on one's interpretation of the numbers representing similarities. We may have only rankings among inter-point distances, in which case the map will be guaranteed only to preserve their rankings. If we have access to *metrical* data, in inches or kilometres, quite a rigid constraint is possible: distances between points in the map will be a constant linear function of the inter-point distances. At least in principle, one could construct such a map with a ruler and compass, although the work would be tedious. Multidimensional scaling systematizes it and turns it over to a computer.

The technique seems a potent form of statistical magic. It isn't, particularly, but it takes some work to show how the trick is done. The Appendix provides an introductory description.

4.6 Companionship and Community

In this section I will show how the methods outlined thus far solve the problems of companionship and imperfect community detailed in Goodman (1977). With the triadic predicate '*x* is more similar to *y* than to *z*', one can distinguish a quality from some constant companion, and deftly avoid the problem of imperfect community. In the next section I will show how this approach can answer various 'circularity' objections that have been raised against materialist analyses of phenomenal qualities (Bradley 1964, 1966; Cornman 1962), and so finally answer one of the remaining objections to our explanation of looks (Section 2.3).

The problems of both companionship and imperfect community arise in systems that attempt to define qualities in terms of a similarity relation holding between particulars. For example, Carnap (1967) takes as his primitive terms *Elementarerlebnisse*—momentary cross-sections of the entire stream of experience—and a relation of part-similarity between *elementarerlebnisse*. He attempts to define qualities (such as whiteness, sweetness, and so on) in terms of those primitives.

Goodman calls systems that proceed in this manner *particularistic*; his own he calls *realistic*, since its primitive elements are qualities (qualia). Instead of facing the problem of abstracting qualities from individuals, Goodman faces the problem of attempting to define individuals ('concreta') in terms of qualities.

A typical strategy in the attempt to define qualities in terms of similarities is to examine the pair lists, and form the largest classes possible in which every member of each class bears the similarity relation to all other members of that class. If our individuals (numbered 1–5) have the qualities:

rg	*g*	*b*	*rb*	*rgb*
1	2	3	4	5

then our pair lists (for part similarity) will be as follows:

1:	1	2		4	5
2:	1	2			5
3:			3	4	5
4:	1		3	4	5
5:	1	2	3	4	5

Individual 1 shares all its qualities with 1, shares quality *g* with 2, shares *r* with 4, and shares both *r* and *g* with 5. One might think it impossible to distinguish the qualities *r*, *g*, *b* in these five individuals, since three of them have more than one quality, and each is similar to others in the group in more than one way.

Often this co-occurrence is no bar to distinguishing the qualities. We form similarity circles directly from pair lists. The procedure is to take all the items on a given row, and test each to see if it matches all the others: if not, drop it. Continue this way with each distinct row. To form the largest class from the first row, each member of which matches *all* the other members of the class, we must drop individual 2, and get {1, 4, 5}—the quality *r*. The second row gives {1, 2, 5}, which requires no deletions, and gives quality *g*. The third row gives {3, 4, 5}—the quality *b*. No further classes can be formed in accord with our rule. In this way the quality classes *r*, *g*, *b* are derived from the pair lists.

Similarity circles yield some of the tools needed to answer Cornman's objection mentioned in Section 4.1. One cannot translate 'I am having a yellowy orange after-image' as 'Something is going on in me like what goes on when I see an orange', because the latter is implied by a sentence such as 'Something is going on in me like what goes on when I see a roughly spherical shape', while the former is not. One must somehow specify that colour is the intended similarity, not shape; but to specify some particular aspect in terms of which the two are similar, it seems that one must already have completed the analysis of the qualities in question.

A Carnapian analysis of similarity circles can sometimes solve this problem. Suppose we have the following items:

1. orange circle	4. orange square	7. orange triangle
2. blue circle	5. blue square	8. blue triangle
3. red circle	6. red square	9. red triangle

Our pair lists will be:

1:	1	2	3	4			7		
2:	1	2	3		5			8	
3:	1	2	3			6			9
4:	1			4	5	6	7		
5:		2		4	5	6		8	
6:			3	4	5	6			9
7:	1			4			7	8	9
8:		2			5		7	8	9
9:			3			6	7	8	9

Now as similarity circles we try {1, 2, 3, 4, 7}, but delete 4 and 7 (neither matches 2) to get {1, 2, 3}—the circles. We can also delete 2 and 3 to get {1, 4, 7}—the orange items. We try {1, 2, 3, 5, 8} but delete 1 and 3 to get {2, 5, 8}—blue things. {2, 3} is already in {1, 2, 3}. From the next row, {3, 6, 9} works fine—red things. From {1, 4, 5, 6, 7} we delete 1 and 7 to get {4, 5, 6}—the squares. And so on. From the pair lists we can get similarity circles, and those will enable us to identify the respect in which an orange after-image is like an orange, and not like a blue circle—it is in respect of the quality {1, 4, 7}.

4.6.1 *Companionship*

Companionship spoils this pretty picture. Carnap's approach does not always work. Whenever two qualities *always* occur together, similarity circles will fail to distinguish the two qualities. Suppose our companionship list is

br	b	bg	g	bgr
1	2	3	4	5

In this list, *r* occurs always with *b* (see Goodman 1977, p. 116). Goodman showed that in this case *r* cannot be distinguished from *b* by using the pair list for part similarity.

The triadic relative similarity predicate does enable us to distinguish the two qualities. To predict what judgements of relative similarity would be made from Goodman's lists, we must make some assumptions that map the shared qualities on to similarities. We assume that things sharing more qualities are more similar to one another than things sharing fewer. We assume that things sharing equal numbers of qualities are equally similar or dissimilar. Finally, we assume that, other things being equal, things are more similar to one another if they have similar numbers of qualities. On this last assumption, a red and blue patch will be judged more similar to a blue and green patch (i.e. one with two colours) than to a solid blue patch.

Using these rules, our rankings of relative similarities will be:

1:	5	3	2	4
2:	1–3	5	4	
3:	5	1	2–4	
4:	3	5	1–2	
5:	1–3	2–4		

The first row implies, for example, that 1 is more similar to 5 than it is to 3 (or any of the others), more similar to 3 than to 2 or 4, and more similar to 2 than to 4. The result is clearer if we name each individual by its properties:

br:	*bgr*	*bg*	*b*	*g*
b:	*br–bg*	*bgr*	*g*	
bg:	*bgr*	*br*	*b–g*	
g:	*bg*	*bgr*	*br–b*	
bgr:	*br–bg*	*b–g*		

In the first row, for example, *br* is most similar to *bgr*, then to *bg*, then to *b*, then to *g*. As in the previous example, the dashes represent ties. (If we drop our third assumption, the two middle items on the first row form a tie. They are equally similar to *br*. Metric information can be recovered even if there are ties in the rankings, so the ordering of *bg* and *b* is not critical.)

From the relative similarities, we can infer relations among the inter-point distances. If more similar points are to be placed closer together, we can infer from the first row that the distance from 1 to 5 is less than the distance from 1 to 3, which is in turn less than the distance from 1 to 2, and so on. Proceeding row by row, we infer the following concerning the inter-point distances:

$$
\begin{array}{llllllll}
15 & < & 13 & < & 12 & < & 14 \\
12 & = & 23 & \& & 12 & < & 25 & < & 24 \\
23 & = & 34 & \& & 35 & < & 13 & < & 23 \\
14 & = & 24 & \& & 34 & < & 45 & < & 14 \\
15 & = & 35 & \& & 25 & = & 45 & \& & 15 & < & 25
\end{array}
$$

These in turn imply the following simple ordering of relative distances. Segments listed in a given row are the same length, and those in lower rows are shorter:

$$
\begin{array}{lll}
14 & = & 24 \\
25 & = & 45 \\
12 & = & 23 & = & 34 \\
13 \\
15 & = & 35
\end{array}
$$

The ordering of relative distances in turn constrains any map of the qualities. A primitive multidimensional scaling can be completed with ruler and compass.

If we wish to map these points so that relative distances correspond to relative similarities, we can proceed as follows (see Fig. 4.4). Since 12 = 23, points 1 and 3 must lie on the same circle centred on 2. Since 14 = 24, 4 lies somewhere on the perpendicular bisector of segment 12. Since 23 = 34, but 13 < 12, 3 must lie within the triangle 124, and once 3 is placed anywhere on the arc of the circle defined by radius 12, the placement of 4 is uniquely determined. The position of 5 is also uniquely determined. Since 15 < 12, we know that 5 must lie within the circle of radius 12 centred on 1. Since 25 > 12, 5 must lie outside the circle centred on 2. Since 15 = 35, 5 must lie somewhere on the perpendicular bisector of segment 13. Since 15 < 13, 5 must be found within a relatively small segment of that bisector. Finally, 25 = 45, and there is only one point along that segment for which all those constraints are true.

The only choice in the construction is the placement of point 3 somewhere along a finite arc. Once that choice is made, the placement of all other points is determined uniquely. Figure 4.4(*b*) shows the effect of a slightly different placement of point 3 along that arc. Any structure we generate will be a pentagon with point 3 inside, and the ordinal positions of the points are rigidly fixed.

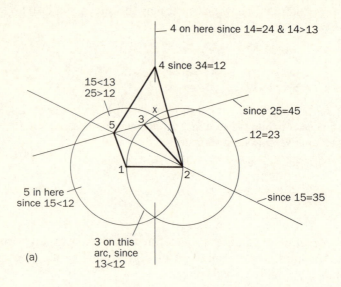

4 on here since 14=24 & 14>13

4 since 34=12

15<13
25>12

since 25=45

12=23

5 in here
since 15<12

since 15=35

3 on this
arc, since
13<12

(a)

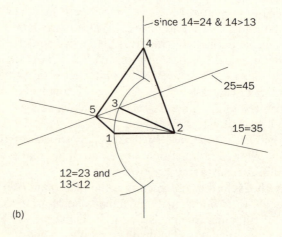

since 14=24 & 14>13

25=45

15=35

12=23 and
13<12

(b)

FIG. 4.4. A solution for companionship

Note: The relative similarities among the five individuals in Goodman's example of the companionship problem constrain the placement of points to forms similar to (*a*) or (*b*).

The structure of relative similarities dictates a spatial order which, when rotated, is approximately as follows:

$$5$$
$$1$$

$$3$$

$$2 \qquad\qquad\qquad\qquad 4$$

Item 2 is as close to 1 as it is to 3. In terms of relative distance we have 2: 1–3, 5, 4, which is monotonic with the judgements of relative similarity. Although we have no atom with just the quality *r*, this arrangement strikingly resembles a portion of the colour triangle. We extrapolate and place a point *r* so as to form an equilateral triangle with points *b* and *g*. The result is as follows:

$$r$$

$$br \qquad\qquad bgr$$

$$b \qquad\qquad\qquad bg \qquad\qquad\qquad g$$

The map identifies *b* and *g* as distinct regions of quality space. We find *bg* between *b* and *g*. We can also show that *br* and *bgr* are both in the *r* direction from *bg*. No one-dimensional map will do. Otherwise the proximity of *br* to *bgr* cannot be reconciled with *b*'s equal distance from both *br* and *bg*.

Adding points to the analysis would serve only to *increase* the constraints on a multidimensional scaling, making it more likely that there is a unique solution. In a way, it is remarkable that a sample of only five points yields such a tightly constrained structure as this.

In short, when analysed in terms of relative similarities, Goodman's classic example of the inscrutability of companion qualities yields a highly constrained spatial structure. If we base our analysis on a two-place part-similarity predicate, we hit a roadblock whenever one quality always accompanies another. In such a circumstance the two qualities cannot be distinguished from one another. The use of relative similarity allows one not only to distinguish the two qualities, but also to place those qualities (and various of their combinations) in an order. One can move directly from a triples list to a map in which distances correspond to relative similarities. We distinguish quality *b* from quality *r* as different *places* in the order. Combinations of those qualities are located appropriately. Some theoretical economy is lost when one moves to a triadic predicate, but the payoff is a solution to the companionship difficulty.

4.6.2 *Imperfect Community*

One might think that it is simple to define qualities using similarities. The obvious idea is to define a quality class as the largest class one can form in which each member is similar to all other members. Goodman showed that such a rule does not succeed in defining quality classes. It does not suffice to show that there is some single quality shared by every member. Consider the collection

br	*rg*	*gb*
1	2	3

Here each individual is similar in some respect to the other two, so that our pair list for part similarity is

1:	1	2	3
2:	1	2	3
3:	1	2	3

In accord with the above rule, we would pick {1, 2, 3} as a quality class. Yet there is no quality common to all three items. Examples like this manifest what Goodman calls *imperfect community*: each individual is similar to all the others, yet there is no quality they all share.

Examples can be constructed by endowing each individual with as many different qualities as there are other members of the collection, and letting a chain of distinct matches run through the entire group. For example, for a four-member imperfect community, we need something like

abc	*bcd*	*cde*	*dea*
1	2	3	4

(see Goodman 1977, p. 118). Again, there is no quality all four items share.

In an imperfect community, each individual is similar to all the others, but in different respects. To define a quality class, we must ensure that each item is similar to all the others in the same respect. There is no obvious way to define these different 'respects' without already having a notion of quality class available. Items 1 and 2 are similar in respect r, while 1 and 3 are similar in respect b; to differentiate these two 'respects' one must already be able to differentiate r from b. So it seems that the attempt to define qualities in terms of similarities is doomed. This problem underlies Cornman's (1962) objection to Smart, mentioned above (Section 4.1).

Suppose we move from a dyadic 'part similarity' predicate to the triadic notion of relative similarity. Can we then rectify an imperfect community? Consider first the three-member example given above. If we employ the same assumptions used above to predict relative similarity judgements from the shared properties of items, the triples list will be:

  1: 2–3
  2: 1–3
  3: 1–2

For example, since br (1) shares one property with rg (2) and one property with gb (3), it will be just as similar to (2) as to (3). A ruler-and-compass multidimensional scaling yields a unique solution. Since we have from the first row that 12 = 13 and from the second row that 12 = 23, these three points must lie on the vertices of an equilateral triangle. The only map consistent with the judgements will be of the form:

  br

  rg gb

An immediate implication is that the quality space is at least two-dimensional, and therefore that the three do not all share just one quality. (They cannot form a single quality class, since we need two dimensions to represent their relative similarities.) Imperfect community is avoided. Furthermore, the three qualities can be individuated in this mapping: each is a segment connecting two points. Our map again mimics a colour triangle (see Boynton 1979, pp. 132 ff.). Each quality corresponds to one of the three directions identifiable from the triangle: quality r is to the upper left, b to the upper right, and g downwards.

Larger imperfect communities are more difficult to plot with ruler and compass, although it can be done, and many yield a unique map. As an example, consider the four-member community:

abc	bcd	cde	dea
1	2	3	4

(see Goodman 1977, p. 118). The triples list for relative similarities, based on the same assumptions as above, is

1:	2	3–4
2:	1–3	4
3:	2–4	1
4:	3	1–2

Here 1 is more similar to 2 than to 3 or 4, since it shares two qualities (*bc*) with 2, but only one quality (*c* or *a*) with 3 or 4. For the same reason, 1 is no more similar to 3 than it is to 4. The list yields a simple ranking of inter-point distances:

$$12 = 23 = 34$$
$$13 = 24 = 14$$

where segments in each row are of equal length, and the segments in the second row are longer than those in the first. These requirements generate a unique spatial structure: the four individuals must be four consecutive vertices of a pentagon (see Fig. 4.5). We start by drawing an arbitrary segment representing 13. We find immediately that 2 must be on the perpendicular bisector of segment 13 (since 12 = 23), while 4 must be on the circle centred on 1 with radius 13 (since 14 = 13). Point 2 must be within that same circle, since 12 < 13. Finally, we know that 24 = 13 and 23 = 34. There are just two placements of point 2 along the perpendicular bisector of segment 13 that could satisfy these constraints; and once 2 is placed, point 4 is fixed uniquely. One placement yields Fig. 4.5; the other would simply flip the figure over. In either case we get the same ordered sequence of vertices of a pentagon.

The analysis in terms of relative similarity reveals a fifth individual one could add to the group and retain an imperfect community, namely *eab*. This individual shows up as the missing fifth vertex of the pentagon. Furthermore, we can distinguish five distinct qualities among four individuals. The four consecutive vertices of a pentagon give us five distinct directions on the plane.

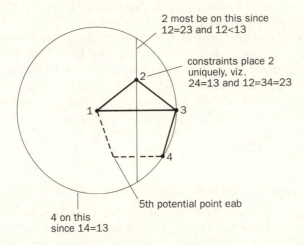

FIG. 4.5. A solution for imperfect community

Note: This set is an 'imperfect community'; each individual is similar to all the others, yet there is no quality they all share. A ruler-and-compass multidimensional scaling distinguishes their qualities as different regions in this structure.

Goodman's examples of imperfect communities are all composed of atoms whose qualities label vertices of regular polygons. For example,

> *ab, bc, ca*
> *abc, bcd, cde, dea*
> *abcd, bcde, cdef, defa*

and so on. Multidimensional scaling of proximities based on such lists can be predicted by counting the number N of distinct 'qualities' among all the items, and then placing the points as consecutive vertices of an n-sided polygon.

In summary, using relative similarity, we can solve the problems of companionship and imperfect community. We can distinguish two qualities that always occur together by the relative similarities of the individuals that manifest those qualities. In a quality space, companion qualities show up in different 'places'. Relative similarities also provide access to the internal structure of imperfect communities. The different respects in which individuals can be similar to one another emerge as distinct directions on the map.

While the triadic relation of relative similarity is more complex than dyadic part similarity, the extra power seems worth the loss in simplicity. We can proceed directly from a triples list to a ranking of relative distances, and then to a map in which proximity corresponds to similarity. The procedure is much simpler than using a dyadic predicate. With the latter one must define betwixtness, define besideness, determine all pairs beside one another, regularize the array, and finally derive some measure for distance. The theory is complete only for linear arrays: even the definition for betwixtness fails for some nonlinear ones.

4.7   Dimensions and Differentiative Attributes

Qualitative properties of sensations were identified as those properties of internal encodings that determine the outcome of discrimination tasks. Some properties of encodings are 'differentiative' ones; each is necessary, and jointly all are sufficient to ensure global indiscriminability of the presented stimuli.

If just one attribute determined the discriminations among a set of stimuli, then encodings of those stimuli could be ordered by that attribute. Any two encodings sharing the same value would encode indiscriminable stimuli. Other differences in the encodings would not make the two stimuli discriminable. If there were two differentiative attributes, then, although encodings might be alike in one of them, they could still differ in the other, thereby ensuring discriminability of the respective stimuli. There would be two independent dimensions along which encodings could vary. For example, things matched in brightness may differ in hue. Indiscriminability would be ensured only if encodings matched in both.

There must be at least one differentiative attribute of encodings for discrimination to be possible. Suppose we find stimuli that match in that respect but are nevertheless discriminable. Then there must be an additional differentiative feature of encodings, since by definition stimuli whose encodings match in all differentiative features are indiscriminable. If we find stimuli that match in the first two respects yet are nevertheless discriminable, there must be at least three differentiative attributes of encodings. In short, if the discrimination pair list is

N-dimensional, then there must be at least N distinct differentiative attributes of encodings. The dimensionality of discrimination pair lists gives a lower bound for the number of differentiative attributes of encodings of stimuli.

It also gives an upper bound. If P is a differentiative attribute of encodings, there are pairs of stimuli such that mismatch in P by itself suffices to make the pair discriminable. Can such a property fail to appear as a dimension of the discrimination pair list? Suppose encodings share N differentiative attributes but fail to share P, and that (consequently) the respective stimuli are discriminable. The supposition implies that the pair list must be more than N-dimensional. The stimuli will by hypothesis share the first N coordinates in the quality space. Since they are discriminable, they cannot be located in the same place. So we must add another dimension, another respect in terms of which stimuli can be discriminated. Since this is true of every differentiative attribute, each makes itself manifest as a dimension in the structure of discriminations.

In short, using discriminations and similarity judgements, we can discover the dimensionality of the order underlying discriminations, and thereby determine the number of differentiative attributes of encodings.

Talk of quality *space* is meant literally and not metaphorically. No scare quotes are needed. Mathematically, a space is an order of more than one dimension (see Russell 1903, p. 372). A perceptual modality with two differentiative attributes generates a two-dimensional order. Stimuli that are the same in one respect may nevertheless differ in the other. Quality space is a *space* because it is a multidimensional order.

The dimensions of quality space correspond to the differing respects in terms of which stimuli are sensed to be similar or different. They represent the attributes to which the differentiator is sensitive. The coordinates of a point within that space represent particular instances of each attribute: a particular brightness, a specific hue, and so on. Sensory qualities are regions or volumes in this space. One can specify a quality more or less precisely; if one employs the laboratory standard of global indiscriminability, a particular quality would correspond to a single point in quality space. Ordinary terminology is not nearly so precise; the ordinary 'red' applies to many things that do not even match in colour. It picks out a large and loosely defined volume of colour space. Comparatives among qualities are differing *directions* within quality space. However one identifies the 'red' region, x is redder than y if x is closer to that region than is y.

A second argument bolsters the claim that a differentiative feature is a *dimension* of quality space. A differentiative feature is itself an order-generating relation. It is a respect in terms of which encodings can be similar or different. For example, one can order all colour sensations by brightness. Brightness *is* an order: the relation 'brighter than' puts colour sensations in a series just as 'less than' does for the natural numbers. Similarly, hue and saturation are order-generating relations. Encodings are qualitatively identical just in case they are the same in all differentiative attributes. If they differ in any, then some task will show their stimuli to be discriminable. So 'same (surface) colour' means same hue, same saturation, and same brightness. Because each term denotes a series, the order has three dimensions.

Differentiative attributes of encodings are dimensions of quality space. Qualitative identity corresponds to identical location in that space. Sameness in some phenomenal respect corresponds to sharing some coordinate (but perhaps not all).

4.8 An Answer to Circularity Objections

We can finally rebuff the various circularity objections that have been dogging the analysis of sensory qualities since Chapter 2. Some properties of encodings are differentiative properties because each is necessary and jointly all are sufficient for global indiscriminability. Unfortunately, to this point that is the only characterization that could be given for differentiative properties, and so the analysis of qualitative identity was threatened with circularity. The fourth major objection to our explanation of edge enhancement effects in Section 2.3 was that it relied on a premiss mentioning some 'paradigm' object. That paradigm must have a particular quality and be perceived to have that quality. To explain sensory qualities by citing such paradigms seems circular.

The analysis of this chapter provides the beginning of an answer to this objection. Ultimately, even the perceived qualities of 'paradigm' objects will receive an analysis in terms of quality space. But to this point, and in accord with methodological solipsism, we have put no weight on—and cannot even formulate—the distinction between those sensory qualities a thing merely 'seems' to have and those it 'really' has. The sensory quality involved in both receives the same analysis. It is analysed as a location within a quality space, the dimensions of which can in principle be determined by multidimensional scaling. For *some* modalities we know enough about the structure of the quality space to be able to explain its dimensionality and provide a meaningful interpretation for its axes. In those modalities we can in principle dispense with all references to paradigm objects that 'really' have the qualities they are perceived to have.

We have the beginning—but only the beginning—of a fully satisfactory answer to circularity objections. The dimensionality of quality space gives us the number of differentiative attributes among encodings, but it does not identify those attributes. Axes may be placed in many different ways. Multidimensional scaling gives their number but not their placement. If the space is three-dimensional, there must be three distinct ways in which encodings of the stimuli can vary, but multidimensional scaling alone cannot identify them.

All that multidimensional scaling yields is a structure of relative distances. That structure is constant under rotations of axes. One needs other resources to identify the axes of quality space. In effect, one must rotate the structure of inter-point distances until one can provide some meaningful interpretation for the chosen axes. In the next chapter I will show how this can sometimes be done.

Some other caveats should be posted. An N-dimensional space employs N coordinates to identify a point. Those N coordinates are not necessarily distances along orthogonal axes. Other coordinate schemes are often more useful. In the common hue circle, for example, a Cartesian coordinate scheme would be very odd. Instead, polar coordinates are used, in which hue is the angular coordinate and saturation is the radius.

Multidimensional scaling also fails to provide a proof that the number of dimensions for a given modality is N. As described in the appendix, adding a dimension will usually improve the overall fit of the model, but soon the improvements become insignificant. With these techniques, finding the dimensionality of a space requires a *statistical* decision. This is not to say that there is no good evidence for choosing some number N over all other numbers. We simply do not have proof.

Multidimensional scaling depends heavily on the stimulus sample chosen, requires an exhaustive series of similarity judgements, and even then sometimes fails numerically. Interpretation of the dimensions produced—identifying the differentiative features of encodings—relies on other techniques, which are yet to be explored. Nevertheless, developments in this chapter show that the project of defining qualities by similarities does not invariably move in a circle. Using nothing more than the notion of relative similarity, one can determine the number of different respects in terms of which things are sensed to resemble or differ. One can distinguish those different respects, separate companion qualities, and rectify imperfect communities.

5

Different Modalities

5.1 Prospects for a General Theory

We would like a *general* theory of sensory modalities: a theory that could be applied to any sensory modality, including ones that humans do not share. It should not restrict itself to data available only from humans (such as magnitude estimation or verbal judgements), but should embrace and employ animal data as well. It could then be applied not only to the familiar human sensory modalities, but also to non-human ones such as electro-reception and echo location. In Nagel's (1986) words, we would like an 'objective' characterization of the subjective character of a sensory modality, one that would in some sense enable creatures who do not have a particular kind of experience to understand what it is like to have that kind of experience. This 'objective phenomenology' would describe the 'structural features' of perception (Nagel 1979*b*, p. 179).

Completing a quality space for a sensory modality satisfies some of these desires. That space precisely describes the 'structural features' of the modality. Relative similarities generate the structure. The spacing of qualities within a given modality is discovered, not invented; it is not a matter of convention or stipulation. It is just a brute fact that classes of stimuli that are pairwise indiscriminable overlap one another. From such overlap comes its order. Another name for a quality space is a *sensory order*: an order of qualities intrinsic to a particular sensory modality (see Hayek 1952).

Multidimensional scaling takes one directly from a triples list of relative similarities to a map in which distances are monotonic on relative similarities. The technique generalizes; its limitations are more computational and practical than theoretical. The unadorned Quinean notion of perceptual relative similarity can be applied to any sensory modality, unlike more specialized predicates such as 'is the same colour as' or 'is louder than'. One can employ stimulus samples without identifying in advance the attributes of stimuli to which subjects are sensitive. A multitude of sensory qualities may underlie such judgements, but we presuppose nothing about their number or identity. In principle, it is possible to obtain relative similarity data from animals, using confusion probabilities or stimulus generalization tests, and so explore non-human modalities as well.

We start with a bare list of items that match, or a similarly austere list of relative similarity judgements. From a sufficiently long list, one can find the number of distinct ways in which the stimuli are sensed to resemble or differ; the number, that is, of independent features that determine the outcome of discriminations. In a 'space' defined by those dimensions, one can plot the position of every item in the sample so that relative distances correspond to relative similarities.

From this small beginning, one can in principle construct the full quality space for an individual. One can assess the degree to which the model fits the original data and the extent of differences between individuals. The dimensions of that space correspond to qualitative attributes: what I have previously called the *differentiative* features of sensory states.

The distinction must be maintained between the theoretical potential of multidimensional scaling and other scaling techniques and their actual practice. In theory, modern psychometric techniques can isolate sensory dimensions and derive a space. In practice, the work is extremely difficult, and in some cases an actual application is technologically impossible. The main difficulty derives from the sheer number of judgements required. Even with only 20 stimuli, one needs to obtain 190 rankings of similarities among pairs to fill out the data matrix.[1] Each such ranking judgement may require many trials. In some modalities each trial is a tribulation. One can present only one odour at a time, for example, so a simple triple requires successive sniffs. One may need to return to a neutral state of adaptation between successive presentations, and to carry out extensive randomized

---

[1] To fill one-half the data matrix for N stimuli, we need $N \cdot (N - 1)/2$ similarity rankings. It is possible to work with partially filled matrices, but with them one is not guaranteed a unique ranking of inter-point similarities, and the risk of degenerate solutions increases.

blocks of trials so as to control for ordering effects. For animal data each relative similarity judgement in effect requires its own experiment. Finally, a sample of 20 stimuli is many orders of magnitude below what one needs for an entire modality. It has been estimated, for example, that the average human can discriminate 10 million distinct colours. Even a 1 per cent sample of this space would require 5 billion similarity rankings. The research proposal would not be funded. In practice, one must work with a small number of stimuli. With small samples the probability of degenerate solutions increases, since there is a greater likelihood that the stimuli will cluster in just a few groups. In short, just as in Carnap's or Goodman's systems, the theoretical adequacy of the constructional methods deriving from psychometrics should be sharply distinguished from the question of whether those methods provide workable engineering.

In spite of all these practical limitations, the theoretical promise of the techniques still beckons. This promise has already been partially fulfilled in sensory domains that have heretofore proven phenomenologically impenetrable, such as the murky modalities of taste and smell. If one were to arrange odours in an order, how would one proceed? In what ways can tastes seem similar or different? These questions are opaque to introspection, and have proven intractable in the past. But multidimensional scaling has already clarified some features of the domain, and its approach seems free of some of the conceptual muddles that have confused the issues in the past.

Investigators have proposed quality spaces for various modalities. This chapter will describe some examples. In some we seem to be converging on interpretable axes; we can provide at least partial explanations for the structure of phenomenal similarities and dissimilarities in that modality. Only when such explanations succeed can one complete the analysis of sensory qualities. In some modalities there are promising developments in just that direction, and I will provide some examples of what it means to *explain* the structure of a quality space.

5.2 The Psychological Colour Solid

Perhaps the most familiar of quality spaces is the *psychological colour solid*. If one attempts to arrange a large sample of colour patches in an order so that more similar ones are always closer to one another than are less similar ones, the resulting order is three-dimensional. Along one dimension we will find variations in *brightness*, ranging from black through the greys to white.[2] If we collect all the patches of a given brightness and attempt to arrange them, we find that we always need a two-dimensional arrangement that is roughly circular. Each such 'hue circle' is best mapped using a polar coordinate system. One coordinate—the second dimension of our order—is *hue*, ranging from purple through the colours of the spectrum, and back to purple. Hues will vary with angles around the circle. The second coordinate for each plane is *saturation*: the distance from the achromatic centre of the hue circle. Colours along such a radius would vary from a non-chromatic grey towards purer and purer samples of the given hue (see Hardin 1985). The series will illustrate differing saturations. It provides the third dimension of the colour solid.

The psychological colour solid should be distinguished from the various *colour order* systems. A colour order system arranges a large number of colour patches ('material samples') in a three-dimensional array for some specific purpose. The exact ordering is dependent on the purpose of the system, so different systems give different orders. One purpose might be simply to provide some systematic notations for different colour names. Another purpose might be to simplify paint mixing and matching.

In contrast, the psychological colour solid is the *quality space* for colours: it is the order, whatever it is, that is intrinsic to relative similarities and discriminations among colours. Colour order systems can more or less accurately represent the psychological colour solid. For a given individual at a given time there is just one colour quality space, although there are many colour order systems.[3] In some respects, none of the existing

---

[2] Stimuli can be ranked by the apparent intensity of the illumination they reflect or radiate, and that ranking yields an attribute that is also sometimes called 'brightness'. To distinguish the two, the technical term for the whiteness–blackness of surface colours is *lightness*.

[3] Different individuals may judge relative similarities differently, and so may have different quality spaces. For example, dichromats have only a two-dimensional colour space (see s. 2.4). Furthermore, changes within an individual over time can lead to changes in the relative spacing of qualities. For these reasons, there is not just one psychological colour solid true of all people at all times, but different ones for different people at different times.

colour order systems are fully satisfactory as representations of colour quality space; all have deficiencies in representing the similarity and discrimination data.

If an order system is to represent colour quality space, distances must be monotonic over similarities. Pairs of colour samples that are equally distant should be equally similar. Few colour order systems attempt to meet this condition. One that attempted a certain kind of equi-spacing is the *Munsell colour solid*, pictured in Fig. 5.1. The vertical axis of this solid, which Munsell named *value*, corresponds to the lightness of the surface, from white to black. Munsell named the distance from that axis in any horizontal plane *chroma*. It corresponds approximately to the saturation of the colour. In a pentagon around that axis were placed five primaries: red, green, yellow, blue, and purple. Since the spacing between them was set a priori, equal distances between Munsell chips do not exactly correspond to equivalent degrees of hue similarity.

Munsell was an artist and art teacher, and he constructed the first version of his colour order system in 1905 (see Hurvich 1981, pp. 274–5). It predates the development of multidimensional scaling and magnitude estimation techniques, although the construction was apparently completed with a kind of precursor to magnitude estimation methods. It has been several times revised, each time with a larger sample, better controls of viewing conditions, or better materials to improve the stability of placements of chips. Multidimensional scaling (MDS) techniques have not been used directly in its construction. The Munsell Colour Company publishes an atlas of the current system using about 1200 colour samples. It is clear why MDS techniques have found no direct practical use in this construction, since even this relatively small number of samples would require over 700,000 relative similarity judgements.

Multidimensional scaling techniques have been used to test the ordering of hues. For example, R. N. Shepard (1962) applied a variant of non-metric MDS (called 'proximity analysis') to a selection of 14 hues of approximately equal brightness. The ranking of similarities among the pairs was produced directly: subjects were asked to rate the similarity of each pair on a scale from 1 to 5. When the resulting rankings were analysed, the result was the structure given in Fig. 5.2. The ordinal position of hues is as predicted by the Munsell system, and the metric is approximately correct. But according to the Munsell system, the five named hues should form a perfect pentagon. Proximity analysis reveals something closer to two opponent axes: red–green and yellow–blue. The result is even more surprising given that *non-metric* analysis produced the map. Only the

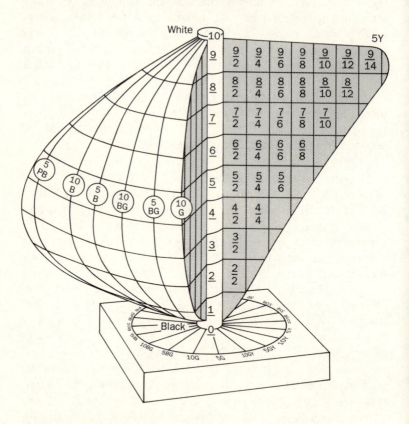

FIG. 5.1. The Munsell colour order system

Note: A quarter of the solid has been removed to show an interior section. The central vertical axis defines the variations in *value*, from black (0) to white (10). The exposed vertical plane is a plane of constant hue (here 5Y). The different hue planes around the axis are labelled 5Y, 10G, 5BG, and so on. Finally, distance horizontally from the central axis is *chroma*, labelled by the denominators of the various fractions.

Source: From Hurvich (1981, p. 274). Reprinted by permission of Sinauer Associates, Inc.

rankings among inter-stimulus similarities were used, not their ratios or sums. If one were to add additional stimuli to the sample, the added rankings would further constrain the solution, and it would more closely approximate the psychological structure of relative similarities among colours.

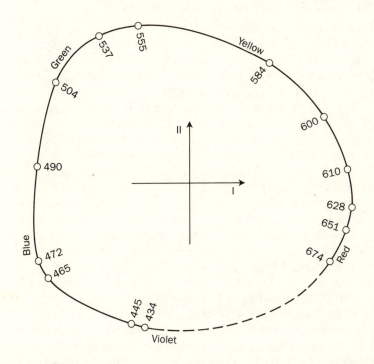

FIG. 5.2. Proximity analysis of hues

Note: Stimuli are labelled by wavelength in nanometres. Proximity analysis placed the points; Shepard drew the curved line connecting them to emphasize the similarity with the hue circle.

Source: From Shepard (1962, p. 236). Reprinted by permission of *Psychometrika*.

At best, the Munsell colour order system can be considered an approximate representation of the quality space for surface colours viewed under controlled conditions. It has the correct topology and ordinal positioning of samples, but the distances between them do not accurately represent similarities. Of course, the system was not constructed to represent the human colour quality space, but to provide an organized set of material standards that would be useful in identifying colours. It is gratifying to find that three dimensions emerge naturally as principles of organization for that set.

5.3 Some Neuro-Phenomenological Distinctions

Clearly, one must distinguish colour order *systems* from the psychological colour *solid* that they more or less faithfully represent. One also must distinguish the psychological colour solid from wavelength mixture space. This second distinction will help one to avoid several classic confusions about sensory qualities.

Wavelength mixture space is derived from the effects of stimuli on three types of transducers. Each dimension represents the number of absorptions in one of the three classes of cones in the retina. A point in that space is an equivalence class with respect to those physical effects on transducers that bear information used in subsequent discriminations.

The dimensions of a quality space have no such ready interpretation. The axes provided by multidimensional scaling have no intrinsic meaning; rotating the 'shape' has no effect on the structure of inter-point distances. Indeed, after one discovers a stable MDS 'shape', one purposefully rotates the axes in the attempt to find interpretable ones. The number of dimensions of the MDS space corresponds to the number of independent ways in which stimuli in that modality can be sensed to resemble or differ, but the dimensions *per se* have no meaning. Indeed, it will be seen that a key step in explaining a quality space is to find interpretable axes. Sometimes one can provide them with a neurophysiological interpretation. Only then can one claim to have determined *what* the differentiative attributes of encodings are, as opposed to knowing simply how many of them there are.

A second contrast between the two spaces concerns the scaling of axes. In wavelength mixture space, equal distances anywhere along any axis represent equal numbers of isomerizations. Furthermore, the *ratios* of distances are significant. Twenty isomerizations are twice as many as ten. Doubling the intensity of a stimulus can therefore be represented by multiplication of its coordinates. In contrast, quality space does not provide any units of measurement. In colour *order* systems, distances along the different axes may not even be comparable. For example, the Munsell order system provides intervals along both the value and the chroma axes, but ten units of chroma cannot be equated to ten units of value. At best, one knows that equal distances should correspond to equal degrees of psychological similarity. But MDS space by itself provides no metric that can be used to measure those distances. There is certainly no common *physical* unit in terms of which that similarity can be measured across the different dimensions.

A third contrast between the spaces follows from the first two. Vector addition is meaningful in wavelength mixture space, but not necessarily in quality space. Because axes in wavelength mixture space represent numbers of absorptions, the effect of mixing two stimuli can be represented by adding vectors. Such addition relies on the fact that ratios are significant, and ten units along one axis represent the same distance as ten along another.

In quality space, however, mixing the qualities associated with two points does not necessarily yield the quality associated with the vector sum of those points. Vector addition *may* be meaningful, but it need not be. If the different axes use different units, for example, or units for which multiplication is undefined, then vector addition is meaningless. It also fails in any quality space that is bounded. One can use special adaptation tricks to create *maximally* saturated colours. Beyond that horizon there are no colours. Suppose we mix two nearby hues that are almost maximally saturated: on vector addition principles we would derive a point outside the maximal saturation horizon; and of course, the mixture does not yield such a point.

The issue is admittedly confusing when considered in colour space. The existence of colour primaries (of which more anon) leads to mixing and matching results that resemble vector addition. Better examples are found in other modalities. A mixture of two odours need not be equally similar to both. The mixture may not be similar to either of its components; it may be found at some seemingly unrelated place in the quality space. Tones provide a second example. Two tones 'sum' to a chord, and not to the tone intermediary between them. A combination of tones must therefore be represented differently than a combination of wavelengths. This question will be further explored in the next section.

In most modalities we have no idea what goes on in the stages between transducer effects and sensations with qualitative properties. There is no good reason to assume that equivalent degrees of difference between the physical effects that two stimuli have on transducers will always yield equivalent degrees of difference between the sensed qualities of those stimuli.

Colour space is not a constant function of wavelength mixture space. Equal distances in wavelength mixture space do not represent equal differences between the colours. To map wavelength mixture space into the psychological colour solid, some segments need to be lengthened or shortened. But mixtures are represented by vector addition only in wavelength mixture space. It follows that mixtures are not always represented accurately by vector addition in quality space.

If one knew how transducers in a given modality code their stimuli, one could construct an analogue of wavelength mixture space for that modality. Generically, wavelength mixture space represents 'identity of effects'; it can also be called a *transducer* space. Distinct dimensions correspond to independent information-bearing effects of stimuli on transducers. If some relevant effects can vary independently of others, then in transducer space the two classes of effects must be represented by distinct dimensions. A point in this space represents an equivalence class with respect to the indicator properties of transducers. If one can scale the various dimensions of transducer space in some common unit, then mixtures of stimuli will be represented by the vector sum of their components.

As hinted above, modalities that contain 'psychological primaries' present some new complexities. *Psychological primaries* for a given domain are the members of the smallest set of qualities (*a*) whose mixtures can match every sensed quality in the domain; but (*b*) each of which cannot be matched by combinations of the others. (Each can be matched only by itself.) From (*a*) it follows that every quality in that domain can be expressed algebraically as some weighted combination of primaries. (Some weights are sometimes zero.) From (*b*) it follows that each primary can be considered phenomenologically 'pure' or 'unique'. One can think of primaries as components of every quality in the modality—except those of the other primaries.

Colour space seems to contain primaries, or 'unique' hues:

they are red, green, yellow, and blue.[4] There is a yellow that is not at all reddish and not at all greenish. But orange or yellow-green or any of the colours between the primaries do not have this character. Orange is both reddish and yellowish. Primaries are pure, and all other hues seem to be mixtures of them.

A necessary condition for the existence of psychological primaries is that one can match any stimulus in the modality by some mixture of the primaries. Such a finding does not itself demonstrate the existence of primaries. Wavelength mixture space shows how almost any three wavelengths can be chosen as 'primaries', and their relative intensities adjusted to match arbitrary stimuli. In this N-dimensional transducer space there will be an indefinitely large class of N-tuples of 'primaries' that would suffice.[5] But not all such N-tuples are considered genuine psychological primaries. They must form a minimal set and yield 'unique' or 'pure' qualities (condition (b)) as well.

The existence of psychological primaries in a given modality is not indicated by any obvious structural features of the transducer space or the quality space. Primaries should also be distinguished from the dimensions of quality space. There are four unique hues, but these define a two-dimensional hue circle. Redness–greenness is one dimension, while yellowness–blueness is another. The unique hues of red and green define only one dimension, because red is encoded as excitation in that system, and green as inhibition. A quality space will have a particular shape. Its dimensionality must be distinguished from the existence of primaries.

What if anything distinguishes red, green, yellow, and blue as primaries in the psychological colour solid? One notes that none of them can be matched by any combination of the others, but of course that is true also (say) of the hues shifted one step to the right of each. None of the facts of relative similarity imply that, although there exists a red that seems not at all orangish, every

---

[4] More precisely, each plane in the colour solid representing colours of equal brightness will contain colours of the four unique hues. Different planes contain unique hues of differing brightness. An exact match is possible with four colours only if the 'domain' comprises colours of equal brightness. Otherwise one can match the colours in hue, but not necessarily in brightness.

[5] Not all N-tuples will do. One necessary condition is that no primary is matched by any combination of the others. Even then, there may be some stimuli outside the 'gamut' of the primaries, just as in wavelength mixture space.

orange seems somewhat reddish. Nothing within the structure of sensory similarities and dissimilarities distinguishes the primaries. Some hues seem to be combinations of others, and some do not. In effect, one finds *privileged directions* within the quality space, directions that provide interpretable components for all the others. This finding provides a second clue to the differentiative attributes, at least in those modalities in which 'psychological primaries' exist. We hunt for some interpretable directions within the quality space. They can be provided by primaries. The differentiative attributes of encodings in those modalities will be those directions that seem to be components of all the others, and do not seem to be mixtures of any others.

The goal is to provide a neurophysiological interpretation for quality space: to anchor the structure of relative similarities by identifying the mechanisms responsible. Many pitfalls lie in the path of providing such an interpretation. To summarize the potential hazards, we should distinguish:

1. a particular sensory quality such as a red colour or a camphoraceous odour;
2. the dimensionality of the quality space in a given modality;
3. the existence and identity of psychological primaries within a modality;
4. the existence of specific receptors that respond only to some particular quality within a qualitative dimension; and
5. the differing physical attributes of stimuli to which different receptors are sensitive.

The distinction between the dimensionality of a quality space and its primaries (if any) has already been mentioned. In many modalities dimensions do not correspond at all to primaries. A given pitch is not a combination of unique pitches; nor is colour saturation a combination of saturations.

Unique hues do not map in any obvious way on to transducers, nor can they be inferred from the properties of visual transducers. One must distinguish psychological primaries (if they exist) from specific receptors (item 4). Although one kind of cone is sometimes (confusingly) called a 'red' receptor, *unique red* does not correspond to that kind, or to its inputs. It is not found in the spectrum at the place where 'red' (long-wavelength) receptors have optimal sensitivity. In fact, no spectral stimulus yields unique red! Instead, unique red is defined in terms of more central qualities: redness with no tint of yellowness or blueness. Such qualities can only be generated with contributions from at least two distinct receptor types.

Other disappointments lurk if one attempts to identify unique red (or any hue) with some non-dispositional property of stimuli. Although wavelengths are related to hues, no non-dispositional wavelength property of a stimulus can be identified with the property 'unique red'. The many combinations of wavelengths perceived to be unique red are grouped together only by their propensity to cause a specific effect in the observer's visual system. They lead to excitation in the red–green system, and baseline activity in the yellow–blue system. The argument for this conclusion is complex (see Hardin 1988, 1984*a*), but some of its initial steps are familiar. Section 2.4 showed how infinitely many combinations of wavelengths could all have the same effect on the visual system. What principle collects all those combinations that present unique red to an observer at a particular time? No non-dispositional collecting principle succeeds. Those combinations all present unique red solely in virtue of their equivalent effects on that observer at that time. Change the observer, or the time, and the collections change accordingly. We cannot assume that there is some non-dispositional physical property common to those stimuli that are sensed (by someone at some time) to be qualitatively similar.

For similar reasons, particular sensory qualities (item 1) need not originate in specific receptors (item 4). For example, although one can sense orange hues, there is no receptor specific to that quality. In fact, there is no receptor specifically sensitive to any particular hue. Hue perceptions always arise from the comparison of outputs from several types of receptors. Somehow this distinction gets lost in other modalities. It is tempting to think, for example, that if one can sniff that minty odour there must be some receptor sensitive specifically to a minty property of odorous gases. Such temptation ignores the distinctions between sensory qualities, physical properties, and specific receptors. The sensed mintiness may be derived from a comparison of outputs from multiple receptors. Even if there were some class of receptors active in all and only the episodes of sniffing minty odours, there need not be a physical property of gases that can be

identified independently of its effects on those receptors, and
which constitutes its minty quality. Many different gases may
have the same effect on olfactory receptors. Perhaps the only way
physically to identify the minty set is by their similar nasal effect.

Finally, a particular dimension of a quality space (item 2) does
not necessarily correspond to a specific receptor type (item 4).
One might find receptors with differing response spectra that all
lie along the same qualitative dimension. Pitch perception
provides a clamorous example. To find receptor cells with distinct
response spectra does *not* suffice to isolate new qualitative
dimensions.

In short, the dimensionality of a sensory order is a topological
feature intrinsic to that order. Each dimension is some respect in
terms of which stimuli in that modality can be sensed to resemble
or differ. There is some fixed number of independent dimensions
of such variation, but quality space does not identify any axes. A
particular sensory quality corresponds to a region within this
space. Psychological primaries, if they exist for the modality,
correspond to distinguishable vectors. If there are psychological
primaries, any quality in the order can be matched by a mixture of
those primaries, and a vector representation of the gamut of
qualities is possible. The search for receptor mechanisms
addresses the distinct question of providing anatomical
underpinnings for the sensory order. Finally, even if one finds
specific receptors, there is no guarantee that one can identify
some non-dispositional property of things to which those
receptors respond. Perhaps the only collecting principle among
the diverse physical causes of receptor activation is just that they
all have equivalent effects on those receptors.

5.4   Spatial Qualia, Chords, and Shapes

One complication has been suppressed thus far in the account of
the quality space that is intrinsic to vision. Experiments in colour
vision typically exert precise control over viewing conditions.
Ambient illumination is specified, and a neutrally adapted
observer views the patches at a specified distance and visual angle.
The patches are directly fixated in the centre of the visual field,
where colour sensitivity is greatest. Under those conditions we
get a three-dimensional psychological colour solid. But this

special case will not suffice to represent the full visual quality space. We should allow variation in any attribute to which discriminations are sensitive, and add a new one if stimuli are discriminable even though they match in all dimensions added thus far. One can discriminate otherwise identical colour patches by their place in the visual field. Colour discriminations themselves vary considerably at different locations in the visual field, and to represent the discriminations possible at different locations one may require different colour solids at different places. At the visual periphery we are all monochromats, and the colour solids at those locations are one-dimensional.

5.4.1 Spatial Qualia

Since two colour patches that match in hue, saturation, and brightness can be discriminated if they have distinct visual locations, we must add at least two additional dimensions, for visual azimuth and altitude. Do we need a dimension for visual depth? The same criterion as before is operative. Suppose we had two patches matched in all five qualitative attributes isolated thus far. The two are presented successively at different depths but at the same visual azimuth and altitude, occupying the same visual angle, and adjusted so that they match in hue, saturation, and brightness. Can they be discriminated or not? If so, we need an additional qualitative dimension, corresponding to visual depth. In any ordinary visual situation (with normal depth cues available) one can discriminate a distant patch from a closer one adjusted to fill the same visual angle (see Kaufman 1974, pp. 326 ff.). For example, one sees the red rug on the floor as manifesting a particular hue, saturation, and brightness *at a particular distance*, although a much larger rug at twice the distance could match the first one in apparent hue, saturation, brightness, azimuth, and altitude. One could discriminate between a six-foot 'stage prop' toothbrush presented at a distance and a normal one presented nearby, even if the two match in colour and shape, and are presented so as to occupy the same visual angle.

An indefinitely large family of different shapes at different distances could present the same two-dimensional visual tableau as the nearby desk. One sees just one member of that family—a particular shape at a distance (see Haber and Hershenson 1980, p. 171). If one can discriminate among the various members of that family—as it seems one can—then visual spatial qualia are three-dimensional. So we get at least a six-dimensional visual quality space, with a three-dimensional colour solid representing the colour discriminations possible at each point within a three-dimensional visual volume.[6]

A similar test applies to other modalities. One hears a distant loud sound as a loud sound *at a distance*, although its intensity could be matched by a faint sound nearby. In fact, its apparent intensity could be matched by a large family of sounds at different intensities and distances. None the less, one hears just that one loud sound at that distance. Auditory depth must be added to pitch and loudness. We will see below that we will also need to add an (oddly distorted) sense of direction to this list.

A simple test for phenomenal depth uses relative similarity. Present otherwise matching stimuli at different depths, and request judgements of their relative closeness. Is the first closer to the second or the third? Submit the proximity judgements to multidimensional scaling. If a close fit can be achieved in a two-dimensional MDS space, phenomenal space is two-dimensional. If we need three dimensions, then we should add phenomenal depth to azimuth and altitude.

Scaling methods provide a test for settling whether qualia have a differentiative feature corresponding to depth. The issue demonstrates again the need to distinguish transducer space from quality space. Often the physical attributes of proximal stimuli are taken as grounds for the claim that there is no sensory quality corresponding to depth. A sample argument might proceed as follows. The receptor surface is two-dimensional, and any pattern of transducer events distributed over a retinal surface could be produced by many different three-dimensional objects at different depths. Those objects would be indiscriminable. Therefore the subjective visual field is two-dimensional, and lacks depth.

One mistake in such arguments is to focus exclusively on one retinal surface. We typically employ two. Their spatial separation is such that the differences ('disparities') between the placement of the images on the two retinas can be used to determine

---

[6] At best, even this structure could only cope with an array of surface colours at-a-moment; if other stimuli are allowed (such as radiant ones, volume colours, or temporally extended presentations) matters become yet more complex. We would need to add new dimensions of variation for features such as glowing colours, glossiness, and apparent motion.

depths.[7] If 'equivalence' is defined with respect to both retinas simultaneously, our family of equivalent configurations collapses. Shapes indiscriminable by one retina will produce distinguishable effects in the other.[8] The more serious mistake in the argument, however, is to treat transducer properties as if they were sensory qualities. Much goes on between the transducers and the stage at which sensory qualities make their appearance, and there is no justification in treating any property of transducers as necessarily reflected in sensation. An analogous argument would conclude (falsely) that no sensory attribute corresponds to variations in wavelength, since many different wavelengths can produce the same effect on any given receptor.

One might wonder why spatial attributes count as *qualitative* attributes of sensation. Typically, one thinks of a visual quale as occurring at a particular place in the visual field. It may seem odd to treat that 'place' itself as a qualitative feature. But one must admit that differences in location can present qualitative differences. The various spatial illusions corroborate the idea. A thing can appear to have spatial attributes that it does not really have. One need only think of the various 'geometrical' illusions, in which various distortions of position and shape occur (see Gregory 1977, pp. 138–42). Just as one invokes a qualitative attribute of sensation to explain why a red car sometimes looks blue, so the various geometrical illusions demonstrate the need for *spatial* qualitative attributes.

Indeed, the difficulty lies not in deciding whether to admit spatial qualitative features, but rather in deciding whether they form a distinct kind of qualitative feature. Does visual depth differ in any fundamental way from hue or brightness? For now we note Carnap's (1967) proposal. One cannot find two colours in the same place simultaneously, but one can find the same colour in two places simultaneously. Facts of this sort may allow a distinction between spatial attributes and the others.

[7] The image of the object occurs in slightly different places in the two retinas. The difference in location is the retinal disparity. The visual system typically employs retinal disparities for depth perception of objects up to 135 m from the eye, although some people are disparity-blind (see Haber and Hershenson 1980, p. 239).

[8] This gives a three-dimensional transducer space for visual locations. We need two coordinates to specify the location of the retinal image of an object in a single two-dimensional retina. To specify the location of the stimulus in both retinas simultaneously, *three* coordinates are needed—azimuth, altitude, and the disparity between the two retinas.

5.4.2 *Chords*

Audition differs structurally from vision. One cannot see two distinct colours at the same place simultaneously, but one can hear two distinct tones at the same place simultaneously. We call them *chords*. Combining two tones does not create some third tone distinct from both, but rather a chord, in which both tones can be discerned. In contrast, mixing two hues yields a third one distinct from both. The hue mixture may resemble its components to a greater or lesser degree, but those components are not discernible as in a chord.

This last claim may be challenged. Can one not see the redness and the yellowness in something that is orange? Even naive observers can reliably rate the degree of redness and yellowness in orange hues, and such ratings form the foundation for the Swedish Natural Colour Order System (see Hård and Sivik 1981). Is there a difference between seeing the red and yellow components of an orange hue and hearing the tonal components of a chord?

The distinction is a real one, and it is easy to make in terms of differentiative attributes. The quality space for surface colours presented under controlled conditions is (probably) six-dimensional. Once one identifies a minimum visual location, there are just three remaining dimensions of discriminable variation among colour patches presented at that location. Any patches seen at that location that match in those attributes—hue, saturation, and brightness—will be indiscriminable. Such a test ensures that our list of differentiative attributes for that stimulus domain is complete.

The same test applied to hearing will produce radically different results. One can discriminate sounds by pitch and loudness, so the auditory quality space is at least two-dimensional. We have already added depth to the list. Contrary to the claims of some philosophers (Strawson 1963, pp. 57–8), one *can* directly localize sounds in space, using only auditory clues. Sounds as experienced with two ears have an intrinsic spatial character. The Italian physicist Giovanni Venturi provided the first recorded demonstration in 1796 (see Murch 1973, p. 206). He blindfolded subjects, sat them in an open field, and asked them to hold their heads still. He then walked around, piping an occasional note on his flute, and asked them to point in the direction of the sound.

Even with more sophisticated methods, errors in localization are surprisingly low, as shown in Table 5.1. An angle of 15° is a bit less than that subtended by one's fist held out at arm's length, so even the largest errors are smaller than one might expect. The spatial order intrinsic to sounds has some peculiarities, however. The space is *anisotropic*, with errors generally increasing as one moves from the sagittal plane towards a position directly opposite one or another ear, but with several dips in the trend. The space also has an *inversion locus* running through it that is not reflected in Table 5.1; that is, subjects quite often make front–back reversals in locating a sound, pointing behind themselves when the sound is actually presented in front (and conversely). They will however point more or less precisely at the reversed spot, so that (for example) a sound 30° off the midline in front will sometimes be localized as 30° off the midline in back (and conversely), with an average error of 15.6° in either case.[9] If one considers the distances from the anterior point to both ears, one can see there is a posterior point that has exactly the same distances to both ears. So the two are often confused (see Gulick *et al.* 1989, p. 320). Table 5.1 gives errors after adjusting for front–back reversals in this way.

TABLE 5.1. Errors in auditory localization

	Position from median plane (degrees)						
	0	15	30	45	60	75	90
Average error (degrees)	4.6	13.0	15.6	16.3	16.2	15.6	16.0

Source: Stevens and Newman (1936).

Topologically, this space has a strange and wonderful structure. It is not readily accessible to introspection, probably because even introspective investigators move their heads too much. A tilt or turn of the head suffices to disambiguate the cues used for auditory localization. Indeed, this 'orienting reflex'

[9] The auditory system uses differences in the timing, intensity, and phase of sounds arriving at the two ears to find their direction. These interaural differences are equivalent for those pairs of positions likely to be reversed. Indeed, Warren (1982, p. 36) notes: 'The question that needs answering seems to be how discrimination between positions in the front quadrant and the back quadrant can be made at all.' The pinna seems implicated; see Warren (1982, pp. 50–3).

typically expires with one's head in an optimal orientation for localizing sounds of interest. Furthermore, sounds that are front–back reversed still seem to come from just one location, and not from both at once; no ambiguity is introspectively apparent.

Front–back reversals are an *auditory spatial illusion*, and show the need for qualitative attributes corresponding to auditory location. Other sorts of auditory spatial illusions are known, of which the most interesting are *binaural beats*. If two tones that are slightly out of phase are presented separately to the two ears, one will hear a sequence of phantom beats that move from side to side. Interaural phase differences are used to localize sounds, and the phantom source will shift position in a way that corresponds with the phase differences between the two tones (Warren 1982, p. 38). One seems to hear a sound at a place where there is no sound.

There is a discriminable auditory azimuth, altitude, and depth. So does auditory space have only five dimensions? Suppose one picks a specific auditory location. We need three spatial dimensions to specify that location, plus others to represent the independent dimensions of variation of sounds at that place. Two additional ones will not suffice, as they would allow one to specify only a single pitch–loudness pair. But two distinct chords that both contain that pitch–loudness pair might be easily discriminable. A chord comprises many pitch–loudness pairs.

In vision we need only a single hue–saturation–brightness triple to specify a surface colour at a given visual location. In audition, many pitch–loudness pairs may be needed at a given auditory location. Sometimes it is said that audition is an 'analytic' modality and vision is a 'synthetic' one. This terminology is somewhat confusing, since in vision it *is* possible to perceive the red and yellow 'components' of some intermediary orange hue. However, with chords a single pitch–loudness match does not ensure indiscriminability, while any stimulus presented under controlled conditions that matches a particular colour in hue, saturation, and brightness will be indiscriminable from that colour. Two indiscriminable chords must match in pitch and loudness for every component tone in each. There is no obvious limit to the number of distinct component tones discernible in a sound. The full spectra of loudness and pitch must be matched for two sounds to be indiscriminable.

This distinction yields another structural difference between the two modalities. An orange hue is similar to red, but it is more similar to those hues between itself and red than it is to red. Similarly, although orange is similar to yellow, it is more similar to yellowy-orange than it is to yellow. These facts explain why orange is 'between' red and yellow. Chords do not show this pattern of resemblances. A chord made up of two notes is not phenomenally 'between' them, nor is it more similar to intermediate notes than it is to its components. A chord is a combination of multiple points in pitch–loudness space. A given wavelength combination is just a single point in hue–saturation–wavelength space, and it does not show the disjoint pattern of relative similarities found in a chord.

Auditory quality space will therefore possess many more than five dimensions. Tones of a single frequency can be discriminated in terms of pitch and loudness. If we add a second tone, we get a stimulus discriminable from any of the single ones. One needs a new pitch–loudness pair for the second component of the sound. If one adds a third tone to the two-tone sound, one gets a new stimulus discriminable from any of the single tones and from any of the two-tone sounds. So we need another pitch–loudness pair for the third component. The same is true as we add a fourth tone, a fifth tone, a sixth tone, and so on. The components are discriminable, and so the combinations reveal additional dimensions of auditory discrimination. Eventually one will reach sounds of such complexity that adding an additional component will fail to produce a result that is discriminable from all the others. Sounds at that limit will be enormously complex.

Introspection does not reveal how many distinct pitch–loudness pairs one must add to specify all discriminations possible among sounds. One requires as many distinct qualitative dimensions as there are ways in which arbitrarily complex combinations of tones can resemble or differ. Audition is sensitive to ratios among some N distinct receptor systems, where N is the number of distinct tones in a combination that can be discerned. N is a very large but finite number.

Colour vision has a closure property lacking in audition. Suppose one attempts to catalogue surface colours presented in laboratory conditions. Once one has three independent dimensions of variation, attempts to find a new colour not already in the set will always fail. The spectral analysis performed by the visual system is extremely crude, and one need only match the ratios among three distinct wavelengths. Visual *metamers* are possible: distinct combinations of wavelengths that nevertheless match. They match because they match in those three critical dimensions. In audition, however, we do not get closure with just three qualitative dimensions. Adding a new tone yields a sound discriminable from all the previous combinations. In audition the spectrographic analysis is extremely fine, and any mismatch among some N frequency components can lead to a discriminable difference. It is practically impossible to find the auditory equivalent of metamers. Almost any difference in the pitch–loudness spectrogram of two sounds leads to a discriminable difference between them.

In a way, it is easiest to think of the pitch of a sound as a component of auditory *location*. At a given auditory azimuth, altitude, and distance there may be some N discriminable pitch–loudness pairs. But at a given auditory azimuth, altitude, distance, and pitch there is just one loudness. Unfortunately, more than one pitch 'dimension' is required, since one can alter the pitch components of a sound at a given auditory place in some N distinct ways simultaneously. We need as many distinct pitch dimensions as there are discriminable ways to alter a combination of tones.

5.4.3 *Shapes*

A chord is a multi-toned stimulus; the visual analogue is a multicoloured shape. How are such shapes treated in visual quality space? If a chord with N tones requires $N \cdot 2$ dimensions, will a multicoloured shape with K distinct colours require a quality space with $K \cdot 3$ dimensions?

The multicoloured aspect of a thing *can* account for its discriminability from others. Ordinary objects with their multifarious qualities are grist for the multidimensional mill. Indeed, our first samples will include such objects. At the start we do not prejudge which attributes of objects are relevant to discriminations, and so we do not know which attributes should be controlled in discriminations or similarity judgements. One can start with any stimuli at all in the comparisons, having no idea of their qualitatively salient properties or the differences that engage discriminations.   Then a vast multidimensional scaling of the triples list could in principle isolate the number of dimensions.

If all sorts of ordinary objects are allowed in the initial sample, it seems likely that several visual attributes that are not on our pristine list of six will emerge as potential ordering relations. For example, an elliptical object might be judged more similar to a circular one than to a square one in virtue of the shapes of the three.   Will shape emerge as a separate dimension of visual quality space?   Goodman (1977) points out that shape predicates are possible for any qualitative order: the shape of a given object in that order is the pattern of simpler qualities it manifests. Visual shape is a pattern of spatial attributes.   A multicoloured object has a distinct pattern of colours, and that pattern can be considered its colour 'shape'.   Rhythm is an auditory temporal shape.

Such complex attributes pose two problems.   First, will 'shape' predicates provide new and additional dimensions of the quality space?   More generally, how are *combinations* of qualities to be analysed?   In some constructions given in Chapter 3, multi-coloured objects (such as one labelled '*rg*') were located in a single place, distinct from that occupied by singly coloured objects (such as '*r*' or '*g*').   Given the construction thus far, will some dimension corresponding to 'multicolouredness' emerge from the scaling?

Suppose that shape predicates initially emerge as ordering relations.   For shape to be a new dimension, one must find a series of stimuli differing in shape but the same in all other respects.   Such a series is possible only if shape *per se* engages some new discriminative capacities.   We may have subjective effects of shapes that cannot be predicted from their effects on all the other discriminative capacities in operation.

While such a finding is possible, it seems unlikely.   More likely is that discrimination of shapes can be wholly explained by discrimination of edges.   The difference between the circle and the ellipse is a difference that can be explained in terms of distances in one direction or another.   Discrimination of distances is in turn explained by discrimination of visual locations. Discriminations among shapes would reduce to discriminations of visual latitude, longitude, and depth.   We would not need any *new* dimension to explain the discriminations.

A second problem with shape predicates is to explain why visual shapes and auditory chords should be treated differently. Both are combinations of simpler qualities. Chords require new dimensions in the quality space, but I have just argued that visual shapes do not. Why is the inference made in one case but not the other?

One difference between them is that multiple tones can be heard at the same place and time, while multiple hues cannot be seen at the same place and time. Multiple colours in a given object can therefore be differentiated by their occupying different places, while the multiple tones in a chord cannot be so differentiated. Again, it helps to think of pitch as another 'location' coordinate. To specify the full qualitative content of the two experiences, additional 'coordinates' are needed for auditory experiences but not for visual ones.

In effect, a 'shape' in any modality will be represented by a *sum* of points within the quality space. An object with just two discriminable visual locations, one red and the other green, will be represented by two points in quality space, one corresponding to the red location and the other to the green. A visual shape is a sum of points, connected spatially. Now orange is both reddish and yellowish. How can one distinguish an object that is wholly orange from one that is half red, half yellow? Briefly, we will find a different pattern of resemblances among the two sums of points. The solid orange object will be more similar to some colours between red and orange (and to some between yellow and orange) than it is to red (or to yellow). So all its points will be clustered in the hue region between red and yellow. The half-red, half-yellow object will not show this pattern of resemblances. It will have some red points and some yellow points, but the red points will not be more similar to colours between red and yellow than they are to red, and the yellow points will not be more similar to colours between red and yellow than they are to yellow. The sum of points representing the multicoloured object has a discontinuity separating two distinct hue regions.

5.5 Taste and Smell

Facts about matching can individuate modalities. Sensations in a given modality are connected by the matching relation. From any sensation in the given modality, it is possible to reach any other by a sufficiently long series of matching steps. Distinct modalities are not so connected. One can get from red to green by a long series of intermediaries, each matching its neighbours; but no such route links red to C-sharp.

While tints and tones are clean crisp stimuli, the chemical senses present a murkier picture. The phenomenal properties of tastes and smells are not clear and distinct to introspection. Henning (1916) proposed one of the first schemes for ordering taste qualities, depicted in Fig. 5.3. It is a tetrahedron, whose four vertices are 'sweet', 'salty', 'sour', and 'bitter'. The 'sweet' vertex represents a taste that is maximally sweet and minimally sour, salty, or bitter. Increasing distance from a given vertex represents an increasing dissimilarity from the associated quality, just as in a multidimensional scaling model. For example, a point pushed from the 'sweet' vertex towards 'sour' would represent a slightly soured sweetness.

Henning claimed that sweet, sour, salty, and bitter are *psychological primaries* for tastes. Each primary is unique: it cannot be matched by any mixture of the other primaries. Every taste could be matched by a mixture of primaries. Actually, Henning's hypothesis was that any given taste results from a mixture of just three primaries. This places every taste on one of the four planes of the tetrahedron: the interior is empty. Henning also claimed that each primary was produced by a *specific receptor*—a receptor that responds to just one chemical quality of a food.

Although a tetrahedron has four distinct vertices—four 'primaries'—it is of course just a three-dimensional shape. We earlier distinguished the dimensionality of the quality space from the number of 'primaries' proposed for that modality. Although we have four primaries, we do not have four independent respects in terms of which tastes can be sensed to resemble or differ. There is no inconsistency. In a tetrahedron, fixing distances from any three of the vertices will uniquely determine the distance to the fourth vertex. If the quality space were as Henning proposed, then, once one knew just how sour, bitter, and salty a given taste was, its sweetness would thereby be given as well. We do not have four distinct dimensions of variation, but only three. Analogously, sampling colours all of the same brightness yields a two-dimensional plane in the colour solid. On it one will find, not two, but four unique hues.

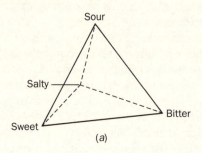

(a)

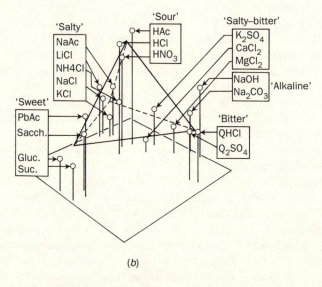

(b)

FIG. 5.3. The Henning taste tetrahedron

Note: Henning thought of the four qualities at the vertices as *psychological primaries* for the taste modality. Part (*b*) shows results of a multidimensional scaling of tastes of simple chemical compounds. It resembles Henning's taste tetrahedron, but adds an 'alkaline' group outside the 'bitter' vertex.

Source: Erickson and Schiffman (1975, p. 395). Reprinted by permission of Academic Press and of the authors.

Susan Schiffman and Robert Erickson have subjected Henning's taste tetrahedron to several tests using multi-dimensional scaling. Their 1971 study used 19 chemicals roughly equated for the intensity of their tastes. Subjects rated the relative similarities of all the possible triples. Schiffman and Erickson then analysed the rankings using non-metric multidimensional scaling. Figure 5.3(*b*) shows the results. A three-dimensional Euclidean model fits the data, and the points roughly describe a tetrahedron. The only exception is the existence of an additional 'alkaline' group outside the tetrahedron, opposite the 'sweet' vertex. Subsequent studies (Erickson and Schiffman 1975; Smith 1985) found very similar similarity structures for other collections of stimuli, using various techniques to obtain the raw data rankings.

Of course, the MDS space does not confirm the existence of the four psychological taste primaries postulated by Henning, as Erickson and Schiffman (1975) take pains to point out. Indeed, the existence of some points outside the tetrahedron is inconsistent with the psychological primaries model. Some contemporary accounts take Henning's four primaries to be separate *modalities*. Instead of a unitary taste modality, we have a sweet sense, a sour sense, and so on; each is given a 'labelled line' to the central nervous system (see Pfaff 1985). Even the question of whether tastes are analytic or synthetic remains contentious (see Erickson 1985; Bartoshuk and Gent 1985). Some argue that a taste such as bittersweet is similar to a chord, in that the separate components do not fuse to form a new quality; while others argue that it is similar to orange, in which a new quality is formed but one can sense its similarities to red and yellow. Multidimensional scaling can contribute data to these debates by clarifying the different ways in which tastes resemble and differ.

Odour perception is the most obscure of human sensory modalities. In his *Sensation and Perception in the History of Experimental Psychology*, E. G. Boring (1942) noted that the study of olfaction at that time was at about the same stage of development that visual science had achieved in 1750. Engen notes many of the still-current limitations. We do not know what molecular attribute distinguishes those chemicals that have an odour from those that do not (Engen 1982, p. 25). We do not know if there are receptors tuned to specific molecular features, and if so what those features are (pp. 27, 30, 32). There are at least seven different classes of theories concerning which molecular properties affect olfactory receptors (p. 7), and no clear resolution is in sight. It is unclear whether one can distinguish changes in intensity of odour from changes in quality (p. 115). It is also unclear whether olfaction treats mixtures of gases in an analytic fashion (as in hearing) or a synthetic fashion (as in vision) (p. 123).

One intriguing unresolved issue is whether *cancellation* of odours is possible. The dispute dates from an early twentieth-century argument between Zwaardemaker and Henning. It is of obvious theoretical relevance in any attempt to understand olfactory quality space. One can cancel the redness in a hue by mixing in sufficient green. The result is not both red and green, but a new colour (which may be achromatic, yellowish, or greenish) in which all the redness has disappeared. Can one similarly cancel the goatiness of some odours by mixing in an odour on the 'opposite side' of olfactory space? Or does one thereby merely add a new component that somewhat masks the old—so we get (say) a fragrant and goaty odour? The issue is still unresolved.

Perhaps the greatest confusion lies in attempts to order the phenomenal properties of odours. A bewildering variety of systems of classification and ordering has been proposed. There are entire volumes devoted to classifying and describing the various systems of classification (see Harper *et al.* 1968). The candidates show much more significant variation than those attempting to model the similarities among colours. The latter are all three-dimensional, and all somewhere contain something resembling the familiar 'hue circle'. In olfaction there is not even agreement on the number of dimensions required. Many of the systems are seven-dimensional, although some systems for classifying biological odours have 12 and others 18 dimensions. Linnaeus's system (1756; see Harper *et al.* 1968, pp. 19–21) employed seven descriptive categories: aromatic, fragrant, ambrosial (musk-like), alliaceous (garlic-like), hircine (goaty), foul, and nauseating.

Some phenomena provide intriguing hints of the structure of olfactory quality space. Deficiencies in odour perception are known as *anosmias* (or, perhaps more properly, *hyposmias*). It seems that there exist anosmias specific to particular classes of odour. One person may be unable to distinguish among alliaceous odours but can discern the different ambrosials, while another may have the pattern of discriminations reversed (Engen 1982, pp. 80–2). These deficits strikingly resemble partial colour vision deficiencies, in which some subjects cannot discriminate reds from greens, while others cannot discriminate yellows from blues. There is no obvious visual analogue for *hyperosmia*, which is an abnormal super-sensitivity to odours, often associated with adrenal insufficiency. Such individuals are estimated to be as much as 100,000 times more sensitive to specific odours than are normals. They can smell sucrose, urea, and hydrochloric acid, which normals can only taste (Engen 1982, p. 92).

Even the normal range of olfactory sensitivity is remarkable. The most sensitive individuals can detect select substances at one-millionth the concentration needed by the least sensitive (Amoore 1977). Another odd fact to be considered by any theory of the molecular attributes of odours is that stereo-isomers (molecules with the same formula but mirror-image structures) sometimes have very different odours. One might smell of spearmint and the other of caraway (Engen 1982, p. 6).

Henning (1915) proposed a system ordering the relative similarities among odours. It was similar to his model for tastes, but had six primaries (arranged in a prism) rather than four. Henning claimed that each odour was a mixture of at most four primaries, so all odour qualities would be located on the planes of the prism. Relative distances to the four primaries showed the relative similarity of the odour to each of the four. Crocker and Henderson (1927) developed a second ordering based on similarity judgements. Theirs was a four-dimensional structure, using four of Zwaardemaker's dimensions—fragrant, burnt, acidic, and caprylic (hircine, goaty). The authors attempted to create an explicit numeric scale for each. They tried to find chemicals whose odours could be ranged, in replicable and equal steps, from less intense to more intense in the given dimension—fragrance, burntness, and so on. The intent was to provide a four-number coordinate for any odour. Unfortunately, the comparison ratings proved unreliable (see Harper *et al.* 1968, p. 30). The entire system used magnitude estimation, and it lacked a rationale for using exactly four dimensions.

Multidimensional scaling promises to cast considerable light on the murky phenomenology of odour perception. Unfortunately, it is primarily useful for *testing* hypotheses of the dimensionality and structure of the olfactory quality space; given the numbers of similarity judgements required, it does not have much use for *discovering* that structure. Odour ratings are particularly difficult to obtain. One must sniff successively, each time waiting patiently for any odour after-effects to disappear.

Schiffman *et al.* (1977) performed a paradigmatic experiment. Twelve university students rated the similarities among odours of 19 chemicals. The stimuli were presented using a special device (an 'olfactometer') that allows one to adjust concentrations. The subjects sniffed each member of a pair in turn, and then marked a line ranging from 'Exact same' to 'Completely different' to indicate how similar the two were. Subjects needed from five to eight hours to complete the needed similarity judgements among the 19 stimuli. When analysed with one variant of non-metric multidimensional scaling, a simple two-dimensional solution emerged. The arrangement had interpretable axes. One ranked the chemicals from the most to least pungent, while the other ranked them from most to least pleasant to smell.

5.6 Explaining Quality Space

Quality space is not a theory, but a datum, which itself requires explanation. Sometimes a multidimensional order is treated as if it were an explanatory theory for a given modality. Some might attempt to explain similarity judgements by postulating an internal space that has various dimensions and inter-point distances. Such an interpretation by no means follows from the data, and is sometimes a gratuitous misinterpretation. A quality space is just an economical *redescription* of the order intrinsic to similarity judgements. That order is often multidimensional, and so (as already mentioned) talk of a 'space' is legitimate. The word is used to mean nothing more or less than a *multidimensional order*. It should not be taken to possess all the rich properties of space as defined in analytic geometry or in physics. For example, one should not presume that an MDS space is dense—that between any two points there is a third. Chapter 3 showed how multidimensional orders can emerge from finite sets, which of course cannot be dense. Metric assumptions are also treacherous. Distances are monotonically related to similarities, but there is no presumption that sums or ratios of distances are interpretable. There may be no common unit to express distances along different axes. Instead, the 'space' of multidimensional scaling is the sparse and empty sort found in graph theory and branches of topology. It is a representation of the order intrinsic to sensory judgements, and is discovered, not postulated.

Of course, one could propose a spatial model as part of an account of a sensory modality. One could postulate orthogonal and densely ordered dimensions emerging somewhere in sensory processing, and propose that placement along these dimensions explains similarity judgements. The point is just that this sort of explanatory model is *not* an implication or assumption of multidimensional scaling efforts. A good analogy is the use of factor analysis in interpreting test scores (see Gould 1981). Factor analysis merely redescribes correlations among test scores, and provides a perspicuous representation of test score correlations. So for example if we find a single factor (call it 'IQ') common to many tests, we have merely redescribed the fact that those tests correlate highly with one another. A factor is not a theoretical entity that explains those correlations. Factor analysis does not demonstrate that there exists a single attribute in people that explains each person's performance on each test and whose variations across people explain the correlations among the tests. Of course there is the problem of explaining the high correlations among all the tests, and one solution to this problem is to postulate a single variable ('intelligence') that does this, and that is presumed to be 'measured' by the IQ factor. But other explanatory models are available.

Since the quality space is discovered, not postulated, we are left with the problem of explaining the quality space. How can one explain the structure of similarity judgements in a given modality? Consider for example the psychological colour solid. We would like to explain facts such as the following:

1. Pink is more similar to red than it is to green.
2. Orange is between red and yellow.
3. There are bluish greens, but there are no reddish greens.
4. The hues can be arranged in a circle.
5. Yellow is least similar to blue; red is least similar to green.

6. Some yellow and blue lights can be mixed to yield a stimulus that appears achromatic.

7. There is an orange that seems just as reddish as it is yellowish. However, red does not seem to be just as much yellow as it is blue. Instead, it seems there is a red (a *unique* red) that is not at all yellowish and not at all bluish.

Within the colour solid we find a hue circle in which red and green are at opposite ends of one axis, yellow and blue are at opposite ends of another, and the two axes are approximately perpendicular to one another. Other hues are placed among those four so that the whole forms a seemingly continuous circle (see Hardin 1985). We would like to answer questions such as: Why is red opposite green? Why can hues on opposite sides of the circle be mixed to yield an achromatic stimulus?

The structure of qualitative similarities and resemblances cannot be explained in purely qualitative terms. Phenomenally, orange is between red and yellow, but one is at a loss to provide a phenomenal explanation for why this is so. An account that employed qualitative terms would presuppose aspects of the very order that we would like to explain. It will not do to claim that orange is between red and yellow because it is just as similar to red as to yellow. Those very similarities require explanation.

One can provide such an explanation by finding a neurophysiological *interpretation* for the quality space.[10] Quality space can be treated as a structural description. It says of quale X, whatever quale X may be, that it is more similar to Y than to Z, less similar to W than to Y, and so on. It says the same sort of thing about W, Y, and Z. One finds a neurophysiological interpretation for this structure when one finds neural states and processes a, b, c that instantiate those variables X, Y, Z. Some neural states and processes stand in just the same pattern of relations as those obtaining among points in the quality space. One thereby gives a neurophysiological explanation for the structure of qualitative similarities and differences.

Or at least one *hopes* to do so. Colour vision is the best understood modality, yet even there the explanation is

[10] I am here using the word 'interpretation' in the sense of 'finding values for the variables'. To provide a neurophysiological interpretation for a quality space is to identify neurophysiological states and processes that stand in the same pattern of relations as those occupied by the points in the quality space.

incomplete. I will also describe briefly the glimmerings of such an explanation for taste.

5.6.1 *Visual Opponent Processes*

One can provide a plausible neurophysiological identification for three axes of the colour solid. By detailing the neurophysiological mechanisms that generate those axes, one can explain many of the resemblances and differences among colours. The axes are generated by *opponent processes*, each of which combines inputs from several receptor types. The three opponent processes are red–green, yellow–blue, and white–black.

Chapter 2 described how wavelength discrimination relies on a comparison of outputs of different receptors. Inhibitory connections could compare the ratios of receptor outputs. Opponent processes carry out such comparisons. Each responds with activity above the norm ('above baseline') for one part of the spectrum, and with activity below baseline for another part. Such opponency could be provided by inhibitory and excitatory synapses. Because the different opponent processes have different patterns of excitatory and inhibitory connections to the three sorts of cones, each will respond positively (or negatively) to different parts of the spectrum. Activity in each opponent process is in this way independent of activity in the others.

The exact connections from cones to opponent processes are still unknown, but one plausible hypothesis is shown in Fig. 5.4. Here the yellow–blue process is inhibited by outputs from the short-wavelength receptors, and excited by outputs from both middle- and long-wavelength receptors. It will respond with activity below its baseline for wavelengths in the short end of the spectrum, corresponding to blue, since there we find the most inhibition and the least excitation. It will, of course, respond identically to wavelength *mixtures* that have just the same effect on the three receptor systems as spectral blue. The yellow–blue opponent process will respond with activity above its baseline for wavelengths in the spectrum corresponding to yellow, since there we get the least inhibition (from the short-wavelength receptor system) and the most excitation.

Axons in the optic nerve form their first synapses at the lateral geniculate nucleus (LGN). Some cells in the LGN respond in just the ways required for the opponent processes. This has been

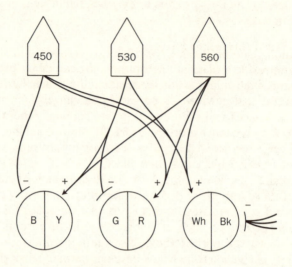

Fig. 5.4. Visual opponent processes

Note: The three types of cones at the top are labelled by the wavelengths to which each is optimally sensitive. The opponent processes are labelled first by their excitatory (+) connections: they are Y–B (yellow–blue), R–G (red–green) and Wh–Bk (white–black). The inhibitory connections to Bk (indicated on the right) proceed from all three types of cones.

Source: Hurvich (1981, p. 132). Reprinted by permission of Sinauer Associates, Inc.

shown by microelectrode recordings of LGN cells in the macaque monkey, whose colour discriminations are very similar to those of humans. Different wavelengths are presented, and the response of a given cell to each is recorded. We find different response spectra in different cells, but three basic forms corresponding to a red–green opponent system, a yellow–blue system, and a white–black system (see DeValois and DeValois 1975, 1988; Hurvich 1981, ch. 12).

Each opponent system provides an interpretable axis for the colour solid. The red–green process provides the axis that runs through the hue circle from red to green. The yellow–blue process yields an independent axis running from yellow to blue. The white–black process sums all three cone processes and thereby tracks the overall intensity of light. It gives the lightness axis, which stacks hue circles of different lightness on top of one another.

The opponent-process model can explain much of the structure of qualitative similarities among colours. Such explanations have been thoroughly described by C. L. Hardin in various publications (see his 1988, 1986, 1985, and 1984*a*), and so I will confine myself to just a few examples. First, we can explain why there is no reddish green, but there is a bluish green. If reds are coded by activity in the red–green system above baseline, then greens are coded by activity in the system below baseline. For there to be a reddish green, one would require activity in the red–green opponent system both above and below its baseline simultaneously, which is physically impossible. For similar reasons there can be no bluish yellows. Hues intermediate in the spectrum between blue and green will affect both the yellow–blue and the red–green system, and so there can be many bluish greens.

The red that seems not at all yellowish and not at all bluish is called a *unique* red. Similarly, a unique yellow is one that is not at all reddish and not at all greenish. The opponent process model can explain why (for example) there is a unique red, but no unique orange. Some stimuli will neither excite nor inhibit the yellow–blue system, but will leave it neutral. When such stimuli are presented, activity in the red–green system alone determines the hue that is seen. If the red–green system is excited, one sees a unique red; if it is inhibited, one sees a unique green. If the red–green system is also responding at baseline, one sees an achromatic colour: some shade of grey, whose intensity is determined by the white–black system. The unique hues are those presented by stimuli that neither excite nor inhibit one of the opponent processes, leaving it neutral. Wavelengths in the spectrum corresponding to orange will stimulate both the red–green and the yellow–blue system, and so there can be no unique orange.

The degree of qualitative similarity between hues is not a constant function of their position in wavelength mixture space. For example, pairs of wavelengths separated by 10 nm do not all show the same degree of similarity. The effects on transducers do not map simply into similarities. We must cite *new* principles to explain the relative similarities. Each opponent system receives inputs from at least two and perhaps all three cone systems, but each weights those inputs differently, so that excitations in the long-wavelength system have a much greater excitatory effect on the red–green system than on the yellow–blue system (see Hurvich 1981, p. 133).

The net result of these coding irregularities is that colour similarities do not map in a constant way on to wavelength similarities or transducer similarities. There are many more 'psychologically equal' hue steps between 580 and 600 nm than between 520 and 540 (see Boynton 1979, p. 256). Nevertheless, the opponent process model can account for many of the irregularities. One would predict that wavelength discrimination would be best in those regions where a change in wavelength produces the greatest change in opponent process outputs. One such region would be located where a change in wavelength produces the greatest change in opponent process *inputs*—that is, where transducer outputs change most quickly. This prediction is largely fulfilled (see Boynton 1979, ch. 8). In regions where the slope of absorption spectra is high, one finds better wavelength discrimination than in those where it is low.

One also would expect good wavelength discrimination in those parts of the spectrum where opponent process outputs flip from excitation to inhibition (or the reverse). Wavelength discrimination functions have two minima, at around 480 and 580 nm, where very small changes in wavelength are discriminable. These are the regions where the two opponent process systems cross their respective zero points. The yellow–blue system has a zero point at 480 nm, and the red–green system at 580 (see DeValois and DeValois 1975, pp. 132, 133). Very tiny wavelength changes are there sufficient to shift the opponent process cell between inhibition and excitation (see DeValois and DeValois 1975, p. 143).

The physiology of opponent processes can explain many other sensory phenomena. It can explain large field effects and the differences in colour discriminations at different retinal locations. Opponent process theory can explain many of the perceptions of colour-deficient observers. Some observers (anomalous tri-chromats) have a three-dimensional colour space, but are much worse at certain discriminations than are normals. Other observers (dichromats) have a two-dimensional colour space. There are two sorts of dichromats, and the two sorts make different kinds of anomalous colour matches. Opponent process theory can provide plausible accounts of these findings (see Boynton 1979, ch. 10; Hurvich 1981, pp. 222–69).

In effect, the opponent process theory provides an *interpretation* for the psychological colour solid. We explain the structure of similarities between colours by identifying the neurophysiological mechanisms responsible for the similarities, and showing how their functioning accounts for that structure. We hunt for mechanisms that can account for the discriminability of stimuli along one or another axis through the quality space. If we find such a mechanism, we have identified one of the features used by the mechanisms of discrimination to make their discriminations. We have, in short, identified one of the *differentiative* features of encodings. We must find as many such distinct mechanisms as there are dimensions of the quality space. Otherwise some variations in relative similarity will remain unexplained. The privileged 'directions' thereby isolated in the quality space need not be mutually perpendicular: we need to ensure only that none can be predicted by the others.[11]

Suppose we have a three-dimensional quality space, and we have isolated neural mechanisms that explain how the system differentiates stimuli using three specific axes. The features to which those mechanisms are sensitive are the differentiative ones. With them we can provide neurophysiological coordinates for the given stimuli within quality space. Previously we knew only how many such differentiative features must be employed in a given modality. The success of the neurophysiological venture *identifies* the differentiative features, and so at last discharges one of the obligations remaining from Chapter 4.

5.6.2 *Comparing Vision and Audition*

Some of the deeper structural features of a modality are best revealed by comparing it with other modalities. It is worth considering the extent to which these deeper features can be explained. For example, why is it possible to arrange hues in a hue *circle*? Why is it that one cannot arrange pitches in a pitch circle? Why does one hear a two-toned chord as a combination of

11 For example, the red–green and yellow–blue axes are not necessarily perpendicular to one another: MDS typically places green closer to yellow than to blue. Even if the red–green and yellow–blue axes are not orthogonal, their combination nevertheless defines a plane.

two tones but see a combination of two hues as a new hue, distinct from both?

Some fundaments of sensory neurophysiology can explain these deeper structural features. For example, when is it possible for a quality space to contain a closed loop (such as the hue circle)? One possible explanation is surprisingly simple: a loop is possible if at least one endpoint of the spectrum stimulates just one type of receptor. One must be able to mix varying proportions of stimuli affecting the endpoints without any differential effect on other receptors. It so happens that the shortest wavelengths to which any of one's receptors are sensitive affect only the S cones; they generate no response from M or L. In contrast, most of the longer wavelengths to which receptors are sensitive affect both the M and L systems, but S not at all. It is therefore possible to take the longest wavelengths to which any receptors are sensitive and mix in gradually increasing proportions of those affecting just the S system. We can get a smooth progression of intermediaries from 100% L, 0% S to 0% L, 100% S. The two endpoints of the spectrum connect, and we have a hue circle.

Audition employs a radically different arrangement of receptors (see Fig. 5.5). While there are only three distinct types of absorption spectra for cones, there are thousands of distinct output spectra for auditory receptors. Sounds are sensed in somewhat the way Hobbes envisioned: by *pushing* the nerves (more precisely, by pushing their cilia). Auditory receptors line the basilar membrane of the ear. Different frequencies cause distortions of the membrane at different places. Cilia on receptors pick up those distortions, and the cell responds with varying degrees of excitation. Receptors at different places along the basilar membrane of the ear therefore respond optimally to different frequencies. In principle, there are as many distinct optimal frequencies for different receptors as there are deformationally distinct places on the basilar membrane (see Warren 1982, pp. 10–22). This yields countless distinct output spectra or distinct receptor 'types'; for almost every audible frequency there is a receptor 'tuned' to that frequency. Furthermore, because of this physical arrangement, the response spectra of receptors that are neighbours along the basilar membrane will overlap considerably.

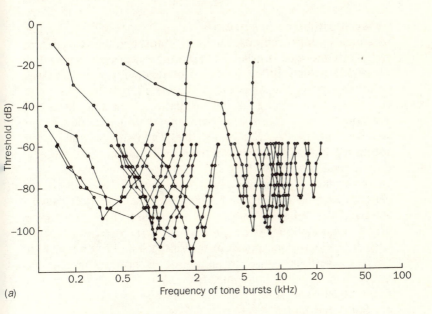

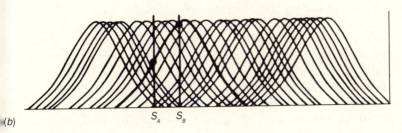

Fig. 5.5. Auditory receptors

(a) Sensitivity functions for auditory receptors at different locations along the basilar membrane of a cat. Recordings were taken from individual auditory nerve fibres. The vertical scale measures the intensity of sound (in decibels) required to generate a response at a threshold level in the nerve.

Source: Kiang (1965, p. 87). *Discharge Patterns of Single Fibers in the Cat's Auditory Nerve*. Cambridge, Mass.: MIT Press. Reprinted by permission of the MIT Press.

(b) Hypothetical response curves (or 'output spectra') for a large number of auditory receptors. The horizontal axis gives the frequency of sound; the height of each curve represents activity level of the given receptor. S_A and S_B are stimuli.

Source: Derived from Erickson and Schiffman (1975, p. 408). Reprinted by permission of Academic Press, Inc. and of the authors.

These simple facts can explain some structural differences between audition and vision. One cannot find an auditory stimulus that affects just one type of auditory receptor. Output spectra, even for receptors at the very lowest and the very highest audible frequencies, overlap those of other (nearby) receptors. If we *could* stimulate the receptors at the endpoints alone without differentially affecting any other receptors, it might be possible to generate a second series of intermediaries connecting the two.[12] We would have a pitch circle. Since, however, it is impossible to stimulate just the receptors at the endpoints of the pitch spectrum, there is only one path from one endpoint to the other. Pitches remain ordered along a line.

The same fundamental facts can explain the difference between hearing a chord and seeing orange. One gets closure among hues after a wavelength mixture has just three independent components; adding a fourth reference wavelength does not yield any new hues. In contrast, a sound containing four tones will be discriminable from almost all those containing just three. So will sounds containing five, six, and so on. Why do just three adjustments suffice for colours, while audition requires a much higher number?

Each frequency in a chord will stimulate many auditory receptors. (There will be one band optimally sensitive to that frequency, but many nearby ones are affected as well.) Typically, the ratios of activation among those receptors cannot be duplicated by any other frequency. In Fig. 5.5(b) one can count ten distinct auditory response curves that overlap frequency A (of stimulus S_A) and frequency B. Cells with such response curves would all respond to both stimuli, but to differing degrees, as dictated by their particular response curves. With so many distinct response spectra, overlapping as they do, a single frequency typically generates a unique pattern of receptor outputs among all the different types it affects. Distinct frequencies can almost be identified by the receptors they stimulate. For example, it might be possible to find a different frequency at a some intensity that has just the effect as S_A does on two, three, or even four distinct receptor types. But almost any such stimulus could

[12] Of course, later stages of the auditory system would have to be sensitive to these odd combinations of receptor inputs. In colour vision we have this sensitivity, and so connect the endpoints of the spectrum with *extra-spectral* hues.

be discriminated from S_A by examining outputs from the total class of receptors that S_A stimulates. Any stimulus that stimulates that same class at the same ratios must have just the same frequency as A.

The plenitude of differently tuned receptors helps one hear the components of chords. Two frequencies A and B in a chord stimulate distinct groups of receptors at different ratios of excitation. There is no single frequency that has just the same effect on the union of those classes, and so the combination can be distinguished from any single frequency. Similarly, addition of a third tone, fourth tone, and so on will recruit more receptors and add more outputs. No single frequency at any intensity could match that joint effect. So, assuming that the system can make use of that information, the receptor arrangement makes it possible to hear the distinct components of the chord.

In contrast, there are only three types of visual receptors, they are broadly tuned, and every wavelength except those at the short end of the spectrum stimulates at least two of the three. One cannot discriminate wavelengths by the different groups of receptors they activate, but only by the differing ratios of excitation among the three receptor types. When we mix spectral red and spectral yellow, there *is* a single wavelength stimulus—one corresponding to spectral orange—that has just the same effect on receptors as does the mixture. The combination yields a quality that matches one already encountered among the single-wavelength stimuli. We get closure after reaching three dimensions of variation.

5.6.3 *Interpreting Taste Space*

Although neural models are best developed for vision and audition, other modalities deserve consideration, if only to test the explanatory strategy. Suppose our goal is to find some neural mechanism that subserves discriminations along one dimension of the quality space for tastes. An obvious first step is to search for a physically interpretable relation that orders points in the same way as that dimension. One can repeat this strategy for each dimension of the space.

Figure 5.6 shows a candidate for the taste space mentioned above. Three interpretable axes capture the ordering of the given stimuli: the molecular weight of the chemical, its pH value, and a hedonic dimension based on ratings of whether the odour is pleasant or unpleasant. The three are independent. One plane in the figure displays the molecular weight and pH axes, and shows how they differentiate the points and capture their relative similarities.

That one can provide interpretable axes does not show that the nervous system is sensitive to them. To explain the quality space, we must isolate the axes to which the nervous system actually responds. We would need to find mechanisms responsive specifically to molecular weight and to pH value. In this regard, the 'hedonic' dimension is objectionable: it is a psychological attribute defined in terms of rankings, and there is no clue as to how the humble neurone could make them.

Figure 5.6(b) illustrates a more direct approach to the capacities of nervous systems. Multidimensional scaling can be applied to any data that yield ranked similarities. One can measure the firing rates of neurones following presentation of various stimuli, and use multidimensional scaling to analyse the similarities among the rates. Part (b) shows such an analysis for neurones in the rat chorda tympani following presentation of various chemical tastes. The solution is three-dimensional, and the arrangement of points within it mimics the taste tetrahedron illustrated in Fig. 5.3. While not definitive, such findings bolster the view that there are neural mechanisms sensitive to the various dimensions of difference found in quality space. They encourage the attempt to provide a neurophysiological explanation for the structure of similarities and differences sensed among those stimuli. Such encouragement is needed, since so little is actually known about the structure of the chemical modalities.

FIG. 5.6. Interpreting taste space

(a) Two interpretable axes in the MDS space for tastes presented in Fig. 5.3. Coordinates provided by molecular weight and pH can convey all the information in the similarity space.

Source: From Schiffman and Erickson (1971, p. 629). Reprinted by permission of Pergamon Press and of the authors.

(b) A multidimensional scaling based on responses of rat chorda tympani neurones to the labelled chemicals.

Source: Erickson and Schiffman (1975, p. 404). Reprinted by permission of Academic Press, Inc. and of the authors.

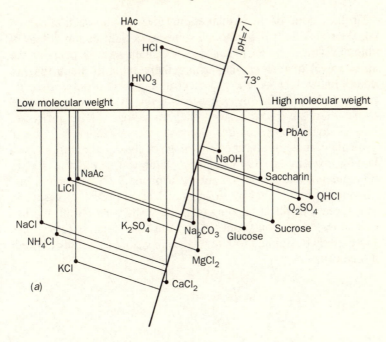

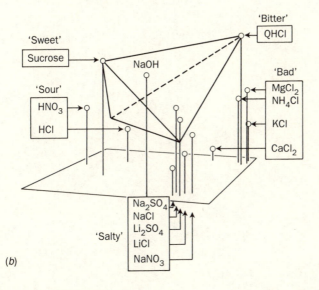

FIG. 5.6. Interpreting taste space

In fact, none of the 'explanations' given in this section can be considered definitive. Although some aspects of the physiology of colour vision in its early stages can explain some aspects of the structure of qualitative similarities, there remains much that we do not know. The isolation of spectral opponent processes should not be taken as in any sense *completing* a neurophysiological explanation of colour vision phenomenology. The processes critical to sensing colours do not occur within the lateral geniculate nucleus, and the physiology of those later stages is still largely mysterious. Only in those later stages will the deeper phenomenal features of colour be explained. Nevertheless, the opponent process theory provides at least a partial success, and any success at all is encouraging. It suffices to derail a priori objections, and holds out hope that the same strategy can successfully be applied to later stages in vision, as well as to other modalities.

6
Defining and Identifying Qualities

6.1 Places in the Sensory Order

We left our methodological solipsist in her lab, just beginning the task of mapping the full structure of visual qualitative similarities. With the developments in the previous chapter, we can suppose she has proceeded to apply similar techniques to all her modalities. While she might begin with judgements of the relative similarities of ordinary objects, eventually it becomes obvious that some of the attributes in terms of which such objects are discriminated (shape, patterns, and so on) can be explained in terms of other, simpler features; so our solipsist begins controlling some stimulus parameters so as to study other dimensions of variation more efficiently. For example, once the structure of relative similarities among tones indicates that variations in azimuth, altitude, and depth are discriminable, our solipsist will fix a location and proceed to study discriminations with respect to pitch and loudness of tones at that location. Since most sensory modalities show sensitivity to spatial differences, encodings in them have some attributes that are relevant to spatial discriminations and others that reflect differences in qualities at those places. We may require a six-dimensional quality space for surface colours, a three-dimensional taste space, a five-dimensional tactile space, and a seven-dimensional olfactory space.

How might our solipsist identify a particular sensory quality? Suppose she wishes to identify the exact qualitative character of her experience when she sniffs a lilac, tastes honey, or feels the warmth of the sun. How might she proceed? The particular smell of the lilac is something that can be encountered in other odours, so it must be characterized more abstractly than by reference to the particular thing that caused it. (Furthermore, the lilac may lose its odour, or sometimes one may be unable to sense it.) The particular odour of the lilac will be more similar to some smells and less similar to others, and the collection of such relative similarities suffices to locate the quality within the order.

Particular qualities correspond to places within the sensory order. The identity is easy to see in the case of colours. Two colours differ if they differ in hue, saturation, or brightness. Sameness in all three yields a single colour. If hue, saturation, and brightness are dimensions of the psychological colour solid, a particular colour quality will be a particular *place* within that solid.

Just as criteria for counting distinct places are imprecise, so are criteria for counting distinct sensory qualities. The most precise specification for the quality would count it distinct from any quality with which it is globally discriminable. So the experience of sniffing some other flower would not have the same qualitative character as that of the lilac if there is any third odour discriminable from one but not the other. This strict criterion identifies distinct sensory qualities with distinct *points* in the sensory order. More commonly, one counts two items as presenting the same sensory quality if they are pairwise indiscriminable, or (even less precisely) if they match. These are correspondingly larger volumes within the quality space (see Westphal 1987, p. 98). Sensory qualities will not necessarily be distinct points within the sensory order, but they may be counted with the same vagueness one uses to count distinct places.

The sensory qualities experienced by the solipsist are places within the sensory order of the solipsist. If she wants to identify what it is like for her to sense some object, she will identify a place within her own sensory order. More formally, qualitative identity among the experiences of a given person was defined (in Section 3.1) by the judgements of that person of which stimuli match which.

Assume for a moment that you are the solipsist, and that you make no prejudgement of whether others have experiences like yours when you sniff the lilac, or, for that matter, whether their 'experience' of the lilac has any qualitative character at all. You could still identify the particular sensory quality you encounter when sniffing the lilac in terms of the other odours that for you match the smell or are relatively similar. The sensory quality you experience is a place within your sensory order.

Although the identity of sensory qualities with places within a quality space follows from the earlier definition of qualitative identity, one can note some independent grounds of support. For one, the identification of a particular sensory quality is in many ways analogous to the identification of a place. To identify a location, one gives either a proper name of a place with which one's interlocutor is familiar, or a set of spatial relations from some collection of such places (north of Fifteenth Street, seven blocks west of the bank, etc.). Similarly, to identify a particular shade, one either presents a matching sample or describes its relations to other shades with which one's interlocutor is already familiar (bluer than aqua, lighter than turquoise, etc.).

The idea of identifying a particular quality with a particular location within an order is also found in Goodman:

On the basis of all such information at our command, we construct a map that assigns a position to each of the described qualia. Quale names may then be treated as indicating positions on this map. Indeed, to order a category of qualia amounts to defining a set of quale names in terms of relative position, and thus eventually (in our system) in terms of matching. When we ask what color a presentation has, we are asking what the name of the color is; and this is to ask what position it has in the order—or in other words to ask which . . . qualia it matches. (Goodman 1977, pp. 200–1)

Qualia identification is a kind of spatial identification, where the 'space' is that defined by the order yielded by qualitative similarities and differences. A structural description picks out a unique node in the order by identifying some property of the relations in which it stands. One can use such descriptions to identify particular qualities.

Identification of a quale can also employ indexicals and ostension ('*this* colour', etc.), but such uses have always seemed problematic. They seem both to be indispensable and to introduce circularity into any analysis. Knowing that Cambridge blue is a lighter blue than Oxford blue does not help one to identify Cambridge blue unless one knows which is Oxford blue. Knowing merely the relations in which the colours stand does not seem sufficient to identify any of them. On the other hand, it seems odd to introduce any sort of indexical into an analysis of a colour quality. One might find some material sample and declare it the standard Oxford blue (as a specific bar was declared the standard metre), but then, what if the material fades? Furthermore, indexicals do not seem to assist the analysis of terms for sensory qualities. It does not provide an analysis of the concept 'metre' (or 'length') to point to the standard metre bar. But one cannot employ the concept without some standard. How can indexicals be indispensable to the use of the term, but no part of its analysis?

This chapter will be concerned with the problems of identifying and defining particular qualitative terms, and with the role of indexicals and of material samples in the identification and definition of sensory qualities. Problems with indexicals will be seen to be the real issue behind the use of 'paradigms' in explaining looks (Chapter 2), and this chapter will provide one potential solution to problems with paradigms. What role do such paradigms or exemplars play in the analysis of sensory qualities?

6.2   Intersubjective Differences

The idea of using paradigms in an analysis of sensory qualities faces a fatal problem: different individuals will require different paradigms for the same quality. Clearly, such paradigms will not work for those whose colour vision is anomalous or deficient: the red–green colour-blind individual will sometimes be unable to discriminate a normal's paradigm of red from a normal's paradigm of green. What is more startling is that such failures can be demonstrated even among individuals all of whom have 'normal' discriminations.

These issues arise when we venture beyond the bounds of methodological solipsism. How might the sensory order derived for one person apply to another person? What sorts of intersubjective comparisons of quality can be made?

One might think that comparisons can be made directly, in terms of the physical parameters of stimuli associated with a given place in the sensory order. We might be tempted to define each 'place' within the space in terms of its stimulus coordinates. A place would be a class of stimuli, and it could be re-identified in the sensory order of different individuals by re-identifying that class. In the psychological colour solid, for example, we might expect that a particular place within it is occupied by monochromatic 540 nm light, another place is occupied by monochromatic 550 nm light, and so on.

Data on individual differences demonstrate that this idea will not work. A given 'place' within the psychological colour solid may be occupied by different classes of stimuli in different people—even among those who are neither colour-anomalous nor deficient in their discriminative capacities. One easy way to show this is to plot the spectral loci for the unique hues. Recall that a unique green is a green that is not at all yellowish and not at all bluish. Taught this definition, and placed in front of a colorimeter, subjects can readily make the adjustments necessary to present themselves with the quality that they will call 'unique green'. Over repeated trials, a given subject's colorimeter setting for unique green (or any unique hue) will be remarkably consistent. But different individuals will consistently arrive at different settings, and the distribution even in the 'normal' population is wider than one might expect. Figure 6.1 shows the unique green loci for a sample of 50 individuals. Although the average is 503 nm, many individuals set the colorimeter as much as 15 nm on either side of the mode. The difference is a large one. Any one of the subjects will see many discriminable colour differences between 490 and 515 nm.

Given the consistency of colorimeter settings over trials, it seems reasonable to suppose that subjects are consistently picking what is for them the same quality—a green that is not at all yellowish and not at all bluish. So each consistently picks out his or her uniquely green place in the colour solid. But different stimuli occupy that place for different people. Hurvich compares the perceptions of the normal to the colour anomalous as follows:

This is not a problem of misnaming . . . For example, the blue, the green, and the yellow that both they and the normal see in the spectrum are probably identical. However, the *wavelengths* that produce the same color experiences, the blue, the green, and the yellow, are, in the two instances, somewhat different. (Hurvich 1981, pp. 223–4)

Hurvich notes that results are what one might expect if different individuals had slightly different calibrations between wavelengths and perceived colours. Such differences may be responsible for some of the disputes on colour naming that occasionally arise between individuals, particularly in the blue–green portion of the spectrum. Undoubtedly the reader has encountered disputes of this sort. Is this colour turquoise, greenish blue, or bluish green? Perhaps the given stimulus maps to different places within the colour solids of the two disputants. An individual who sees 515 nm light as unique green will see a 503 nm stimulus as a bluish green. One who sees the 490 nm stimulus as unique green will see a 503 nm stimulus as a yellowish green. The dispute is not over words, but rather over the differing stimulus calibrations for their respective colour solids (see Hurvich 1981, pp. 222–3).

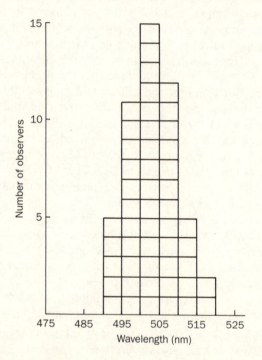

FIG. 6.1. Loci for unique green

Note: Fifty subjects selected the wavelength that would appear to be a green that was not at all yellow and not at all blue. Individuals in the middle of this distribution would see wavelengths at either end as markedly yellowish or bluish.

Source: From Hurvich (1981, p. 223). Reprinted by permission of Sinauer Associates, Inc.

A simple analogue for this sort of intersubjective difference is provided by the one-eye adaptation experiment mentioned in

Chapter 2. If you close one eye, stare at some bright colour for 30 seconds, and then blink your eyes successively, you will note shifts in the chromatic appearance of most things. The adaptation difference between the two eyes vanishes quickly, so the effects will soon disappear. While they last, however, these adaptation effects are similar in several ways to the purported differences between people. Discriminations made with the adapted eye will match those made with the unadapted eye. Any two items that present different hues to the unadapted eye will present different hues to the adapted eye. Matching items will continue to match as well.[1] But the apparent hue of everything shifts.

Such a finding seems fatal to the project of defining sensory qualities in terms of a location within a sensory order. A nearby book presents different hues when viewed first through the adapted eye and then through the unadapted eye; yet on both occasions the book is discriminable from the same set of things. How then could we define the hue presented by the book in terms of the class of stimuli with which it is discriminable? Such a definition would fail. We cannot mention a class of stimuli when we define a sensory quality, since on other occasions or in other people a different class could present the same quality.

Other examples of this sort of intersubjective comparison are possible. One interesting technique can be used to control for the influence of the macular pigment of the eye on an individual's colour perceptions. The macula (or 'yellow spot') is a central region of the retina that contains a non-photosensitive yellow pigment. The extent to which the macula is pigmented varies greatly among individuals, and this differential pigmentation yields systematic differences in the hue perceptions of different individuals. Light must travel through the retina before reaching the receptors, and so the effect of a pigmented area is similar to that of wearing goggles with a very slight yellow tint. Again, almost all pairs discriminable for 'normals' will be discriminable for those with heavily tinted maculae, and conversely. But those with heavily tinted maculae will have hue perceptions that are everywhere tilted towards yellow.

---

[1] Discriminations will not be identical through the adapted and unadapted eyes, although it takes laboratory tests to demonstrate the differences. One loses some ability to discriminate saturation differences. Two stimuli discriminable through the unadapted eye because of differences in saturation may not be discriminable through the adapted eye. Other caveats are mentioned in s. 6.4.

A filter in front of the eye absorbs wavelengths in certain ratios and so alters their effects on receptors. In 1927 W. D. Wright invented an ingenious method to control for such effects. It uses three primary and two target wavelengths. Between the first and the second primary we have one target, and between the second and the third we have the other. The subject starts by adjusting the intensities of the first two primaries to match the first target. We fix the intensity of the second primary at that level. The subject then attempts to match the second target with a mix of the second and third primaries, leaving the second primary at that fixed level and adjusting only the intensity of the third primary. Because some fixed amount of the second primary is used in both matching tasks, we can equate X units of the first primary to Z units of the third. The intensities of the three primary wavelengths in all subsequent matching tasks by that subject are thereafter adjusted by the ratio $X : Y : Z$. These units give equal stimulating power at the retina (see Boynton 1979, pp. 147–8).

Suppose we find such ratios for several people and then have each use the normalized primaries to match an achromatic white stimulus. Since for a given person the units represent equal effects at the receptors, the differences in the chromaticity coordinates of the white stimulus will show the differences in pre-receptoral absorptions. The results are plotted in Fig. 6.2. This shows the loci for the achromatic 'white' points for 55 observers. Compared with the midpoint of the distribution, individuals in the lower left use much more blue light to produce their 'white', while those in the upper right use much more yellow. The differences are quite large and would be noticeable by anyone in the distribution. Mixtures in the lower left will look quite bluish, while those in the upper right will look yellowish.

The absorption spectrogram of the macular pigment is known, and this yellow shift across different observers can be quantitatively predicted by assuming that different individuals have different densities of the pigment (Wyszecki and Stiles 1967, pp. 420–1). Presumably individuals in the lower left of the distribution in Fig. 6.2 have more heavily tinted maculae, and so require more blue to produce their 'white'. Folk wisdom has it that some people see the world through rose-tinted glasses. Here at last we have hard scientific evidence that some people see the world through *yellow*-tinted maculae.

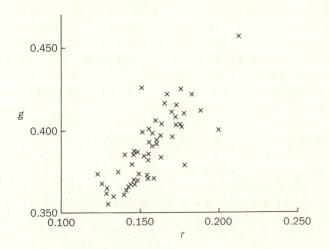

FIG. 6.2. Loci for achromatic white

Note: Amounts of normalized *r* and *g* primaries needed by 55 observers to match an achromatic white. The primaries are normalized in units representing equal stimulating power at the receptors. To an observer in the center of the distribution, mixtures in the lower left would look bluish, while those in the upper right would look yellowish.

Source: From Wyszecki and Stiles (1967, p. 420). *Color Science*. Copyright © 1967 by John Wiley & Sons. Reprinted by permission of John Wiley & Sons, Inc.

A given stimulus maps on to different places in the colour solids of different individuals. One cannot use stimulus coordinates to identify the same place within the colour solids of different people, since the stimuli that present that quality differ for different people. Yet in both of the examples just given, discriminations are (almost entirely) undisturbed: things that match for one person will match for the other. It seems that the quality of every stimulus is shifted in one person relative to others.

The same phenomenon can be demonstrated in one person across different times. The easiest example again refers to the macular pigment. It seems fairly well established that the macula yellows as one ages (see Wyszecki and Stiles 1967, p. 420). If so, then all of us undergo a very slow shift towards the yellow in the wavelength coordinates of our respective colour solids. The shift proceeds so slowly that the effect of any given 24 hours is imperceptible. Things that matched in hue ten years ago (and that did not fade or change in hue) also by and large match in hue today.[2] Nevertheless, a given wavelength looks yellower today than it did ten years ago. All the things it matches also look yellower. This could be seen if one could compare the mixture of primary wavelengths one used to match it ten years ago with those one uses today. Call the first mixture A and the second B. Ten years ago A looked white and B would have looked yellow; today B looks white and A would look blue.

The case mimics a hypothetical one described by Sydney Shoemaker in a different context. While considering possible spectrum inversions in an individual named 'Fred', he notes:

As Gilbert Harman and David Lewis have pointed out to me, what I have described of Fred's behavior is compatible with there having been over the thirty years a change in Fred's color experience so gradual that the change from one day to the next would not be noticeable (as Lewis put it, a rotation of the color circle so slow that it took thirty years to go 180 degrees) . . . (Shoemaker 1982, p. 361)

In actuality, we do not have a rotation of the colour solid, but rather a very slow migration of the entire solid, through a space defined by stimulus coordinates, and in the direction given by a yellowing of the macular pigment with age. This is not an example of spectrum inversion, since discriminations change in a detectable way. Nevertheless, the example demonstrates a dissociation between stimuli and the colour qualities they present which is similar to the sort discussed in cases of spectrum inversion.

What are we to say of these cases? In them the quale attached to a particular stimulus differs for different people, or gradually changes within a person over time. Nevertheless, different people seem to share the same sensory order, and it does not appear to change appreciably within a given person over time. It seems clear that one cannot define a 'place' in the quality space in terms of stimulus coordinates, since those stimulus coordinates differ among different people, and the coordinates of stimuli needed to present the same quale to a person change over time.

---

[2] Again, some abilities to discriminate hue and saturation differences *do* change, although the changes are detectable only in laboratory tests.

6.3 Problems with Paradigms

Even if the facts would allow one to identify sensory qualities with classes of stimuli, logic would forbid it. There might be a world in which everyone experiences unique yellow at just the same wavelength in the spectrum. Nevertheless, even in that world one could not mention that wavelength in any analysis or definition of 'unique yellow'.   The reasons first became apparent in the discussion following J. J. C. Smart's proposals to provide 'topic-neutral' translations for phenomenal reports.

Smart faced the problem that claims such as 'I have a yellowy-orange after-image' or 'I have a sharp stabbing pain in my knee' seem to ascribe some phenomenal property to some mental state. Rather than attempt to identify such phenomenal properties with physical properties, Smart argued that such claims only appear to ascribe some property to some particular.[3] He proposed that such claims characterize internal states and processes only as being similar in some respect to what goes on when one perceives some thing that has certain properties. The reports are 'topic-neutral' because they do not say what those states and processes are; they only say that they are *like* other states and processes. So 'I have a yellowy-orange after-image' is analysed as

What is going on in me is like what is going on in me when my eyes are open, the lighting is normal, etc. etc., and there really is a yellowish-orange patch on the wall. (Smart 1963, p. 94)

'This is red' means roughly that

A normal human percipient would not easily pick this thing out of a heap of geranium petals, though he would easily pick it out of a heap of lettuce leaves. (Smart 1963, p. 79)

And 'I have a sharp pain' is analysed as

What is going on in me is like what goes on when a pin is stuck into me. (Smart 1963, p. 96)

I argued in Chapter 2 that psychophysiological accounts of perceptual effects share some elements of this topic-neutral strategy. In effect, the claim that '*x* looks red to *S*' is analysed as

---

[3] Kim (1972) pointed out that a topic-neutral analysis of such reports is not the only way Smart might have avoided the difficulty with phenomenal properties. If such reports are analysed adverbially, the temptation to say that they ascribe some property to some particular vanishes.

'What is going on in S is like what goes on when S sees something y that is red'. The object y in this schema was called a 'paradigm': it is red and perceived to be red. One way to explain why something looks red is to show how it leads to sensory states and processes that are relevantly similar to those that occur when one perceives the redness of some paradigm red thing.

Cornman (1962) argued that the formulation 'what is going on in me is like what goes on when . . . ' fails to provide translations unless the respect in which the goings-on are similar could be specified, and furthermore that one could not specify the different respects in which internal goings-on might be similar unless one employed a vocabulary describing phenomenal properties. Chapter 4 showed how to answer this objection. One *can* isolate the differing respects in which two things are similar even if one's only primitive term is the triadic predicate for relative similarity. One can then identify the differing respects in terms of which what is going on in me now is like what goes on at other times.

There are other objections to any analysis of sensory qualities that mentions paradigm objects. Jackson (1977a) gives one that is simple and decisive. He points out that, if we analyse 'x is red' as 'a normal human percipient would not easily pick x out from a heap of geranium petals, but would easily pick x out from a heap of lettuce leaves', then 'x is red' implies that geranium petals (and lettuce leaves) exist. As he says, 'x cannot be hard to pick from the non-existent' (Jackson 1977a, p. 136). This implication is disastrous, since it would require geraniums to exist if anything red exists. It seems easy to imagine a universe in which just one thing is red—a firetruck, say. It is in no way necessary that a universe contain a geranium petal in order for it to contain a red firetruck. But this would follow from Smart's proposal.

The problem generalizes. One cannot mention any paradigm object or exemplar in an analysis of a sensory quality, since instances of that quality could exist even though the mentioned paradigm does not exist. Call this the *Paradigm Existence* objection. It is troublesome. Dictionaries quite often mention paradigms in their entries for colour terms, for instance. Blue is the colour of the sky; orange is the colour of the citrus fruit indigenous to northern India. These cannot be *definitions* for the colour terms. It seems possible that our planet could totally lack an atmosphere, yet there would still exist some blue things in the universe. That nearby book cover could still be orange even if the fruit had never evolved.

One might think this difficulty could be evaded by expanding the list of objects to be included as paradigms. As Jackson points out, this does not work:

For it is evident that the truth of 'x is red' does not entail the existence of *any* of these things: things might have been red although the world contained no pillar boxes, no blood, no geraniums, no ripe tomatoes, and so on and so forth. (Jackson 1977a, pp. 136–7)

It will not do to make the similarity claim counterfactual—that is, to analyse 'x is red' as 'if geranium petals exist, x would be hard to pick out from geranium petals'. That analysis would imply the implausible claim that, in any possible world in which geranium petals exist, they are red.

A second objection is related to this problem with counterfactuals, and will be called the *Contingent Attachment* objection. Briefly, a particular sensory quality is only contingently attached to whatever class of stimuli is in this world perceived to have that quality. For example, it is a contingent matter that geranium petals are red. One cannot analyse 'x is red' as 'x is similar in colour to geranium petals', since the definition would imply that necessarily any red thing is similar in colour to geranium petals. This claim is hard to sustain if geranium petals might not have been red. A similar objection can be lodged against any putative paradigm. 'Oxford blue' cannot be defined in terms of a standard material object (similar to the standard metre), since that object may fade or otherwise change in colour. Indeed, as mentioned in Section 6.1, for the same reason 'metre' cannot be defined in terms of the standard metre bar.

Contingent attachments imply that one cannot mention stimulus classes when analysing a sensory quality. Suppose there were a world in which everyone perceived unique green when viewing monochromatic light with a wavelength of 503 nm. We still cannot define 'unique green' as 'the colour similar to that perceived when viewing light of 503 nm', since it is only a contingent matter that that stimulus class is attached to that quality.

The third problem—the *Paradigm Specification* problem—is to decide what to use as a paradigm. To identify a paradigm successfully, it seems that one must employ the very term to be analysed. Otherwise one could not ensure that the paradigm is an instance of the intended quality. The problem was first identified by Bradley (1963), who wrote that any such analysis

> will either contain a term admitted by both parties to the dispute as denoting what is *prima facie* a phenomenal property, or it will not. If it does, then the 'analysis' involves circularity; if it does not, then the *analysans* does not imply the *analysandum*, for the reason already given. (Bradley 1963, p. 389)

Either the description of the paradigm retains some qualitative terms (and so the analysis is circular), or it does not employ any qualitative terms, in which case the analysis fails.

These three objections show that one cannot treat the topic-neutral formulations as analyses of phenomenal reports. One cannot define 'red' or 'pain' in terms of exemplars of the respective qualities. A close reading will lead one to doubt whether Smart intended his topic-neutral formulations to be taken as analyses. While that intent seemed clear in the 1959 article, it was subsequently modified, and eventually Smart explicitly denied that the topic-neutral formulation was meant to provide a definitional equivalence:

> I must make it clear that I am not producing the phrase 'What is going on in me is like what goes on in me when . . . ' as a *translation* of a sensation report. It is rather meant to give in an informal way what a sensation report purports to be about. . . . my intention is simply to indicate the way in which learning to make sensation reports is learning to report likenesses and unlikenesses of various internal processes. (Smart 1963, p. 96)

This leaves unresolved the question of how we are to understand the use of paradigms. What is the topic-neutral account if not an analysis?

I said above that a sensory quality is to be identified as a place within the sensory order. It now seems clear that analyses of sensory qualities should not mention any stimuli. The sensory order has only a contingent attachment to stimuli. The relations of qualitative similarity and indiscriminability define an order of qualities and give it a certain intrinsic shape, but places in that shape cannot be defined by classes of stimuli. The entire shape can 'move' with respect to its stimulus coordinates. One person may have the unique green locus at 503 nm, while in another it may be at 515 nm. A particular place in the colour solid is not necessarily attached to any particular class of wavelengths.

6.4 What Generalizes?

How then can one make any sort of comparison of colour perceptions of different individuals? We would like to go beyond the limits of methodological solipsism. Our solipsist can construct a quality space that for her defines the order and spacing of qualities. She can identify particular qualities by the stimuli that present them to her. How can this perspective be broadened to take into account the sensory qualities of others?

Suppose that two methodological solipsists work independently at the matching and relative similarity tasks necessary to provide a full catalogue of their sensory qualities. What might they find if they compare notes? Direct comparisons of stimuli leading to various phenomena may prove fruitless. There is no stimulus that every person perceives as unique red. But intersubjective comparisons may still be possible. Various relations hold among the stimuli presented to one of the solipsists, and those relations define the sensory order for that solipsist. While the particular stimuli that stand in those relations differ from person to person, the pattern of relations can be generalized. The *structural* properties—properties of the relations—will generalize.

Suppose one solipsist finds a stimulus x that he or she perceives as a green that is not at all yellowish and not at all bluish. One might expect that we can generalize to the other with the form:

There is a stimulus x perceived by every person y as a green that is not at all yellowish and not at all bluish.

One problem is that person y must have normal colour discriminations: some dichromats and all monochromats will fail to find any stimulus that presents a unique green. To simplify the formulations for the remainder of this section, let us confine the universe to those with 'normal' colour discriminations, so excluding anomalous trichromats, dichromats, and monochromats.[4] Even with this restriction, the generalization above does not succeed. We need a generalization of the form:

For every person y there is a stimulus x perceived by y as a green that is not at all yellowish and not at all bluish.

[4] There will be considerable variations in discriminations within the range considered 'normal'. The latter is a statistical concept, denoting a distribution, not a particular set of individual discriminations.

The order of the quantifiers must be switched. For each (normal) person there is a stimulus perceived to have qualities related in such and such a way to other qualities. For different individuals it will be a different stimulus. It is the pattern of relations among stimuli that will generalize across individuals, not the particular identities of the stimuli that satisfy that pattern. The occupants of a particular place in the pattern vary from person to person.

Once we identify the wavelength combinations presenting unique hues to a person, we can state many facts about that person's colour perceptions in terms of those unique hues. (Again, it should be understood throughout the remainder of this section that our domain includes only those with 'normal' discriminations.) For example:

1. Any spectral stimulus can be matched in hue by mixing no more than two of the unique hues and adjusting their relative intensities.

2. Unique blue and unique yellow can be mixed to cancel and give an achromatic white.

3. The relative intensities of the unique hue wavelengths needed to match spectral colours define functions known as *chromatic response functions* (see Hurvich 1981, pp. 57–61). These functions show the same form for anyone with normal colour discriminations, although a given curve may be shifted up or down the spectrum for different individuals.

4. The stimuli that yield unique hues do not change in hue as their intensity increases. All other wavelengths have an apparent change in hue as their intensity increases.

The same *pattern of relations* obtains in other people, although the particular stimulus that occupies a particular place in the pattern varies from person to person. For example, suppose we find that for some person y, λ_1 is the wavelength mixture that presents unique blue, and λ_2 presents unique yellow. Then for person y some combination of λ_1 and λ_2 will yield achromatic white. But that pair may not be complementaries for another person x. To x, λ_1 may be a slightly greenish blue, and λ_2 may be a slightly greenish yellow, and their combination will always appear somewhat greenish to x, no matter how their relative intensities are adjusted. So we cannot say

λ_1 and λ_2 are such that, for any person x, λ_1 combined with λ_2 yields an achromatic white for x.

Instead, we must say

> For any person x there are wavelength mixtures y and z such that y combined with z yields an achromatic white for x.

Once the unique hues for an individual are identified, one can describe much of the structure of that person's colour perceptions. The various hues can be defined by their relations to those four unique hues, for example, and the gamut of that individual's hue perception is fixed. But none of this generalizes if one attempts to characterize the unique hues by the spectral wavelengths that present them.

The pattern of relations generalizes, but not the particular *relata*. If we were to diagram the qualitative relations obtaining among stimuli for two people, and leave the points unlabelled, we would (with some caveats to be noted below) find roughly the same diagram. The labels—the physical parameters of stimuli at a given point—would probably differ. Statements couched in terms of the physical parameters of stimuli will not generalize across people.

Of course, structural properties generalize only among those with 'normal' discriminations. This is the first caveat to the claim made above. A dichromat or a monochromat has a quality space with a different structure: it loses one or two dimensions compared with the 'normal'. Second, even if we confine ourselves to 'normal' trichromats, the structural match from person to person is not perfect. There will be slight discrepancies in various parts of the structure diagram for different people, and even for one person over time.

These discrepancies arise from minor differences in individuals' abilities to discriminate different parts of the spectrum. A difference between two individuals in the locus for even one of the unique hues will create minor differences in their discriminations. Suppose one individual sees 503 nm as unique green, and another sees it as a bluish green. Although the differences would be detectable only in a laboratory, we would expect one individual to make fewer discriminations between 503 nm and the wavelength corresponding to blue, and more between 503 nm and the wavelength corresponding to yellow. As noted earlier, this intersubjective difference is like the hue shift one can see when one eye is selectively adapted. While it is hard to find pairs of things that match when viewed through one eye but do not match when viewed through the other, adaptation can be shown to affect the discriminability of some pairs of stimuli, and so one would find minor differences in the structure diagram produced in the two cases.

Similar differences are found in the discriminations of 'normal' trichromats. For almost any pair of such people there is some portion of the spectrum in which one person has better discriminations than the other. Discriminability seems related to the rate of change in the outputs of the opponent processes (see Boynton 1979, pp. 260–6). As mentioned earlier, stimuli near the 'zero' point of one or the other opponent process tend to be highly discriminable, since the change from excitation to inhibition is salient. Suppose the exact wavelength at which the zero point is reached (e.g. at which a unique hue is presented) is shifted in one individual relative to the other. Both are best at discriminating wavelengths near their respective zero points, and since those points differ we will find that each can discriminate some pairs of wavelengths the other cannot.

Of course, most of the structure of 'normal' colour discrimination generalizes successfully. Among normal trichromats, orange is always between red and yellow, red and green are complementaries, there is a bluish red but not a yellowish blue, and so on. These structural facts define the ordinary hue circle, and suffice to identify the red–green and yellow–blue axes in different individuals. It helps too that our ordinary colour terms do not name minimally discriminable points, but regions or volumes of colour space. With them we can identify corresponding places in the colour solids of two individuals, even though the correspondence is not exact. The process is analogous to identifying corresponding parts in the skeleton or anatomy of different people. In each we can pick out the femur and the nose, even though those parts rarely have identical shapes in different people. The ones that correspond stand in the same place in relation to other parts of that person.

The concept of a 'unique yellow' (or of any particular qualitative content) is the concept of a place in the pattern of relative similarity relations holding for an individual. Because properties of those relations generalize across observers, the same place can be identified in others as well. Different stimuli may be sensed by different individuals as unique yellow, but the hue is identified by the place it occupies in the individual's quality space. 'Unique yellow' is defined by its qualitative relations with other sensory states, and properties of those relations generalize across individuals.

6.5 Intrinsic and Extrinsic Properties

Can an analysis of sensory qualities as places within a quality space make sense of the various distinctions mentioned thus far? We need an analysis that can clarify the notion of generalizing structural properties, cope with the differences in stimuli that in different people present the same quality, and somehow explain the role that exemplars play in learning the meaning of qualitative terms.

We can make a start by noting a geometrical distinction. Some features of a space are *intrinsic* features, and some are *extrinsic*. Intrinsic features of a space are (intuitively) those that geometers confined to its surface could discover. Such geometers would be limited to measuring distances between points on the surface, and so intrinsic features are those that follow just from the inter-point distances of the space. Extrinsic features are those that can only be determined by measurements extrinsic to the surface (see Sklar 1977, pp. 36–8).

A quality space is defined by inter-point distances. It is constructed from relative similarities in such a way that distances between points are monotonic on relative similarities. The triples lists provide the 'distances' between any two points. Any features resting entirely on inter-stimulus similarities are geometrically intrinsic features of the space.

The 'shape' of a surface is a geometrically intrinsic feature of that surface: it can be derived from the distances between points on the surface. Besideness relations among points are also intrinsic. Shape and location are also *invariant* features of the surface: they are independent of whatever coordinate scheme is used for measurement. One can employ different sorts of coordinate schemes for assigning numbers to places on the surface. One can orient the axes for such schemes in different ways. Different coordinate schemes do not alter the shape of the surface. If the coordinate scheme is adequate for measurement purposes, one can draw the same conclusions about its shape.

The most famous example of an intrinsic feature of a surface is its *Gaussian curvature*. This can be derived purely from the inter-point distances on the surface. Gauss showed that this curvature (whether it is positive or negative) is also an invariant feature of the surface (see Sklar 1977, pp. 32–8). It does not depend on the coordinate scheme chosen. Any family of curves meeting certain minimal conditions can be used as a coordinate scheme. The curvature of the surface can still be derived.

Any feature that can be derived from the pair list for discriminabilities or the triples lists for relative similarities will be an intrinsic feature of the quality space. The shape of the overall space and the location of a given quality within the space both follow from those inter-point distances, and so are intrinsic features of the space. That orange is between red and yellow is a geometrically intrinsic feature of the psychological colour solid. The placement of orange is a function of the relative similarities—distances—of red, orange, and yellow, and it could be derived no matter what coordinate scheme one used to name the colours, provided that scheme is monotonic and maps the space. If the psychological colour solid has a bulge in the purples—as the Munsell colour order system suggests it has—then that bulge would be an intrinsic feature of the colour solid. Any colour order system that modelled the structure of relative similarities among colours would have that same bulge.

Many features of the psychological colour solid are not intrinsic features. For example, many different *coordinate schemes* for it have been proposed: different axes and units for labelling each point within the space. We have the Munsell system of hue, value, and chroma; the NCS system of components of unique hues; the Ostwald system of colour triangles, and so on. These different systems will give different coordinates for a given point in the psychological colour solid.

The association of a particular stimulus class with a given location in quality space is also an extrinsic feature of the quality space. While the shape of the space and the location of a point within it are intrinsic to the space, the stimuli that happen to be sensed as having that particular quality may vary from person to person. The entire shape could be shifted with respect to stimulus coordinates without altering any of its intrinsic features. One can imagine changing all the tri-stimulus coordinates of points in the psychological colour solid without changing its shape. The connection between the quality space and its stimulus coordinates is a contingent one, and the same shape can have different extrinsic properties.

I argued above that a particular sensory quality can be identified with a particular place in the sensory order. A particular shade of orange is a particular place between red and yellow in the psychological colour solid. Now places in the psychological colour solid are intrinsic features of the space. They are defined purely by inter-point distances, and are independent of whatever coordinate scheme is chosen to label the points. It is then a short step to suggest that an analysis of sensory qualities should mention only intrinsic features of the quality space: extrinsic features can be no part of the analysis.

This suggestion implies that the meaning of a colour predicate can be given only in terms of its relations to other colour predicates. The place of the colour in the psychological colour solid is defined by those relations, and it is only its place in the solid that is relevant to its identity (see Westphal 1987, p. 98). The stimuli that happen to be perceived to have that quality cannot be mentioned in any definition of the term.

The definition for 'unique green' cannot mention any particular stimuli, since the stimuli that present that quality to Jack may not present it to Jill. The term must be defined purely in terms of its relations to other places in the psychological colour solid. For example, 'unique green' is a green that is not at all yellowish and not at all bluish. Different stimuli may yield this quality for Jack and for Jill, but this latter fact is an extrinsic characterization of the given place in the colour solid. We are allowed (and need) only intrinsic characterizations.

Of course, the other colour terms in the definition of 'unique green' must in turn be eliminated. The suggestion is that all the definitions for colour words merely state their relations to one another. In that way, the given 'place' is specified purely in terms of intrinsic features; no stimuli are mentioned in any definition of a colour term. We specify a structure of relations holding among a group of names, but in no other way do we specify the referents of those names.

The English word 'orange' probably derives (via Old French, Spanish, Arabic, and Persian) from the Sanskrit 'narangi', naming the well-known fruit tree indigenous to northern India. But 'orange' cannot be *defined* as 'the colour of the narangi fruit', for three reasons: (1) others might find that those fruits consistently appear reddish; (2) narangi fruits might not have been orange; and (3) an orange thing could exist even if narangi fruits did not. Those arguments force one to deny that 'orange' can be defined by an exemplar. But it seems that anything that is orange has a colour between red and yellow. Orange is intrinsically between red and yellow.

Philosophers sometimes use 'intrinsic' to mean 'necessary', so that the intrinsic properties of a thing are those it has necessarily. Intuitions differ dramatically over which features of colours (if any) are intrinsic in this sense. But the standard examples of necessary features are also geometrically intrinsic ones. For example, it seems that orange is necessarily somewhat reddish and somewhat yellowish. It is intrinsically (geometrically) located between red and yellow. Furthermore, orange necessarily is neither greenish nor bluish. It is intrinsically on the opposite side of green and blue. Of course, many facts concerning the place of orange in the psychological colour solid would not be considered necessary properties of orange or of orange things. For example, the most saturated orange is less saturated than the most saturated red (see Hurvich 1981, p. 84). Is this feature of its location a necessary property of 'orange'? We are spared the need to find an answer. If qualities are places in a quality space, their analysis will mention only intrinsic features of that space. There is no requirement that it mention all of them, and so we need not designate any particular subset of the geometrically intrinsic features of a quality as constituting its analysis. The proposal is safe if all the features one would normally take to be necessary are also geometrically intrinsic ones. The reader can pick his or her favourite necessary features; they will all be intrinsic features of the location of that quality in a quality space.

Colour adaptation phenomena demonstrate the distinction between intrinsic and extrinsic features. A strong chromatic adaptation in effect shifts the entire colour solid in tri-stimulus space. A stimulus that formerly engendered an impression of saturated red will (after red adaptation) engender a different, less saturated one; and will (after green adaptation) engender one of supersaturated red. Such shifts show that identity criteria for a particular quale cannot be framed to include particular stimuli (since all those stimulus coordinates can be changed). But even after the shift, what makes that quale a quale of pale red (as opposed to saturated red) is just its place in the solid—that it is closer to the white axis than is the spectral locus. One can still provide identity criteria for qualia in terms of matching, but the particular stimuli needed to fix the reference of a qualia term have changed.

The intrinsic–extrinsic distinction also can accommodate the individual differences mentioned in Section 6.2. Jack may experience unique green at 503 nm in the spectrum, while Jill finds hers at 515. In identifying unique hues, one can identify the same respective place in the colour solids of two individuals, although the respective stimuli associated with that place differ considerably. The particular stimulus coordinates of that place are extrinsic features, which differ in the two individuals. 'Green' presumably means the same for both, but different things look uniquely green to the two of them. If we are to specify the qualitative content of 'green', we can only say something like: 'the complement of red, the colour which when added to blue makes it more like turquoise', and so on. Such specifications mention no stimuli.

The idea of providing purely intrinsic characterizations of sensory qualities also bears on the issue of functionalism and qualia. Functionalism can be minimally construed as the proposal to define psychological terms by their relations to stimuli, to responses, and to one another. I suggest that definitions of qualitative terms cannot include all three of these relations. The colour solid has various intrinsic features constituted by the relations that colours bear to one another. The structure is not attached to any stimulus. Definitions for qualia terms ought to be framed purely in terms of place in the quality space, leaving out any mention of relations to stimuli.

Such definitions would be compatible with the possibility of 'spectrum inversion' (or, more broadly, of 'qualia inversion'). In effect, a spectrum inversion is a total shift in the stimulus classes assigned to places within a given quality space. Perhaps the assignment of stimulus classes to a given quality is no part of the definition of terms for those qualities. To anticipate slightly, such an assignment is rather used to *fix the reference* of the terms. The latter is not achieved purely within the scope of psychological theorizing. Fodor's (1980) version of methodological solipsism is perhaps relevant as well to the definition of sensory qualities: reference-fixing is no part of the bargain.

So, for example, colour terms would be defined only in terms of the qualitative relations they bear to one another. Paradigms play no part in the definitions; no stimuli or exemplars are mentioned anywhere. Consequently the entire structure lacks reference. One must fix the reference of any such words *indexically*. In the next section I will argue that the role of exemplars is to fix the reference of qualitative terms. This role differs from that of giving the meaning or sense of a term. The sense of such terms is purely a matter of their relations to one another—of their location within the quality space. The entire space can be rotated or shifted with respect to coordinates provided by stimuli.

6.6 Reference-Fixing

Kripke introduces his distinction between *giving the meaning* of a term and *fixing the reference* of the term with a discussion of the relation between the term 'metre' and the standard metre bar (Kripke 1980, pp. 53–60). It will be seen that the relation between colour terms and colour exemplars is very similar to this relation.

Suppose S is the standard metre bar in Paris. Can we define the term 'metre' in terms of its length? Of course, at different times S may be different lengths, so to be precise we pick some particular time t_0. Suppose we define 'one metre' as 'the length of S at t_0'. Kripke points out that

the 'definition', properly interpreted, does not say that the phrase 'one meter' is to be synonymous (even when talking about counterfactual situations) with the phrase 'the length of S at t_0' . . . (Kripke 1980, p. 56)

Elsewhere he says 'the description used is not synonymous with the name it introduces but rather fixes its reference' (Kripke 1980, p. 96). The phrases are not synonymous for the same reason that 'red' cannot be *defined* as 'the colour of geranium petals'. If our claim gives the meaning of 'one metre', then anything that has the length of S at t_0 is one metre long. Just as it seems to make sense to suppose that geranium petals might not have been red, it also seems to make sense to suppose that the bar could have been other than one metre long at time t_0. It might have been heated, chilled, or chipped. The length of S at t_0 might have been a different length than one metre. But it makes no sense to suppose that one metre might be a different length than one metre. Hence the reference to the length of S at t_0 does not give the meaning of 'one metre'. Furthermore, just as there could exist red things even if geranium petals did not exist, so there could exist things one metre long even if S did not exist.

Although a man proposing that a metre is the length of S at t_0 does not thereby give the meaning of 'metre', he is certainly doing something, described by Kripke as follows:

he's using this definition not to *give the meaning* of what he called the 'meter', but to *fix the reference*. . . . There is a certain length which he wants to mark out. He marks it out by an accidental property, namely that there is a stick of that length. Someone else might mark out the same reference by another accidental property. But in any case, even though he uses this to fix the reference of his standard of length, a meter, he can still say 'if heat had been applied to this stick S at t_0, then at t_0 stick S would not have been one meter long.' (Kripke 1980, p. 55)

One distinction between giving the meaning and fixing the reference of a term is that in the latter there is no synonymy claim. A second is that reference-fixing involves no necessary truths. Anything that has the same length as S had at time t_0 is one metre long. But it is not a necessary truth that S is one metre long at t_0. Finally, the reference for 'metre' fixed by the length S had at t_0 can be used to describe different lengths S might have had at t_0.

To fix the reference of 'one metre' differs markedly from *defining* it by introducing a description. If we view 'one metre = the length of S at t_0' as a claim that defines or gives the meaning of 'one metre', then we treat 'the length of S at t_0' as a description, and claim that anything satisfying that description is necessarily one metre long. On the reference-fixing view, 'the length of S at t_0' functions not as a description, but more like a name. It picks out a particular length—the one that S had at t_0. Anything having that length is one metre long. Since one identifies the particular length that S in fact had at t_0, one can use that very length to describe different lengths S might have had at t_0.

Kripke advances several other more controversial claims concerning reference-fixing. For example, he argues that, if the claim 'one metre = the length of S at t_0' fixes the reference of 'one metre', then it is an *a priori* truth (Kripke 1980, p. 56). Furthermore, such reference-fixing is claimed to make 'one metre' a 'rigid designator'—a designator of the same thing in all possible worlds in which that thing exists (p. 55). Although the terminology is provocative, we need not wade into the swamp of exegetical obscurities that surrounds these claims (see Schwartz 1977, and Loux 1979). Instead, we need only note how the distinction between giving the meaning and fixing the reference of a term can clarify the role of exemplars in defining and identifying sensory qualities.

For one, when we propose that 'red is the colour of geranium petals', we can admit immediately that 'the colour of geranium petals' is not coextensive with 'red' in all possible counterfactual situations. In particular, geranium petals might have been a different colour. The claim does not give the meaning for 'red' but merely serves to fix its reference. It says that red is the colour that geranium petals in fact have—or, better, that it is the colour that some particular ostended geranium petals had when ostended. It is accidental that geranium petals are red, but we can nevertheless use them to pick out that colour. This deals with the Contingent Attachment difficulty. That geranium petals might not have been red defeats only the synonymy claim, not the reference-fixing claim.

For similar reasons, Paradigm Existence poses no difficulty in using exemplars to fix the reference of terms. Things could be red even if there were no geranium petals for them to resemble. They would be red in that counterfactual situation if they had the colour that geranium petals in fact have.

So (1) there is no synonymy claim for 'red' and 'the colour of geranium petals'; (2) there is a particular kind out there, and 'the colour of geranium petals' is used to pick it out; (3) it is in no way a necessary truth that the ostended geranium petals were red at time t_0—they might have been some other colour, or might not have existed at that time. The description identifying geranium petals does not mean the same as 'red'. 'Red' refers to the colour that geranium petals happened to have at that time. The sense of the term is given entirely by the location of the quality in the colour solid. Any mention of a paradigm is used simply to fix the reference, not to provide a synonymous description.

We can see that Smart was correct in hesitating to call his topic-neutral accounts *translations* of phenomenal reports. Instead, he says 'It is rather meant to give in an informal way what a sensation report purports to be about' (Smart 1963, p. 96). A topic-neutral formulation of the sort 'what is going on in me is like what goes on when . . .' is best construed as fixing the reference of the phenomenal term. It does indeed identify 'what the report is about' and is much more closely tied to how such reports might be learned than is the typical analytic definition.

On Kripke's account of reference-fixing, the length 'one metre' is picked out by an accidental property that stick S happens to have at a particular time. He notes that 'Someone else might mark out the same reference by another accidental property' (Kripke 1980, p. 55). The same is true of exemplars used to identify sensory qualities. Consider Smart's difficulties in attempting to analyse 'I am in pain' as 'What is going on in me is like what goes on when I am stuck with a pin.' He says the problem is that

pains have nothing in particular to do with pins . . . There is indeed no need to learn the word 'pain' by having a pin stuck into one. A child may, for example, be introduced to the word 'pain' when he accidentally grazes his knee. But sensation talk must be learned with reference to some environmental stimulus situation or another. Certainly it need not be any *particular* one, such as the sticking in of pins. (Smart 1963, p. 96)

One can fix the reference of the term 'pain' by using different exemplars. None of them are attached to the *sense* of the term, and any one of them will do. Furthermore, we do not require that everyone employ the same exemplar. Jack can fix the reference of 'pain' via experiences of pins, and Jill may have learned it through contact with hot burners. As long as the same quality is manifest in both experiences, the reference of the term can be fixed through either experience.

The word 'pain' can pick out a class of states in virtue of their qualitative similarity to states that one has learned to call 'pain'. Someone who has never experienced pain could not identify pain qualitatively; identification could only proceed by its typical causes and effects. But once one has felt a pain, one's mechanisms of internal discrimination have a feature to latch on to, and future states can be identified as pain by being qualitatively similar to that initial paradigm. Terms for such states can wend their way into public discourse because people share similar mechanisms of internal discrimination, and will mostly agree on which sensory occurrences are qualitatively similar and which are not. If Jack finds two sensations to be qualitatively similar, then so will Jill. Reference to a class of qualitative states succeeds intersubjectively (and across generations) only because such agreement is widespread. As long as individuals (and generations) have a shared sense of qualitative similarity, it does not matter that the term is passed along from speaker to speaker with distinct sensory episodes serving as exemplars.

Finally, the idea that exemplars are used exclusively to fix the reference of terms for sensory qualities explains how terms characterized purely relationally could refer. Earlier I argued that 'orange' *means* 'a colour just as similar to red as it is to yellow, and more similar to either than it is to green or blue'; 'yellow' *means* 'the complement of blue'; and so on. Each colour term is *defined* by features that are intrinsic to the colour quality space; the meaning of any such term is a matter only of relations to other terms. One cannot mention any stimuli in attempting to elucidate their meanings. Such 'definitions' leave the entire relational structure floating free of any reference. To give it reference, some terms must be tacked down somewhere. Exemplars serve this function. 'Red' just means something like 'the complement of green . . .', but to fix its reference one must point to an exemplar and say 'that's one'. With a few such exemplars the entire structure of colour terms is tacked down.

Several odd facts need to be reconciled in any analysis of sensory qualities. Each term is relationally defined, but without exemplars the entire structure of definitions lacks reference. No stimulus can be mentioned in any definition of a qualitative term. Different people may employ different exemplars for a term. Relatively few ostensions during the learning of colour words enable one subsequently to identify thousands of colours. I suggest that all these facts can be accommodated by a simple analysis. The meaning of such terms is given solely by characterization of features intrinsic to a quality space. Their reference is fixed through the use of exemplars. Such reference-fixing is possible because we all have similar mechanisms of internal discrimination, and will mostly agree on which pairs match and which do not.

6.7 Qualities and Natural Kinds

We can clarify the analysis proposed for sensory qualities by contrasting it with the Kripke–Putnam view of natural-kind terms. There are some resemblances between the two accounts, but it is important to see why one cannot treat sensory qualities straightforwardly as natural kinds.

According to Kripke and Putnam, some general terms like 'gold', 'water', and 'tiger' have their extension fixed not by a cluster of definitional necessary and sufficient conditions, but by a reference-fixing technique similar to the one used for 'one metre'. Briefly, the extension of the term 'gold' is determined by selecting some samples or paradigms of gold, and specifying that 'gold is the substance instantiated by the items over there, or at any rate, by almost all of them' (Kripke 1980, p. 135). The 'almost all' proviso is to deal with the possibility that some fool's gold is found in the samples. The formulation has some minor variants. Gold is anything that is the *same substance* as most of those samples, or is the *same kind* as most of the samples, or shares the *same nature* as the samples.

In the standard examples, to fix reference to Q, one picks a sample of paradigm Q items and then proclaims that Q is anything that is the same substance or has the same nature as most of the items in that sample. Reference is 'fixed' in these ceremonies by the combination of ostended paradigm and some relation such as 'same substance as' or 'same kind as'. For example, according to Putnam (1973), water is anything that is the same liquid as (or has the same nature as) this stuff here (pointing to a sample of water). The paradigm is not part of a definition: it is used merely to pick out which class is meant.

The use of a similarity relation such as 'same nature as' is one element of interest in this analysis. For Putnam the 'nature' of a thing is whatever underlying mechanism explains its observable properties. The notion is theoretical. The nature of a thing is ultimately determined by scientific investigation. In 'Meaning and Reference', Putnam says

The key point is that the relation same$_L$ [for 'x is the same liquid as y'] is a theoretical relation: whether something is or is not the same liquid as this may take an indeterminate amount of scientific investigation to determine. (Putnam 1973; in Schwartz 1977, p. 122)

So, in any possible world, we have a sample of *water* before us if and only if whatever explains the observable properties of the sample before us also explains the observable properties of the stuff that was ostended during the reference-fixing ceremony (see Newton-Smith 1981, p. 169).

Reference-fixing requires some similarity relation between the originally ostended paradigms and later samples. In natural kinds this relation is the theoretical one of sharing the same nature or being of the same kind. Among sensory qualities the needed similarity relation is provided by qualitative similarity. That relation is rooted in our sensory mechanisms. It is the same relation that orders the qualities in a quality space and whose limit is qualitative identity. One can imagine fixing the reference of a new colour term by ostending a paradigm and proclaiming that anything indiscriminable from it is that colour. We need not search in any abstruse theory for the needed similarity relation: it is built into our sensory systems. As Quine puts it,

Without some such prior spacing of qualities, we could never acquire a habit; all stimuli would be equally alike and equally different. These spacings of qualities, on the part of men and other animals, can be explored and mapped in the laboratory by experiments in conditioning and extinction. Needed as they are for all learning, these distinctive spacings cannot themselves all be learned; some must be innate. . . . it can be said equally of other animals that they have an innate standard of similarity too. It is part of our animal birthright. (Quine 1969, p. 123)

Instead of relying on a theoretical notion of 'sameness in kind', past paradigms of sensory qualities are related to later presentations by the innate sense of qualitative similarity. Stability in similarities is required if reference-fixing is to succeed. If the current presentation in one minute seems to match the past paradigm for red and in the next seems to match the past paradigm for green, one will have some difficulty deciding which term (if any) applies. If the judgements never stabilize, one cannot ascribe it any particular colour.

Furthermore, as Quine notes, a common vocabulary for sensory qualities is possible only if different members of the language community share such an innate spacing of qualities. Those whose sense of 'same colour' diverges markedly from the norm (as does the dichromat's) for that reason will fail to pick out the referent of a given colour term. One who cannot discriminate reds from greens judges them the same colour, and for that very reason cannot be relied on to learn the extension of the terms 'red' or 'green'. Reference-fixing fails. Similarly, if people rarely agreed on whether two presentations match or on which member of a pair some third one most resembles, then the classes of subsequent presentations picked out as similar to the ostended paradigms would differ from person to person. No common vocabulary would be possible. The term's half-life in the common tongue would be brief. Reference-fixing relies on our sharing the same quality space, retaining it over time, and transmitting it across generations.

Qualitative similarity must be distinguished from the deeper, theoretical 'similarity of kinds'. One can sensibly ask whether the class of presentations similar in the former sense constitutes a kind in the latter sense. Is the class of all red presentations a *physical* kind? There are good reasons to think the answer is 'no' (see Hardin 1984a, 1988). The presentations are similar only in so far as they are sensed by us to be similar. The structure of the colour space is generated from within; no physical kinds that one can specify without reference to the observer will yield that structure. So there is no non-dispositional physical kind comprising just the red things. The idea of using a similarity metric and a few paradigms to fix the reference of qualitative terms should not be taken to imply that qualities constitute theoretically significant kinds.

There is a second distinction between natural kinds such as gold and sensory qualities such as red. Among the former, reference is fixed to *things*. To what is reference fixed when one fixes the reference of 'red'?

With colour terms, the link between later presentations and the ostended exemplars is established by the *qualitative* similarity of the occasions. One can if one likes form the class of objects whose presentations are qualitatively identical with the presentation of some exemplar on occasion t_0, and in that way fix reference to a class of things. 'Red' would then have as its extension the class of things whose presentations are qualitatively similar to one of the presentations of an ostended exemplar. Reference would be fixed to things by the similarities among the sensory effects of those things.

The only difficulty is that, within the class of things whose presentations are qualitatively similar to one of the ostended red exemplars, one is likely to find some things that, in ordinary parlance, merely 'looked' red on that occasion, but are 'really' blue. So it seems that reference is actually fixed to a class of *presentations* of things. We identify all those occasions on which some thing looked just the same as one of the ostended red exemplars.

This class of qualitatively similar presentations will include some episodes during which things merely 'looked' red. The problem of picking out the class of red things might be taken as one of showing how to identify and delete the latter presentations (of things merely appearing to be red) from the others, which 'really' are red. This is a complicated question which is tangential to the argument. Some doubt that there is any real distinction to be made. The latter will be pleased to note how colour science proceeds without paying any attention to the distinction. As long as one can identify and describe the conditions determining when two presentations match, there seems little need to distinguish the occasions on which a thing presents its 'real' colours from those on which it presents 'merely apparent' colours.

Along with all these distinctions between qualitative terms and natural kinds, we should note some difficulties with the reference-fixing account of qualitative terms. For one, a thing can be red without being indiscriminable from any red exemplar ever ostended, as long as it is relatively more similar to the red exemplars than to others. Ordinary colour terms identify not *points* in the colour solid (e.g. the minimal elements differentiable by global indiscriminability) but *regions* (see Westphal 1987, p. 98). The analysis thus far also requires as many paradigms as there are discriminable colours.

A simple way to deal with both difficulties is to link presentations to the ostended paradigms using the relation of relative similarity instead of qualitative identity. We pick exemplars of several different colours. Then the reference for 'red' is fixed as the class of things that are more similar to the red exemplars than to any of the other exemplars. This proposal is close to Quine's suggestion (1969) that one define kinds using a paradigm and a foil. The extension of 'red' must be learned inductively. It is no small feat to establish where 'red' leaves off and 'orange' (or 'purple') begins. One solution is to pick 'foils' at the outer limits of the red region in the colour solid. Then something is *red* if it is more similar in colour to the paradigms than the paradigms are to the foils (see Quine 1969, pp. 119–20).

With this device, the different paradigms of red need not be mutually indiscriminable, but can sample a gamut within that region of the colour solid. Relative similarity with respect to them can be used to delimit the red region of the space.

A third difficulty arises precisely from the need to fix reference to a range of colours rather than to a particular point. Reference-fixing must fail for fully determinate hues. We cannot fix the reference of 'unique green' by ostending samples, since for different people different samples are perceived as unique green. No sample will suffice for everyone. One cannot learn 'unique green' by ostension. These problems infect other hue names, particularly for the binary hues midway between unique ones. Perhaps even ordinary names such as 'turquoise' and 'aquamarine' are affected. Perhaps one cannot ostend an exemplar of turquoise (the colour, not the mineral), since some will see the sample as a greenish blue, and others as a bluish green. Individual differences defeat reference-fixing for names of at least some particular hues. How can reference-fixing succeed if reference is not fixed?

'Unique green' names a green that is not at all yellowish and not at all bluish. Perhaps we learn how to apply 'unique green' by first learning 'green' and then learning the relations 'yellower' and 'bluer'. One can fix reference to the green *region* of the colour solid, since intersubjective differences are not so large that a gamut of samples will fail to include the differing qualities presented to normals. Furthermore, relations such as 'yellower' and 'bluer' can be learned even if one person perceives the entire array of samples as (say) yellower than does the other person. So, although 'unique green' cannot have its reference fixed by ostension to a paradigm, ostension to samples and to series *can* fix the reference of 'red', 'green', 'yellower', and 'bluer'. Using those terms, 'unique green' can be defined.

Precise terms for particular hues can be learned only after one learns vague terms for hue gamuts. For speakers to share a common colour vocabulary in spite of the remarkably large differences among those with 'normal' colour discriminations, 'green' must denote a region of colour space, and not a single point. If we had only terms for particular hues, we could not point to a sample that serves for everyone; nor would a sample fix the extension of terms to be applied to later presentations. But the regions denoted by common hue terms are broad enough to encompass individual differences. We need not all hit the bull's eye from a hundred yards: the task instead is to pick off the barn from ten paces with a shotgun. Individual differences in marksmanship will not appreciably affect the outcome. Once one has identified the region corresponding to green, the region corresponding to blue, and some ordering relations among the hues, one can proceed on that basis to define terms that are much more precise.

A final problem arises from the need to identify particular qualitative dimensions (see Quine 1969, p. 120). For example, in our initial baptism, red things are proclaimed to be those whose presentations are relatively more similar in colour to such-and-such paradigms than the paradigms are to some foils. How can this reference to 'similarity in colour' be eliminated?

The same reference-fixing strategy can be used. Colour is that aspect of the appearance of things that can vary even if the things are of the same size, shape, distance, position, and texture. Many of these latter attributes will presumably reduce to colour differences among discriminably distinct visual locations, while colour differences themselves will redeploy as three independent aspects of hue, saturation, and brightness. In the latter system, hue is that aspect of a presentation that can vary independently of saturation, brightness, visual latitude, longitude, and depth. Each of these aspects (presuming we have the correct list) should in turn be defined in the same way. For example, visual latitude is that aspect that can vary independently of hue, saturation, brightness, longitude, and depth.

One can learn these relations inductively by sampling *series* of exemplars. For example, one might first present a series of things that differ only in hue, next a series of things that again differ only in hue, but all of which differ in size, shape, and so on from the things used in the first series. In this way one can learn the relation 'differing only in hue' and thereafter reliably apply it to objects that differ in hue as well as shape (or whatever). Indeed, such exemplary series are required if one is to learn the differences between the scientifically defined dimensions of visual experience—between hue and saturation, for example. Otherwise one cannot fulfil the instruction 'pick the two items that have the same saturation but different hues' even though one knows that saturation is that aspect of colour that is independent of hue and brightness.

7

Summary and Conclusion

7.1 A Summary

My goal has been to show that some presentations of sensory qualities *can* be explained, and that those explanations survive the various philosophical objections raised against them. I proposed that we initially adopt an attitude of methodological solipsism, concentrating on the sensory qualities presented in the experience of just one subject. Explanations of perceptual effects proceed by showing that the thing (or distal stimulus) presenting a particular sensory quality in a particular situation has the same physical effect on some stage of the sensory system as some paradigm object that has and is perceived to have that quality (ss. 2.2–2.4). To turn this basic strategy into a genuine non-question-begging explanation, we need to establish the following claims.

1. We show that, if the two objects (or distal stimuli) have the same physical effects on particular cells of the sensory system, and those effects are the ones that bear information for later stages of sensory processing, then the two objects will be globally indiscriminable: there will be no third object discriminable from just one of them (ss. 2.4, 2.5).
2. Establishing global indiscriminability of two stimuli suffices to show that the encoding of one is qualitatively identical with the encoding of the other (ss. 3.1, 3.2).

So we can show that the experience of the object that seems to be *P* is qualitatively identical with that of the paradigm object that is perceived to be *P*. Thus far this explanation is circular, since it relies on our accepting the premiss that some paradigm object presents the quality *P*—the very quality whose instances require explanation. Eventually, though, the reference to paradigms is eliminated from the explanation. To do this we need to identify which properties of encodings are qualitative ones, so that a sensory quality can be analysed in a non-circular way. This latter step is achieved through the construction and interpretation of a quality space, as follows.

3. Sense impressions are an ensemble in a channel subserving discriminations. The qualitative attributes of sense impressions are information-bearing properties of those states: they sort them into different 'types' in the ensemble. Furthermore, they are *differentiative* properties: the ones bearing the information on which discriminations turn (s. 3.3).

4. The number of independent differentiative properties of encodings can be determined purely from the structure of the lists of which stimuli are indiscriminable and which are not. Those pair lists define a space—a multidimensional order—that I have called a 'quality space' or 'sensory order'. The number of distinct qualitative attributes of encodings in a given modality will fall out as the number of *dimensions* of the quality space (ss. 4.2, 4.3).

5. More workable constructions employ relative similarity, or triples lists of the form: *x* is more similar to *y* than to *z*. These yield the order of qualities much more directly than two-place similarity predicates. The use of relative similarity can solve Goodman's problems of companionship and imperfect community, and has been elaborated into the methodology of multidimensional scaling (ss. 4.4–4.8).

This approach can be fruitfully applied to *any* sensory modality (ss. 5.1–5.5). Sensations in a given modality resemble one another or differ from one another in different ways. The dimensionality of the quality space gives the number of distinct ways in which those sensations can vary. It does not determine what those dimensions of variation are. To get the latter, we need to proceed as follows.

6. In some modalities the structure of the quality space can be explained (or partially explained) neurophysiologically. In effect, one provides a neurophysiological 'interpretation' of the sensory order, identifying the neural mechanisms subserving discriminations in a particular dimension of variation. We identify particular neurophysiologically privileged 'axes' through the quality space: the ones in terms of which discriminations are actually made (s. 5.6).

With this, we can give a neurophysiological explanation of the structure of qualitative similarities in the given modality. We can explain facts that are phenomenally impenetrable, such as the dearth of reddish greens, the circular form of hue quality space, or the linear form of the space for auditory pitches. Only if this latter step is completed can one claim to have identified the differentiative attributes of encodings. With them one can eliminate the need to refer to paradigm objects in an explanation of perceptual effects, since one can analyse the sensory quality presented by that paradigm object as follows.

7. A particular sensory quality is a particular *place* in the sensory order. A point in the space is an equivalence class with respect to global indiscriminability. A quality is a region or volume in the space, comprising a gamut of such points (s. 6.1).

Sensations in any modality have some finite number of distinct dimensions of qualitative variation. To identify the particular qualitative content of a particular sensation, one specifies its relative location in each of these dimensions. For example, to identify a particular colour, one specifies where it is in the series of hues, where it is in the series of saturations, and where it is in the series of lightnesses. In effect, one gives a 'coordinate' for each dimension. A sensation that has the same relative location in each of the dimensions of variation will present exactly the same qualitative content. Those that differ qualitatively must differ in at least one respect.

Up to this point, developments are solipsistic. To include the variations in sensory qualities among different people, the analysis is elaborated as follows.

8. A place in the sensory order is abstract in the same way that a sensory quality is abstract. In particular, it cannot be identified by naming any particular stimuli, even those that consistently present the given quality for a given person. A given stimulus sometimes presents different people with different sensory qualities. Even if discriminations are isomorphic, a given sensory quality has only a contingent attachment to any particular stimulus (ss. 6.2, 6.3).

9. Nevertheless, the structure of the quality space in a given modality will (by and large) generalize across individuals. The same structure diagram will work for the sensations of different people, although the particular stimulus 'labels' to be attached to

a particular place vary from person to person. Which stimulus labels are attached to a particular place in the quality space is a geometrically extrinsic feature of that space (s. 6.4).

10. For these reasons, a given 'place' can only be defined in terms of geometrically intrinsic features of the quality space: its distance relations to other places. A definition that gives the meaning of a qualitative term can only mention its relations to other such terms. Paradigms (or, more generally, any mention of stimuli) are used for a different reason: to secure the reference of such terms (ss. 6.5–6.7).

7.2 Spectrum Inversion

The last three points yield a new answer to the old problem of spectrum inversion. Spectrum inversion is possible if two states could be functionally identical yet qualitatively distinct. The two states might be found in two individuals, or in one individual at two different times. As Ned Block puts it, the inverted spectrum 'hypothesis' is the hypothesis that

though you and I have exactly the same functional organization, the sensation that you have when you look at red things is phenomenally the same as the sensation that I have when I look at green things. If this hypothesis is true, then there is a mental state of you that is functionally identical to a mental state of me, even though the two states are qualitatively or phenomenally different. So the functional characterizations of mental states fail to capture their 'qualitative' aspect. (Block 1980a, pp. 257–8)

On standard accounts, the 'functional role' of a psychological state is defined by its causal relations to other psychological states, to stimulus inputs, and to behavioural outputs. One describes the 'job' or 'role' a state plays in the system as a whole by detailing all of such relations. A state in one system has the same functional role as a corresponding state in another system if the two stand in the same pattern of relations to other internal states, stimuli, and behaviour. If all of their states correspond in this way, the two systems are 'functionally isomorphic'.

The analysis proposed for qualitative terms departs from standard functionalism. I have argued that any analysis of such terms must drop all reference to stimuli. We cannot mention oranges—or any other stimuli—when trying to define 'orange'. Such references are extrinsic to the quality space. They name contingent attachments. Similar considerations would lead us to drop all mention of particular behaviours. 'Pain' cannot be defined in terms of pin pricks or of wincing. The result is that definitions of qualitative terms must confine themselves to intrinsic features of the quality space. They must proceed purely in terms of the relations of discriminability and relative similarity that give the quale its place in the quality space. 'Orange' could only be defined as something like 'a hue that is somewhat reddish and somewhat yellowish, and is about as yellow as it is red; the complement of blue–green'. All the other colour terms in such a definition would receive definitions of the same sort.

Such an analysis is not necessarily circular. Each qualitative term would be associated with a structure description: a description of the properties of the relations it bears to other qualitative terms. Such structure descriptions can in some cases achieve singular reference. In fact, the human colour space seems to contain 'landmarks' that can be identified in purely relational terms (see Harrison 1973, Clark 1985d, Hardin 1988). Unique hues can be identified, and some pairs of them are relatively more similar than others. One can identify a locus through the colour space along which humans can make the greatest number of discriminations. Once a few such landmarks are identified, one can identify other regions in the space by their relations to those landmarks. Singular reference would be achieved.

Of course it is logically possible that a quality space fail to contain any such identifiable landmarks. The structure may be relationally symmetric (or, in Carnap's phrase, 'homotopic'), so that two or more points in it stand in exactly the same pattern of relations to other points, even when those 'other points' include all of the elements of the structure (Carnap 1967, p. 26). Even if, as a matter of fact, the human colour space is asymmetric, and, in that sense, cannot be inverted, it could have been symmetric. Does that possibility defeat the proposed analysis?

It certainly creates problems for standard functionalist accounts. If the 'functional role' of a state extends all the way outwards to the stimuli that cause it and the behaviour it helps produce, then it seems easy to describe cases in which two states might serve the same functional role, yet be qualitatively distinct. But there is an ambiguity in the notion of 'functional role' or 'functional definition'. In any complex system, the functional role of a part can be described in terms that are relatively 'proximal' or relatively 'distal'. If one describes only the parts that are immediately next to the given part, its immediate inputs, and the effects it has on its immediate successors, then one describes what can be called the 'proximal' functional role of the part. If the system works in a consistent fashion, one can trace the more remote antecedents and consequences of that proximal role, perhaps all the way outwards to peripheral stimulus inputs and behavioural outputs. If so, one describes the 'distal' functional role of the part: its particular contribution to the input–output regularities of the system as a whole.

According to the analysis I have proposed, qualitative terms can only be defined by their proximal functional roles: by the relations of qualitative similarity and discriminability defining the quality space. Their distal roles—their connections to particular stimuli—are too variable and contingent.

It is easy to imagine cases in which the distal functional role of a part changes, even though its proximal role is undisturbed. Suppose that in your house there is one fan to force air through the heating system, and another one up in the attic, to cool the house in the summer. One day the fan motor in the heating system burns out, and you replace it with the motor of your attic fan. The brushes and contacts in that motor have the same proximal roles they always had. (Otherwise the motor would not work correctly.) But distally—traced out to more remote antecedents and consequences—they now play a totally different role in your household. They serve as part of a heating system and not a cooling system. The 'stimuli' that turn on the motor are totally new, as are its effects on the temperature of the house.

The standard varieties of spectrum inversion discussed in the literature are all cases in which the *distal* functional roles of qualitative states change. You look at a ripe orange and experience the colour quale orange. In cases of inversion, that quale comes to be associated with new stimuli, either in other people, or in you at other times. Looking at oranges would no longer generate the orange quale. But this would be nothing but a change in distal roles. The place of orange in the quality space is unchanged. Orange is still somewhat reddish and somewhat yellowish, and it is still the complement of blue–green. We simply have new stimuli associated with all the points in the quality space. The possibility is no longer disturbing, or even informative, since (as argued in Section 6.2), detectable variants of it are known to occur.

Consider the human psychological colour space as a solid. Its shape and the placement of all the qualia in it are defined by the relations of relative similarity and discriminability. In spectrum inversion, that structure—the pattern of relations among qualia—does not change. The only change is that new stimuli become associated with points in that structure. It is transplanted into new surroundings, like our attic fan moved to the furnace. If 'functional roles' include attachments to stimuli, such an inversion is fatal to the analysis. But it is perfectly consistent with an analysis that defines qualia in proximal terms: by the relations of discriminability and relative similarity yielding the quality space.

Block recognizes the possibility of describing functional roles in these two different ways. He describes what he calls 'long-arm' functional roles as ones that 'reach out into the world of things' and 'short-arm' functional roles as ones that are 'purely internal' (Block 1990, p. 70). He goes on to ask:

Why can't the functionalist identify intentional contents with long-arm functional states and qualitative content with short-arm functional states? The result would be a kind of 'dualist' or 'two factor' version of functionalism. My response: perhaps such a two factor theory is workable, but the burden of proof is on the functionalist to tell us what the short-arm functional states might be. (Block 1990, p. 70)

I argue for a 'two factor' account. The short-arm (proximal) functional roles that define qualitative contents are all and only those that define the place of a quale in its quality space. They are the relations of discriminability and relative similarity that define the intrinsic spacing of qualities.

Could some new variety of spectrum inversion defeat the proposed analysis? One would need to imagine that the same qualitative state could come to serve different proximal roles, or that different qualitative states could be found to have identical proximal roles. This is very different from the standard sorts of spectrum inversion. One would need to imagine that orange—that very same quale—would no longer resemble its current neighbours. Orange—not the experience caused by looking at oranges, but orange itself—must cease to be somewhat reddish and somewhat yellowish. It must continue to be the quale it is, though it could no longer resemble the qualia it does. Perhaps the quale orange comes most closely to resemble blue. In a series of hues ordered by relative similarities, that very same quale would now be placed over *there*, among the blues and greens.   Or perhaps orange becomes a unique hue, so that one can pick out a pure orange—an orange hue that is not at all reddish and not at all yellowish.

These latter inversions seem to me to be incoherent. Orange, whatever it is, is somewhat reddish and somewhat yellowish, no matter what stimuli in turn present red or yellow. It cannot be bluish. The relations among the qualitative terms *define* them. One could not have a unique orange, or an orange that is more similar to blue than to a yellowy red.

A problem of sorts arises for this analysis only if a quality space is homotopic. Suppose its structure shows the requisite symmetry, so that two points stand in the same pattern of relations to all the other points in the structure. As noted above, it seems logically possible that some sentient species somewhere has such a quality space.   Does that possibility defeat the claim that qualia are defined by their place in a quality space?

If the quality space were homotopic, then we could provide structural descriptions for particular qualitative terms, but not structural *definite* descriptions. We could not say 'Orange is *the* colour that stands in such and such relations . . . ', since two distinct points in the structure could satisfy the same description. One must admit that there is a sense in which this would constitute a failure in our definitions of particular qualitative terms, but I will argue that it would be an odd and limited kind of failure, one that we can (and, for some terms, do) accept.

First note that from its structure, we could determine that the quality space is homotopic. We would know, after all, that there are *two* points that satisfy the same pattern of relations to all the other points in the structure. They have structure descriptions of the same form. We do not confuse the two points or treat them as one. Furthermore, if we could attach a reference to a single variable in such a description, we could immediately disambiguate it. The two points do not stand in the same relations to the *same* relata; they merely stand in patterns of relation that have the same form.   With a single reference unambiguously fixed, the entire structure would lock in place, and we could identify the two points. At worst, then, the possibility of a homotopic space would show that the analyses do not on their own achieve singular reference. We would know that there are two points, but not know which is which.

In the previous chapter, I argued that paradigms are essential to the learning of colour terms (s. 6.6). Words for colours can only be defined in terms of one another. The entire structure lacks reference unless it is somewhere tacked down, by ostending a few samples. The tactic succeeds because most human beings share a sense of which presentations are similar to which.

If there are terms that function in this manner, one need not require their definitions to individuate. The indexical element would be essential to securing reference, and the term could function even though one could not provide a set of definitional necessary and sufficient conditions picking out its extension. The failure of the definition to secure a unique reference would not impede the use of the term. Indeed, it has been argued that precisely such failures can occur with natural-kind terms such as 'gold', 'water', or 'lemon'. Such terms can have a place in the language even if we cannot frame a definition that suffices to fix a unique reference. So, for example, Putnam (1970) argued that all of the currently proposed necessary and sufficient conditions for 'lemon' could turn out to be false. One can imagine revising *all* of our beliefs about the nature of lemons. For complete revisions in our 'definitions' to be possible, the term must achieve reference independently of its definitional conditions. To individuate, we require an indexical. The stuff must be the same substance as this (pointing to an exemplar). If qualitative terms gain a footing in the language in a similar way, by exploiting an innate sense of qualitative similarity and ostension to samples, then we would expect use of an indexical to be essential to securing their reference.

There are other examples of terms for which we seem to tolerate definitions that may, in odd, counterfactual situations, fail to secure unique reference. Consider spatial terms such as 'left' and 'right', 'clockwise' and 'counter-clockwise', and their cognates. Does a clockwise spiral have all the relational properties of a counter-clockwise spiral? In a sense, yes—the two have structure descriptions of the same form—but in another sense, no—points on them do not bear all the same relations to the same points. They are incongruent counterparts (see Van Cleve and Frederick, 1991). If playful aliens tampered with your semantic memory, you might find yourself in a situation in which you could not determine which is which. (You also would not know which of your hands is your left hand.) But from the structure descriptions you could determine that there are two different spirals, and once a mark is made on either one, they could be distinguished by the relations that other points bear to that mark. The relation between red and its inverse in a homotopic quality space is logically analogous. The thought experiment fails to show that the two cannot be distinguished by their relational properties, or that there is some intrinsic difference between them that is ignored by the analysis. Our definitions might fail to secure unique reference, but the problem could be solved with a single ostension. If the terms function as suggested, some use of indexicals is essential anyway.

In short, the proposed analysis is consistent with the logical possibility of spectrum inversion. Qualitative terms are to be analysed purely in terms of their proximal functional roles: the relations of discriminability, relative similarity, and qualitative identity that assign each a place in the quality space. The analysis drops all mention of relations to stimuli and to behaviour. We can then readily admit that a particular stimulus might present different people with different qualia. If qualitative terms function by exploiting the similarity relations built into one's sensory mechanisms, combined with ostension to exemplars, then we can allow for the counterfactual possibility of a homotopic quality space. Such a possibility at most implies that the definitions would not on their own secure unique reference, and that ostension would be needed. But if the terms function as suggested, this implication is neither unexpected nor damaging.

7.3 Subjective and Objective

As a conclusion, it is fitting to return to Nagel's worries concerning subjective and objective, and to consider to what extent they are allayed or exacerbated by this account.

For Nagel a view is relatively subjective to the extent that it is determined by particularities of the subject: his or her biological make-up, history, position in the world, and so on. A view is relatively objective to the extent that it leaves those particular facts behind and frames generalizations that include both the world and the previous (and more subjective) viewpoint within its scope. The problem is that conscious mental processes seem to be *essentially* subjective. It seems that their characteristics are not more fully revealed when one abandons the subjective viewpoint of the creature that has them, but in some sense can be understood only from that subjective viewpoint. Nagel (1979*b*) uses the example of echo location in bats (see also Farrell 1950). In some sense it seems that what it is like to be a bat can be understood only by bats or by creatures similar enough to bats to have similar experiences.

How would the theory developed above attempt to construct a bat phenomenology? One would proceed by constructing bat psychophysics and studying the structure of its discriminations. One can test such capacities among non-verbal creatures by making receipt of food (for example) dependent on a selective response to one of two stimuli and then successively decreasing differences between the stimuli (see Jacobs 1981). To what differences is the creature sensitive? While technically difficult, experiments to answer these questions (even for bat echo location) are possible.

And, I would argue, they would give an answer of sorts to the question, What is it like to be a bat? An ability of the bat to discriminate two stimuli shows that what it is like to be a bat experiencing one of them is not phenomenally the same as what it is like to be a bat experiencing the other. The structure of the pair list will reveal necessary conditions for qualitative similarity from the bat's point of view. The qualitative likenesses and differences among experiences of the bat could be identified from the structure of its discriminations. Using the techniques described in Chapters 4 and 5, we could learn not merely that there exist likenesses and differences among the sensory states of the bat, but what those likenesses and differences are. We can ascertain the number of distinct attributes of sensory states to which discriminations are sensitive, and rule out rival hypotheses giving a different dimensionality to the sensory space. Finally, a developed neurophysiology could identify the axes through that space in terms of which the bat actually makes its discriminations. Such a development would enable us to identify the differentiative attributes of the sensory encodings of the bat: the ones in terms of which *it* senses things to resemble or differ. We get what seems to be an 'objective' characterization of what it is like to be a bat.

Such a feat must be possible for us even to recognize that bat echo location (or any alien sensory modality) would differ phenomenologically from our sensory modalities. The reason we know that there is a problem concerning what it is like to be a bat is simply that the bat can discriminate stimuli that to us are indiscriminable (sizes, distances, and shapes when your eyes are closed) and will fail to discriminate stimuli that to us are perfectly distinct (e.g. colours). Since we can establish such facts, we have a purchase on alien phenomenology; and if the constructions above are sound, then in principle nothing bars a certain degree of understanding of its sensory phenomenology.

For example, suppose we first attempt to determine the spatial discriminations possible in echo location. Can the bat discriminate depth as well as azimuth and altitude? It turns out that it can. What are its errors in localization at different coordinates? How far away is the echo-location horizon? Does the bat ever make front–back reversals? Once these details are established, one could ascertain the discriminations possible at a particular echo-located region. Can the bat discriminate distinct sizes if they are stationary? Can it distinguish between different species of moth of the same size? With answers to these questions, it would be possible to detail the structure of the echo-location modality, and then imagine how it resembles or differs from other sensory modalities. For example, echo-location spatial discriminations might resemble those possible when one is near brief flashes of dim light in a dark warehouse. Perhaps they more closely resemble the spatial discriminations one can make among bursts of voices in a dark room, or perhaps they are closer to those mediated by touch if one tries to assemble an engine in the dark. Bat spatial discriminations might resemble any of these, and at least in principle one could establish which of them it most resembles, and the ways in which it differs from all of them.

To what extent would such an understanding answer Nagel's worries? Such a description would not enable us to experience the world the way the bat does, so in that sense it would not answer the question, What is it like to be a bat? Perhaps 'knowing what it is like to be a bat' uses the word 'know' in the sense of 'knowing how', so that answering the question is a matter of acquiring certain abilities: to make discriminations, recognize, and remember things in the way a bat does (see Lewis 1988). If so, providing a description—even a full description of the quality space—will not suffice to answer the question. It does however suffice to defeat Nagel's claim (in 1979*b*) that no objective characterization of the experience of the bat is possible.

Nagel claimed that a new discipline of 'objective phenomenology' is needed if we are to understand subjective phenomena. He writes:

Though the subjective features of our own minds are at the center of *our* world, we must try to conceive of them as just one manifestation of the mental in a world that is not given especially to the human point of view . . . The first requirement is to think of our own minds as mere instances of something general . . . We must think of mind as a phenomenon to which the human case is not necessarily central . . . (Nagel 1986, p. 18)

Nagel also characterizes this project as one in which we would 'be able to think of ourselves from outside—but in mental, not physical terms' (Nagel 1986, p. 17). It would employ 'subjective universals' of which some instances could be found in one's own experience.

Mapping the quality space of a sensory modality has some of these features. The idea is not limited to any particular modality, but provides a general framework applicable to any modality, including non-human ones. It allows one to think of human sensory modalities as particular instances of a widespread phenomenon. The delineation of the human psychological colour solid is aptly described as a matter of 'thinking of ourselves from the outside, but in mental, not physical terms'. Those structures of relative similarities are subjective and phenomenal facts of a sort, but described from a more objective standpoint, enabling a creature lacking the experiences to understand something of what it is like to have them. Finally, we proceed almost entirely by detailing the *structural* features of experience: the properties of the relations they bear to one another. As Nagel says,

It should be possible to investigate . . . the quality-structure of some sense we do not have, for example, by observing creatures who do have it—even though the understanding we can reach is only partial. But if we could do that, we should also be able to apply the same general idea to ourselves, and thus to analyze our experiences in ways that can be understood without having had such experiences. (Nagel 1986, p. 25)

This is an excellent description of comparative sensory psychophysics. It has discovered and (to some extent) explained not only the well-known echo location in bats, but also electro-reception in fish (see Bullock 1973), magnetic field detection in carrier pigeons (see Baker 1981), and other modalities.

The philosophical problem posed by sensory qualities is that no objective understanding or explanation of them seems possible: it seems that they can only be understood in their own subjective terms, and that none of the current sciences provide any help in attempting to understand them. But suppose our understanding of the quality space of bat echo location were even better than our current understanding of human colour vision. Would we then understand what it is like to be a bat? There is perhaps a sense in which we would not 'understand' what it is like: knowing all that would not enable us to make the discriminations that the bat makes, or directly to sense the similarities it senses. Yet we would understand something of what it is like; we would have secured one sort of 'objective phenomenology' for the bat. Indeed, it seems apt to describe Fechner's intent in creating psychophysics as one of creating a kind of 'objective phenomenology'. He announced the programme of the new discipline in 1851, after some ten years of agonizing philosophical thought about materialism, consciousness, and the brain (see Boring 1950). Many of Fechner's worries bear a striking resemblance to Nagel's. Psychophysics answers at least some of them.

Appendix
Multidimensional Scaling

Chapter 4 illustrated various ways of deriving the number of dimensions of an order from the structure of similarities between its members. Those methods relied on recognizing various configurations in the data, and seemed unsystematizable. It was noted that the statistical techniques known as multidimensional scaling (MDS) provide a generalizable method for extracting dimensionality from relative similarities. They take one from a set of 'proximities' among stimuli—which might be as simple as rankings of relative similarities—and generate a spatial representation of the stimuli which is such that distances between stimulus points in that space are a monotonic function of their relative similarities. MDS can determine both the number of dimensions required for a space and the coordinates of each stimulus point in that space.

For example, from a map of the United States it is easy to measure inter-city distances. Multidimensional scaling proceeds in the reverse direction: given a table of inter-city distances, it reconstructs the map. Axes on the reconstructed map have no obvious meaning; one could not determine which direction is north, for example. Instead, the map would merely represent the relative distances among the cities.

Just as in the ruler-and-compass types of multidimensional scaling, similarity data constrain the ordering of stimuli. The constraints are more or less rigid depending on how one interprets the numbers representing similarities. If our inter-city distances are not just rankings, but measurements in miles or kilometres, quite a rigid constraint is possible: distances between points in the map will be a constant linear function of the inter-city distances.

Types of Data

There are two major classes of multidimensional scaling, depending on the constraints one assumes to apply to one's data. If one requires that the actual metrical values of those numbers be significant (so that '0.8' is twice the value of '0.4', and so on), then one uses some variant of *metric* multidimensional scaling. It would be used, for example, if we start with inter-city distances in miles or kilometres. In metric multidimensional scaling, the ratios among distances in the final space are intended to represent the ratios among similarities in the initial data.

More often, the ratios among the initial similarities are not significant (or available), and instead only the ranking of the similarities is significant. That 0.8 is twice 0.4 is in this case ignored; instead, it is only the ordinal position—that 0.8 is *more than* 0.4—that is used. Instead of starting from a table of inter-city distances in miles, we would start from facts of the form: New York is closer to Washington than to Chicago; Chicago is closer to Atlanta than to New York; Atlanta is closer to Washington than to Chicago; and so on. The resulting spatial representation will be constrained to respect the rankings of similarities, but not their ratios. These techniques are known as *non-metric* multidimensional scaling. Dimensions and coordinates are retrieved in non-metric MDS; it is non-metric in that only the ordering of inter-point distances is significant, not their ratios.

Since it is difficult to collect metric forms of similarity data, non-metric forms of multidimensional scaling are in practice more important, and I shall focus exclusively on them. In particular, non-metric MDS can be applied directly to triadic relative similarity judgements. One needs a ranking of all the similarity pairs s_{ij}, and to get this one can use a collection of triples judgements. Conventionally, similarity pairs s_{ij} are ordered in such a way that the minimal rank is assigned to the most similar pair, and increasing ranks indicate increasing differences. Each triadic similarity judgement gives a ranking of two similarity pairs: if S_i is more similar to S_j than to S_k, then we know that s_{ij} is less than s_{ik}. We get no information on the ranking of s_{jk} compared with s_{ij} or s_{ik}; to assess the latter one must ask the distinct question of whether S_j is more similar to S_i than to S_k. In effect, one must present each stimulus and rank its similarities to all of the others.[1]

Suppose we are interested in the relative similarities of tastes among four kinds of food: potato, spinach, lettuce, and tuna. We have respondents rate the relative similarities between potato and each of the other three, between spinach and each of the other three, and so on. From such judgements we build up a ranked triples list of the form (for example)

p:	s	l	t
s:	l	p	t
l:	s	p	t
t:	l	p	s

Each row indicates the ranking of similarities for the given item. So potatoes were judged more similar to spinach than to lettuce, more similar to lettuce than to tuna, and more similar to spinach than to tuna.

From such a complete polling of judgements, it is possible to derive the

[1] In fact, this is the chief drawback of these scaling techniques: the sheer number of similarity judgements required from the subject (see s. 5.1).

ranking of similarities among the pairs:

ls	sp	lp	tl	tp	ts
1	2	3	4	5	6

indicating that the lettuce–spinach pair is the most similar of the group, followed by spinach–potato, and so on. If one examines the above triples list one will find that this is the only possible ranking of pairs that is consistent with the relative similarities. For example, we know from the third row of the triples list that the *ls* pair is more similar than the *lp* pair, and the first row implies that *lp* is more similar than *tp*, so we can infer that *ls* is more similar than *tp*. Recall that the lowest rank is assigned to the most similar pair, and larger numbers mean that the pairs are less similar. (For this reason, the numbers making up the raw data are sometimes called *dissimilarities*.) We finally fill in the proximity matrix:

	p	s	l	t
p	–	2	3	5
s	2	–	1	6
l	3	1	–	4
t	5	6	4	–

Multidimensional scaling can be applied directly to matrices of such a form (although typically data matrices are much larger). A solution can be found in two dimensions in which the order of the distances between points is isomorphic to the order of similarities given above (see Fig. A1). This provides coordinates for each item and their inter-point distances. The axes of the space are not assigned any meaning. Although interpretable axes ultimately can be identified, here the axes merely represent two dimensions in terms of which relative similarities can be represented. (As argued in Chapter 5, the job of providing interpretable axes for such spaces is one that should be turned over to the psychophysiologists. Only when they are successful is the quality space complete.)

Distances among these points reflect the order of similarities among the items. There is no metric claim—no claim (for example) that spinach is twice as similar to lettuce as it is to tuna. Only the order of similarities is significant. Nevertheless, one can see that, with many points and many triples of relative similarity to consider, the ordering among the inter-point distances will tightly constrain the spatial representation.

Non-metric MDS is well suited for data gathered using the triadic relative similarity predicate. Other similarity measures can be used (see Davison 1983, pp. 40–54). The most straightforward is simply to ask people directly to rate the degree of similarity between a pair, using some numeric categories such as 1–9 for most to least similar. A variant requires subjects to mark the degree of similarity on a line from least to

(a)

Data matrix

	Potato	Spinach	Lettuce	Tuna
Potato		2	3	5
Spinach	2		1	6
Lettuce	3	1		4
Tuna	5	6	4	

(b)

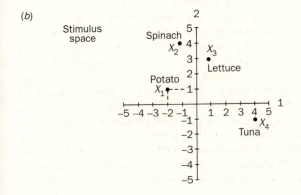

Stimulus space

(c)

Coordinates

Row	1	2
X_1	–2	1
X_2	–1	4
X_3	1	3
X_4	4	–1

Distances

Stimulus		X_1	X_2	X_3	X_4
Potato	X_1	0.00	3.16	3.61	6.32
Spinach	X_2	3.16	0.00	2.24	7.07
Lettuce	X_3	3.61	2.24	0.00	5.00
Tuna	X_4	6.32	7.07	5.00	0.00

Example of classical multidimensional scaling (CMDS)

FIG. A1. Multidimensional scaling of four foods

Note: (*a*) The 'data matrix' table shows the rankings given to the relative similarities of four foods. The most similar pair was spinach–lettuce; the least similar was spinach–tuna. (*b*) The 'stimulus space' is the map generated by multidimensional scaling representing the relative similarity rankings. One hopes to find axes that are interpretable. (*c*) The 'coordinates' table simply shows the coordinates for the four foods in the stimulus space. 'Distances' are derived from those coordinates.

Source: From Schiffman *et al*. (1981, p. 60). Reprinted by permission of Academic Press and of the authors.

most. In a 'magnitude estimation' procedure one stipulates a value (100, say) for the similarity of some pair, and requires subjects to rate the similarities of other pairs relative to that standard. For example, the lettuce–spinach pair might be stipulated as possessing a similarity of 100, and a subject might rate the spinach–potato pair as having a similarity of 80. These three techniques have the advantage that they are relatively easy to employ, but the disadvantage that they cannot be applied to non-humans. Some investigators also question the validity of the numbers that subjects assign to stimuli.

Better similarity measures rely on various sorts of conditional probabilities. These provide a somewhat more general version of the Quinean idea of receptual neighbourhoods mentioned in Section 4.4.1. For example, one can associate different responses $R_1, \ldots, R_n$ with each of the stimuli $S_1, \ldots, S_n$. This 'association' may be a matter of conditioning an animal or simply providing a label for each stimulus to the human. Then come trials in which one attempts to elicit the different responses to the different stimuli. Thereafter one derives a matrix of conditional probabilities $p(R_i | S_j)$. The sum of the probabilities of confusing S_j for S_i (i.e. $p(R_i | S_j) + p(R_j | S_i)$) can be used as an index of the similarity of S_j and S_i (see Davison 1983, p. 50). The same approach can be used in straightforward stimulus generalization tests, or to assess tasks in which the different stimuli are sorted into different categories. Again, the probability of confusing two stimuli is used as a measure of their similarity.[2]

How MDS Works

One way or another one obtains a matrix of similarities. How can the spatial order of the stimuli be derived from that matrix?

If we knew the coordinates of each point, all of the inter-point distances could readily be calculated. If we *guess* the coordinates for each point, we can calculate what the inter-point distances would be for that guess. Those inter-point distances can be compared with the original proximities, and some measure of the 'goodness of fit' between the two can be derived. In the non-metric variants that interest us, the measure of goodness of fit in one way or another compares the rankings of the inter-point distances to the rankings of the original similarities.[3] We can also

---

[2] Stimulus generalization and confusion probabilities are probably monotonic on stimulus similarity, but the apparent assumption here that they are related by a linear function has been challenged (see Gregson 1975, pp. 93–5). Similarity measures may not satisfy all the axioms of probability theory, so adopting any probability measure as a measure of similarity is a substantive commitment.

[3] We need some explicit function to measure goodness of fit, but it happens that different choices of that function do not significantly alter the final results (see Shepard *et al.* 1972, p. 8).

calculate the effect of moving a point in a particular direction and for a certain distance on the inter-point distances and hence on the overall 'goodness of fit'. Some assignment of coordinates will optimize that fit; it will provide a global minimum of mismatches. How do we find that optimal assignment?

The problem can be attacked with numerical analysis. Details are beyond the scope of this book, although the algorithm is described in the next section. In soft focus the picture is this. We provide some starting configuration—some initial estimate of the coordinates needed. This initial configuration may be random, a simple linear ranking of points, or something invented by the investigator. We then assess the goodness of fit between distances and proximities. The fit may be improved by adding a dimension to the spatial representation; that is, by adding a new coordinate to every point, and adjusting distances accordingly. It may be improved by changing the values of coordinates already present. The typical algorithm will test whether fit can be significantly improved either way. If so, the next round of adjustments is made, distances are again computed, goodness of fit is checked, and the iteration continues. If not, we have found at least a local minimum, and the algorithm terminates.

An example is given in Fig. A2. This depicts a non-metric analysis of rankings of inter-city distances in the United States. Initially we assume a one-dimensional order with a random arrangement of points along the line. *SSTRESS* is the measure of 'goodness of fit'. One can see that in the first iteration we move to a two-dimensional order. Each arrow represents the movement of the given point in one iteration. The algorithm in effect searches for the directions in which points should be moved in order to decrease the stress measure, and continues moving them about until the stress measure no longer declines significantly. The final derived configuration is startlingly close to the original, although it is rotated 45° clockwise. (Of course, the orientation of the map is irrelevant to the inter-city distances; recall that the axes have no intrinsic meaning in MDS spaces.)

FIG. A2. Iterations in multidimensional scaling (overleaf)

Note: The task is to generate a map of US cities, given only their relative distances. In the first iteration (part (*a*)), cities were placed along a line. Arrows show how the points moved in the second iteration of the algorithm, which added a second dimension. Iterations continue in parts (*b*) and (*c*). The arrows show how the points moved up through the eighth iteration. The arrowheads in part (*c*) show the final configuration. The entire map is tilted 45° on the page. In the last step, producing the map in part (*d*), we rotate the axes to give interpretable (here, conventional) ones.

Source: From Schiffman *et al.* (1981, pp. 7–9). Reprinted by permission of Academic Press and of the authors.

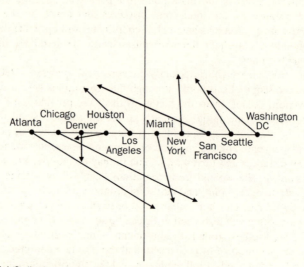

(a) Ordinal analysis of flying distances, iterations 1 and 2: *SSTRESS*=0.727,0.454

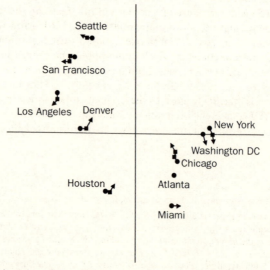

(c) Iterations 6,7, and 8 in ordinal analysis of flying distances: *SSTRESS* =0.080,0.065,0.052

FIG. A2. Iterations in multidimensional scaling

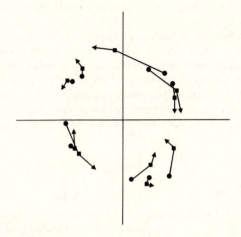

(b) Iterations 3,4, and 5 in ordinal analysis of flying distances: SSTRESS=0.267,0.137,0.100

(d) Final result

FIG. A2. Iterations in multidimensional scaling

MDS Algorithms

For those still sceptical of the premises underlying methods of multidimensional scaling, it is worthwhile considering in more detail how the algorithms function.

One does not use dissimilarities directly in the estimation algorithm, except to generate an initial configuration. Instead, one uses some monotonic transformation of the dissimilarities to get what are called *disparities*. If s_{ij} is the dissimilarity between i and j, we use some function $f(s_{ij})$ to get the (estimated) disparity. Disparities are usually symbolized with the Greek letter δ, so the estimated disparity for the pair ij is δ_{ij}. The function f must be a monotonic transformation of the dissimilarities s_{ij}; that is,

$$f(s_{ij}) \leq f(s_{jk}) \quad \text{if} \quad s_{ij} \leq s_{jk}$$

or

$$\delta_{ij} \leq \delta_{jk} \quad \text{if} \quad s_{ij} \leq s_{jk}.$$

The idea is to estimate coordinates for the points i, j, k, etc., so that the *distances* d_{ij}, d_{jk}, etc., are as close as possible to the disparities. Disparities are always a monotonic function of dissimilarities. We estimate coordinates so that distances between points will be as close as possible to disparities. When we are finished, therefore, the distances between points will be a monotonic function of the dissimilarities.

'Goodness of fit' can be evaluated by comparing the estimated disparities between points to the estimated distances between points. Just as in regression and factor analysis problems, a sum-of-squares measure is appropriate, since it is only the absolute value of differences that is important, not their direction. So we evaluate the difference between our current estimate of the disparity for a pair ij and the current estimate of the distance between points i and j. The distance between points i and j is a function of their estimated coordinates; in the three-dimensional Euclidean case it is

$$[(x_1 - x_2)^2 + (y_1 - y_2)^2 + (z_1 - z_2)^2]^{1/2}.$$

Each of the summed factors is the difference between the respective first coordinates, second coordinates, and so on of the two points. We are not limited to a Euclidean formulation: we can employ different distance functions (Minkowskian, etc.) if desired.

The goodness of fit for a single pair ij is some variant of

$$(\delta_{ij} - (\text{estimated distance})_{ij})^2.$$

This reflects the absolute value of the difference between the estimated disparity for the pair and the estimated distance between the points. The overall goodness of fit for a proposed coordinatization is the sum of such terms for all possible pairs *ij*. It helps to standardize the stress measure in one way or another, so that data-sets that start with higher numbers for their initial dissimilarities do not automatically have higher stress in their solutions. One way to standardize is to divide the sum of squares by the sum of squared estimated distances (Davison 1983, p. 88). Another way is to use standardized distances so that the square of their sum equals one (Davison 1983, p. 107). In any case, the critical point is that goodness of fit is assessed by summing differences between estimated disparities and estimated distances for all the pairs.

Once we fix our distance measure, the problem is to find the function that assigns a disparity to each dissimilarity. Coordinates are simply adjusted so that distances between points will overall have a close fit to those disparities. We solve for a function that minimizes stress. Numerical analysis methods are employed. The process is iterative, and it continues until further iterations do not contribute significantly to goodness of fit.

The function that gives disparities from dissimilarities (and that determines the adjustment of coordinates) is not some simple arithmetic function of the dissimilarities such as product or square root. It is a mapping from dissimilarities to disparities in which the image of each particular dissimilarity can be adjusted independently. At a given stage, we may alter only two or three of the disparities assigned to particular dissimilarities.

Within each iteration there are two distinct stages of analysis, a non-metric stage and a metric stage. In the non-metric stage we adjust the current estimator of disparities to ensure that they are monotonic over dissimilarities. The stage is non-metric because only the ordinal position of disparities is adjusted; their sums and ratios are ignored. In the metric stage we adjust coordinates so that the estimated distances will be as close as possible to those disparities. This stage is metric because distances are a function of the sums and ratios of coordinates.

In somewhat more detail, these two stages work as follows. In one way or another we generate an initial assignment of coordinates to points. From those initial coordinates we derive an estimate of distances between every two points. Let us call this iteration zero. All subsequent iterations will have a non-metric and then a metric stage.

In the non-metric stage we adjust the estimates of disparities so that they are monotonic over dissimilarities. For the estimate of disparities we use the distance estimates from the previous iteration. These estimates are examined to see how well their ranking corresponds to the ranking of the original dissimilarities. Some pairs of disparities will violate the rankings found among the pairs of dissimilarities. We adjust the disparities that are out of order. There are various ways to do this; one simple technique is simply to replace each member of a pair that is out of order with the average of the pair (see Schiffman *et al.* 1981, p. 353). We adjust only those disparities that are out of order. However it is done, this stage ends when the estimated disparities are such that

$$\delta_{ij} \leq \delta_{jk} \quad \text{if} \quad s_{ij} \leq s_{jk}.$$

That is, it ends when the current estimate of disparities is monotonic over the original dissimilarity data.

In the metric stage of the iteration, we start with the estimate of disparities from the just completed non-metric stage, and adjust coordinates of the points so that their distances correspond as closely as possible to those disparities. We are given some function to calculate inter-point distances from their coordinates, we are given the ideal inter-point distances to achieve (i.e. the disparities), and we are given some function (the stress measure) to assess the degree of correspondence between disparities and the inter-point distances. We simply push around coordinates so as to minimize stress. We can determine the direction in which to push the coordinates by numerically determining the direction in which movement has the largest impact on the stress measure. We might need new 'directions' to do this, and so give birth to new dimensions. This approach is a *steepest gradient* approach; we push in the direction that has the most impact on the stress measure.

The metric phase minimizes the discrepancy between the current estimate of disparities and the current estimate of distances. It arrives at some minimum stress measure for the current estimates of both. We compare that stress measure with the one achieved at the previous iteration. If it is not significantly better (where 'significantly better' can be defined by the investigator), further iterations will not improve the overall fit, and we stop. Otherwise iterations continue. We compute inter-point distances using the newly adjusted coordinates, and in the next round use those distances as the current best estimate for disparities.

Adjustments of disparities within the non-metric stage and of coordinates within the metric stage will tend to be largest in the first iterations, and fall steadily. Stress will fall most dramatically in the early iterations, and less and less quickly as the adjustments in disparities and in coordinates become smaller. While theoretically there is an iteration at which stress would cease to fall at all and could not be further improved, in practice the decrease in stress becomes insignificant very quickly. The investigator picks some arbitrary cut-off level to determine when iterations cease. In practice, one must also set some maximum number of iterations, in case the algorithm fails to converge on a solution quickly enough. One needs then to try a new starting configuration, to alter the stress criterion for a solution, or to increase the number of iterations allowed.

Strengths and Weaknesses

Multidimensional scaling satisfies many of the theoretical desiderata
mentioned in Chapter 4. It does not rely on some list of conditions
sufficient to infer dimensions. It can be applied to data-sets that contain
no clue to their similarity structure, and will generally succeed in
extracting that structure. It embodies explicit checks between the derived
space and the original data.

Some of its weaknesses include computational problems associated
with gradient techniques in numerical analysis. In the first place, there is a
possibility of degenerate solutions, particularly if one does not have
enough distinct data-points. This happens if one's data-points cluster into
just a few groups such that every point within a group is highly similar to
all the other points in that group. In practice, one can avoid this problem
by using a sufficiently large sample of stimuli. Secondly, gradient hunting
algorithms can get trapped in 'local minima', in which a solution that
appears superior to any of those in its immediate neighbourhood is
nevertheless not the best one possible—the global minimum is lower. A
typical strategy to avoid local minima is simply to carry out the analysis
repeatedly with many different starting configurations. Finally, because
these procedures are iterative, there is always the possibility that a
solution with the required goodness of fit will not be found within a
practicable number of iterations. In spite of these problems, a given
solution will generally be found no matter what the starting configuration,
and so it is in practice easy to work around the problems of local minima
and convergence failures.

How does multidimensional scaling identify the number of dimensions
in the order? Essentially, we start with a one-dimensional initial configuration, and add dimensions if they improve the goodness of fit between the
final space and the original similarity data. With N stimuli, the maximum
number of dimensions needed to represent all proximities is $N - 1$, but
typically one deals with far fewer. In multidimensional scaling there is no
rigid criterion determining when to stop adding dimensions. Adding a
dimension will almost always improve the fit somewhat. There are
diminishing returns in doing so, however; the improvement after a certain
number of additions becomes insignificant. To decide how many
dimensions are needed in the space, one must employ some statistical
criterion. The problem is similar in many ways to determining how many
factors to extract in a factor analysis. Additional factors will almost always
help, but the contributions soon become insignificant. Admitting a large
number of factors also makes it much more difficult to interpret each one.
As their number increases, the benefits—a better fit to the data—fall, and
the costs—complexity and difficulties in interpretation—rise. When the
costs outweigh the benefits, it is time to stop.

References

Achinstein, Peter (1974), 'The identity of properties', *American Philosophical Quarterly*, 11(4): 257–75.

Alston, William (1971), 'Varieties of privileged access', *American Philosophical Quarterly*, 8(3): 223–41.

Amoore, J. E. (1971), 'Olfactory genetics and anosmia', in L. M. Beidler (ed.), *Handbook of Sensory Physiology*, iv, *Chemical Senses*. New York: Springer-Verlag, 245–56.

—— (1977), 'Specific anosmia and the concept of primary odors', *Chemical Senses and Flavor*, 2: 267–81.

—— Johnston, J. W. Jr., and Rubin, M. (1964), 'The stereochemical theory of odor', *Scientific American*, no. 210: 42–9.

Anastasi, A. (1971), *Psychological Testing*, 3rd edn. New York: Macmillan.

Armstrong, D. M. (1963), 'Is introspective knowledge incorrigible?' *Philosophical Review*, 72: 417–32.

—— (1968), *A Materialist Theory of the Mind*. London: Routledge & Kegan Paul.

—— (1969), *Bodily Sensations*. London: Routledge & Kegan Paul.

—— (1970), 'The nature of mind', in C. V. Borst (ed.), *The Mind–Brain Identity Theory*. London: Macmillan, 67–79.

—— (1982), 'Recent work on the relation of mind and brain', in Guttorm Floistad (ed.), *Contemporary Philosophy: A New Survey*, iv, *Philosophy of Mind*. The Hague: M. Nijhoff.

—— (1980), *The Nature of Mind and Other Essays*. Ithaca, NY: Cornell University Press.

—— (1984), 'Consciousness and causality', in D. M. Armstrong and Norman Malcolm, *Consciousness and Causality*. Oxford: Basil Blackwell, 103–92.

Baier, Kurt (1962), 'Smart on sensations', *Australasian Journal of Philosophy*, 40: 57–68. Reprinted in Borst (1970).

—— (1964), 'The place of a pain', *Philosophical Quarterly*, 14: 138–50.

Baker, R. Robin (1981), *Human Navigation and the Sixth Sense*. New York: Simon and Schuster.

Barlow, H. B. (1972), 'Single units and sensation: a neuron doctrine for perceptual psychology?' *Perception*, 1: 371–94.

—— (1983), 'Perception: what quantitative laws govern the acquisition of knowledge from the senses?' in C. Coen (ed.), *Functions of the Brain*, Wolfson College Lectures. Oxford: Oxford University Press, 11–43

Bartoshuk, L. M., and Gent, J. F. (1985), 'Taste mixtures: an analysis of synthesis', in Donald W. Pfaff (ed.), *Taste, Olfaction, and the Central Nervous System: A Festschrift in Honor of Carl Pfaffmann*. New York: Rockefeller University Press, 210–32.

Bealer, George (1978), 'An inconsistency in functionalism', *Synthese*, 38: 333–72.

Bechtel, William (1983), 'A bridge between cognitive science and neuroscience', *Philosophical Studies*, 44(3): 319–30.

—— and Richardson, Robert (1983), 'Consciousness and complexity: evolutionary perspectives on the mind–body problem', *Australasian Journal of Philosophy*, 61: 378–95.

Beck, Jacob (1972), *Surface Color Perception*. Ithaca, NY: Cornell University Press.

Berkeley, George (1709), *An Essay towards a New Theory of Vision*. London: J. M. Dent, 1910.

Bindra, Dalbir (ed.) (1980), *The Brain's Mind: A Neuroscience Perspective*. New York: Gardner Press.

Blakemore, Colin (1975), 'Central visual processing', in Michael S. Gazzaniga and Colin Blakemore (eds.), *Handbook of Psychobiology*. New York: Academic Press, 241–68.

—— and Campbell, F. W. (1969), 'On the existence of neurons in the human visual system selectively sensitive to the orientation and size of retinal images', *Journal of Physiology*, no. 203: 237–60.

Block, Ned (1978), 'Troubles with functionalism', in C. Wade Savage (ed.), *Perception and Cognition: Issues in the Foundations of Psychology*, Minnesota Studies in the Philosophy of Science, ix. Minneapolis: University of Minnesota Press, 261–326. Reprinted with revisions in Block (1980*b*).

—— (1980*a*), 'Are absent qualia impossible?' *Philosophical Review*, 89(2): 257–74.

—— (ed.) (1980*b*), *Readings in the Philosophy of Psychology*, i. Cambridge, Mass.: Harvard University Press.

—— (1980*c*), 'Troubles with functionalism', in Block (1980*b*), 268–305.

—— (1982), 'Functionalism', in L. J. Cohen (ed.), *Logic, Methodology and Philosophy of Science*, vi. Amsterdam: North-Holland, 519–40.

—— (1983), 'The photographic fallacy in the debate on mental imagery', *Nous*, 17: 651–62.

—— (1990), 'Inverted Earth', in James E. Tomberlin (ed.), *Philosophical Perspectives*, iv, *Action Theory and Philosophy of Mind*. Atascadero, California: Ridgeview Press, 53–79.

—— and Fodor, Jerry (1972), 'What psychological states are not', *Philosophical Review*, 81(2): 159–81.

Boër, Steven, and Lycan, William (1980), 'Who, me?' *Philosophical Review*, 89: 427–66.

Boller, F., and Spinnler, H. (1968), 'Unilateral brain damage and visual memory for colors', *Neurology*, 18: 306–7.

Boring, E. G. (1942), *Sensation and Perception in the History of Experimental Psychology*. New York: Appleton Century.

—— (1950), *A History of Experimental Psychology*, 2nd edn. New York: Appleton Century.

Borst, C. V. (ed.) (1970), *The Mind–Brain Identity Theory*. London: Macmillan.

Boynton, Robert M. (1979), *Human Color Vision*. New York: Holt, Rinehart and Winston.

Bradley, M. C. (1963), 'Sensations, brain processes, and colours', *Australasian Journal of Philosophy*, 41: 385–93.

—— (1964), 'Critical notice: philosophy and science realism', *Australasian Journal of Philosophy*, 42: 262–83.

—— (1966), 'A note on a circularity argument', *Australasian Journal of Philosophy*, 44: 91–4.

Brandt, Richard B. (1960), 'Doubts about the identity theory', in Sidney Hook (ed.), *Dimensions of Mind*. New York: New York University Press.

—— and Kim, J. (1967), 'The logic of the identity theory', *Journal of Philosophy*, 64: 515–37.

Brindley, G. (1970), *Physiology of the Retina and Visual Pathways*, 2nd edn. Baltimore: Williams and Wilkins.

Broad, C. D. (1927), *Scientific Thought*. London: Routledge and Kegan Paul.

—— (1949), *The Mind and Its Place in Nature*. London: Routledge & Kegan Paul.

Brown, Mark (1983), 'Functionalism and sensation', *Auslegung*, 10: 218–28.

Bullock, T. H. (1973), 'Seeing the world through a new sense: electroreception in fish', *American Scientist*, 61: 316–25.

Bunge, Mario (1980), *The Mind–Body Problem: A Psychobiological Approach*. New York: Pergamon Press.

Burdick, Howard (1974), 'On the problems of abstraction and concretion', *Nous*, 8: 295–7.

Burnham, Robert W., Hanes, Randall M., and Bartleson, C. James (1963), *Color: A Guide to Basic Facts and Concepts*. New York: John Wiley.

Burtt, Edwin Arthur (1954), *The Metaphysical Foundations of Modern Science*. Garden City, NY: Doubleday.

Campbell, Keith (1969), 'Colours', in *Contemporary Philosophy in Australia*. London: Allen & Unwin.

—— (1982), 'The implications of Land's theory of colour vision', in L. J. Cohen (ed.), *Logic, Methodology and Philosophy of Science*, vi. Amsterdam: North-Holland, 541–52.

—— (1984), *Body and Mind*, 2nd edn. London: Macmillan.

Carnap, Rudolf (1966), *An Introduction to the Philosophy of Science*, ed. Martin Gardner. New York: Basic Books.

—— (1967), *The Logical Structure of the World*, 2nd edn., tr. Rolf A. George. Berkeley: University of California Press.

—— (1970), 'Theories as partially interpreted formal systems', in Baruch A. Brody (ed.), *Readings in the Philosophy of Science*. Englewood Cliffs, New Jersey: Prentice-Hall, 190–9.

Carterette, E. C., and Friedman, M. P. (eds.) (1975), *Handbook of Perception*, v, *Seeing*. New York: Academic Press.

Chevreul, M. E. (1839), *De la loi du contraste simultané des couleurs*, tr. Charles Martel and reprinted as *The Principles of Harmony and Contrast of Colours*. London: George Bell, 1890.

Chisholm, Roderick (1983), 'On the nature of the psychological', *Philosophical Studies*, 43: 155–64.

Churchland, Patricia S. (1980*a*), 'A perspective on mind–brain research', *Journal of Philosophy*, 77(4): 185–207.

—— (1980*b*), 'Language, thought, and information processing', *Nous*, 14: 147–69.

—— (1982), 'Mind–brain reduction: new light from philosophy of science', *Neuroscience*, 7(5): 1041–7.

—— (1983), 'Consciousness: the transmutation of a concept', *Pacific Philosophical Quarterly*, 64: 80–95.

—— (1986), *Neurophilosophy: Toward a Unified Science of the Mind–Brain*. Cambridge, Mass.: MIT Press.

—— and Churchland, Paul M. (1983), 'Stalking the wild epistemic engine', *Nous*, 17: 5–18.

Churchland, Paul M. (1979), *Scientific Realism and the Plasticity of Mind*. Cambridge: Cambridge University Press.

—— (1984), *Matter and Consciousness*. Cambridge, Mass.: MIT Press.

—— and Churchland, Patricia S. (1981), 'Functionalism, qualia, and intentionality', *Philosophical Topics*, 12: 121–46. Reprinted in John I. Biro and Robert W. Shahan (eds.), *Mind, Brain, and Function*. Norman: University of Oklahoma Press, 1982.

Clark, Austen (1980), *Psychological Models and Neural Mechanisms*. Oxford: Clarendon Press.

—— (1983*a*), 'Hypothetical constructs, circular reasoning, and criteria', *Journal of Mind and Behavior*, 4(1): 1–12.

—— (1983*b*), 'Functionalism and the definition of theoretical terms', *Journal of Mind and Behavior*, 4(3): 339–52.

—— (1984), 'Seeing and summing: implications of computational theories', *Cognition and Brain Theory*, 7(1): 1–23.

—— (1985*a*), 'A physicalist theory of qualia', *The Monist*, 68(4): 491–506.

—— (1985*b*), 'Psychological causation and the concept of psychosomatic disease', in Douglas Stalker and Clark Glymour (eds.), *Examining Holistic Medicine*. Buffalo, NY: Prometheus Books, 67–106.

—— (1985*c*), 'Qualia and the psychophysiological explanation of color perception', *Synthese* , 65(2): 377–405.

—— (1985*d*), 'Spectrum inversion and the color solid', *Southern Journal of Philosophy*, 23(4): 431–43.

—— (1986), 'Psychofunctionalism and chauvinism', *Philosophy of Science*, 53: 535–59.

—— (1989), 'The particulate instantiation of homogeneous pink', *Synthese*, 80: 277–304.

Conee, Earl (1984), 'A defense of pain', *Philosophical Studies*, 46: 239–48.

—— (1985), 'The possibility of absent qualia', *Philosophical Review*, 94(3): 345–66.

Coombs, C. H. (1964), *A Theory of Data*. New York: John Wiley.

Cornman, James (1962), 'The identity of mind and body', *Journal of Philosophy*, 59: 486–92.

—— (1971), *Materialism and Sensations*. New Haven, Conn.: Yale University Press.

Cornsweet, Tom (1970), *Visual Perception*. New York: Academic Press.

Crane, H., and Piantanida, T. (1983), 'On seeing reddish-green and yellowish-blue', *Science*, no. 221: 1078–80.

Critchley, M. (1965), 'Acquired anomalies of color perception of central origin', *Brain*, 88: 711–24.

Crocker, E. C., and Henderson, L. F. (1927), 'Analysis and classification of odours', *American Perfumery and Essential Oil Review*, 22: 325–56.

Culbertson, James T. (1982), *Consciousness: Natural and Artificial*. Roslyn Heights, New York: Libra.

Danay, R. M. (1983), 'Alien concepts', *Synthese*, 56: 283–300.

Davies, Martin (1983), 'Function in perception', *Australasian Journal of Philosophy*, 61: 409–26.

Davis, Lawrence (1982), 'Functionalism and absent qualia', *Philosophical Studies*, 41(2): 231–51.

Davis, Stephen (ed.) (1983), *Causal Theories of Mind: Action, Knowledge, Memory, Perception and Reference*. New York: DeGruyter.

Davison, Mark L. (1983), *Multidimensional Scaling*. New York: John Wiley.

Dember, W. N. (1960), *The Psychology of Perception*. New York: Holt, Rinehart and Winston.

Dennett, D. C. (1969), *Content and Consciousness*. London: Routledge & Kegan Paul.

—— (1971), 'Intentional systems', *Journal of Philosophy*, 68(4): 87–106.

—— (1982), 'How to study human consciousness empirically, or: nothing comes to mind', *Synthese*, 53: 159–80.

—— (1987), *The Intentional Stance*. Cambridge, Mass.: MIT Press.

—— (1991), *Consciousness Explained*. Boston: Little Brown.

DeRenzi, E., and Spinnler, H. (1967), 'Impaired performance on color tasks in patients with hemispheric damage', *Cortex* (Milan), 3: 194–217.

DeValois, R. L., and DeValois, K. K. (1975), 'Neural coding of color', in E. C. Carterette and M. P. Friedman (eds.), *Handbook of Perception*, v, *Seeing*. New York: Academic Press, 117–66.

———— (1988), *Spatial Vision*. Oxford: Oxford University Press.

—— and Jacobs, G. H. (1968), 'Primate color vision', *Scientific American*, no. 162: 533–40.

—— and Morgan, H. C. (1974), 'Psychophysical studies of monkey vision, II: Squirrel monkey wavelength and saturation discrimination', *Vision Research*, 14: 69–73.

———— Polson, M. C., Mead, W. R., and Hull, E. M. (1974a), 'Psychophysical studies of monkey vision, I: Macaque color vision and luminosity tests', *Vision Research*, 14: 53–67.

———— and Snodderly, D. M. (1974b), 'Psychophysical studies of monkey vision, III: Spatial luminance contrast sensitivity tests of macaque and human observers', *Vision Research*, 14: 75–81.

Dretske, Fred I. (1981), *Knowledge and the Flow of Information*. Cambridge, Mass.: MIT Press.

—— (1988), *Explaining Behavior*. Cambridge, Mass.: MIT Press.

Elugardo, Ray (1983), 'Functionalism, homunculi heads, and absent qualia', *Dialogue* (Canada), 22: 47–56.

Enç, Berent (1976), 'Identity statements and micro-reductions', *Journal of Philosophy*, 63(11): 285–305.

—— (1983), 'A defence of the identity theory', *Journal of Philosophy*, 80(5): 279–98.

Engen, Trygg (1982), *The Perception of Odors*. New York: Academic Press.

Erickson, Robert P. (1985), 'Definitions: a matter of taste', in Donald W. Pfaff (ed.), *Taste, Olfaction, and the Central Nervous System: A Festschrift in Honor of Carl Pfaffmann*. New York: Rockefeller University Press, 129–50.

—— and Covey, E. (1980), 'On the singularity of taste sensations: what is a taste primary?' *Physiology and Behavior*, 25: 527–33.

—— and Schiffman, Susan S. (1975), 'The chemical senses: a systematic approach', in Michael S. Gazzaniga and Colin Blakemore (eds.), *Handbook of Psychobiology*. New York: Academic Press, 394–426.

Evans, Ralph M. (1948), *An Introduction to Color*. New York: John Wiley.

—— (1974), *The Perception of Color*. New York: John Wiley.

Farrell, Brian A. (1950), 'Experience', *Mind*, 59: 170–98.

—— (1970), 'On the design of a conscious device', *Mind*, 79: 321–46.

—— (1977), 'On the psychological explanation of visual perception', *Synthese*, 35: 353–79.

—— (1983), 'The correlation between body, behaviour, and mind', in A. Gale and J. A. Edwards (eds.), *Physiological Correlates of Human Behavior*. London: Academic Press, ch. 2.

Farrell, Robert (1974), 'Michael Dummett on the structure of appearance', *Synthese*, 28: 233–49.

Feigl, Herbert (1963), 'Physicalism, unity of science, and the foundations of psychology', in P. A. Schilpp (ed.), *The Philosophy of Rudolf Carnap*. LaSalle, Ill.: Open Court.

—— (1967), *The 'Mental' and the 'Physical': the Essay and a Postscript*. Minneapolis: University of Minnesota Press.

—— (1970), 'Mind-body, not a pseudo-problem', in C. V. Borst (ed.), *The Mind–Brain Identity Theory*. London: Macmillan, 33–41.

Fodor, Jerry A. (1968), 'Functional explanation in psychology', in M. Brodbeck (ed.), *Readings in the Philosophy of the Social Sciences*. New York: Macmillan.

—— (1980), 'Methodological solipsism considered as a research strategy in cognitive psychology', *Behavioral and Brain Sciences*, 3(1): 63–72. Reprinted in Fodor (1981).

—— (1981), *RePresentations*. Cambridge, Mass.: MIT Press.

Fogelin, Robert J. (1984), 'Hume and the missing shade of blue', *Philosophy and Phenomenological Research*, 45: 263–72.

Freedman, S. J. (ed.) (1968), *The Neuropsychology of Spatially Oriented Behavior*. Homewood, Ill.: Dorsey Press.

Frisby, John P. (1980), *Seeing: Illusion, Brain and Mind*. Oxford: Oxford University Press.

Galileo Galilei (1623), *Opere Complete di Galileo Galilei*, iv, *Il Saggiatore*. Florence: Edizione Nazionale, 1842.

Gazzaniga, Michael S., and Blakemore, Colin (eds.) (1983), *Handbook of Psychobiology*. New York: Academic Press.

Geldard, Frank A., and Sherrick, Carl E. (1986), 'Space, time, and touch', *Scientific American*, no. 255: 91–5.

Geschwind, N. (1965), 'Disconnection syndromes in animals and man', *Brain*, 88: 237–94, 585–644.

—— and Fusillo, M. (1966), 'Color naming defects in association with alexia', *Archives of Neurology* (Chicago), 15: 137–46.

Gilchrist, A. L. (1977), 'Perceived lightness depends on perceived spatial arrangement', *Science*, no. 195: 185–7.

—— (1979), 'The perception of surface blacks and whites', *Scientific American*, no. 240: 112–25.

Globus, G., Maxwell, G., and Savodnick, I. (eds.) (1976), *Consciousness and Brain: A Scientific and Philosophical Inquiry*. New York: Plenum Press.

Goldman, Alvin (1976), 'Discrimination and perceptual knowledge', *Journal of Philosophy*, 73: 771–91.

—— (1977), 'Perceptual objects', *Synthese*, 35: 257–84.

—— (1985), 'The relation between epistemology and psychology', *Synthese*, 64(1): 29–68.

Goodman, Nelson (1972a), 'Order from indifference', in Goodman (1972b), 423–36.

—— (1972b), *Problems and Projects*. Indianapolis: Hackett.

—— (1977), *The Structure of Appearance*, 3rd edn. Boston: Dordrecht Reidel.

Gould, Stephen Jay (1981), *The Mismeasure of Man*. New York: W. W. Norton.

Gouras, P. (1985), 'Colour coding in the primate retinogeniculate system', in David Ottoson and Semir Zeki (eds.), *Central and Peripheral Mechanisms of Colour Vision*. London: Macmillan.

Graham, C. H., and Hsia, Yun (1958a), 'Color defect and color theory', *Science*, no. 127: 675–82.

—— —— (1958b), 'The spectral luminosity curves for a dichromatic eye and a normal eye in the same person', *Proceedings of the National Academy of Sciences*, 44: 46–9.

—— Sperling, H. G., Hsia, Y., and Coulson, A. H. (1961), 'The determination of some visual functions of a unilaterally color blind subject', *Journal of Psychology*, 51: 3–32.

Gregory, R. L. (1977), *Eye and Brain*, 3rd edn. London: Weidenfeld and Nicolson.

Gregson, Robert A. M. (1975), *Psychometrics of Similarity*. New York: Academic Press.

Grice, H. P. (1975), 'Method in philosophical psychology (from the banal to the bizarre)', *Proceedings and Addresses of the American Philosophical Association*, 48: 23–53.

Griffin, Donald (1981), *The Question of Animal Awareness*, 2nd edn. New York: Rockefeller University Press.

—— (1984), *Animal Thinking*. Cambridge, Mass.: Harvard University Press.

Guilford, H. P. (1954), *Psychometric Methods*. New York: McGraw-Hill.

Gulick, W. L., Gescheider, G. A., and Frisina, R. D. (1989), *Hearing: Physiological Acoustics, Neural Coding, and Psychoacoustics*. Oxford: Oxford University Press.

Gustafson, Donald (1964), *Essays in Philosophical Psychology*. New York: Anchor Books.

Haber, R. N., and Hershenson, M. (1980), *The Psychology of Visual Perception*, 2nd edn. New York: Holt, Rinehart and Winston.

Hård, Anders, and Sivik, Lars (1981), 'NCS—Natural Color System: a Swedish standard for color notation', *Color Research and Application*, 6(3): 129–38.

Hardin, C. L. (1983), 'Colors, normal observers, and standard conditions', *Journal of Philosophy*, 80: 806–13.

—— (1984a), 'A new look at color', *American Philosophical Quarterly*, 21(2): 125–33.

—— (1984b), 'Are scientific objects coloured?', *Mind*, 93: 491–500.

—— (1985), 'The resemblances of colors', *Philosophical Studies*, 48: 35–47.

—— (1986), 'Qualia and materialism: closing the explanatory gap', presented at the June 1986 meeting of the Society for Philosophy and Psychology at Johns Hopkins University, Baltimore.

—— (1988), *Color for Philosophers*. Indianapolis: Hackett.

—— (1990), 'Color and illusion', in William G. Lycan (ed.), *Mind and Cognition: A Reader*. Oxford: Basil Blackwell, 555–66.

Harper, Roland, Bate Smith, E. C., and Land, D. G. (1968), *Odor Description and Odor Classification*. New York: American Elsevier.

Harrison, Bernard (1973), *Form and Content*. Oxford: Basil Blackwell.

Harvey, J. (1979), 'Systematic transposition of colours', *Australasian Journal of Philosophy*, 57: 211–19.

Hausman, Alan (1979), 'Goodman's perfect communities', *Synthese*, 41: 185–238.

Hayek, Friedrich A. (1952), *The Sensory Order*. Chicago: University of Chicago Press.

Hempel, Carl G. (1952), 'Fundamentals of concept formation in empirical science', in O. Neurath, R. Carnap, and C. Morris (eds.), *International Encyclopedia of Unified Science*, ii(7). Chicago: University of Chicago Press.

—— (1953), 'Reflections on Nelson Goodman's *Structure of Appearance*', *Philosophical Review*, 62: 108–16.

Henning, H. (1915), 'Der Geruch, I', *Zeitschrift für Psychologie und Physiologie der Sinnesorgane*, 73: 161–257.

—— (1916), 'Die Qualitatenreihe des Geschmacks', *Zeitschrift für Psychologie und Physiologie der Sinnesorgane*, 74: 203–19.

Hilbert, David R. (1987), *Color and Color Perception: A Study in Anthropocentric Realism*. Stanford, Cal.: Center for the Study of Language and Information.

Hobbes, Thomas (1651), *Leviathan*. Oxford: Clarendon Press, 1909.

Hook, Sidney (ed.) (1960), *Dimensions of Mind*. New York: New York University Press.

Horgan, Terence (1984), 'Functionalism, qualia, and the inverted spectrum', *Philosophy and Phenomenological Research*, 44: 453–70.

Hornsby, Jennifer (1984), 'On functionalism, and on Jackson, Pargetter and Prior on functionalism', *Philosophical Studies*, 46: 75–95.

Horst, P. (1966), *Psychological Measurement and Prediction*. Belmont, Cal.: Wadsworth.

Hsia, Y., and Graham, C. H. (1965), 'Color blindness', in E. H. Graham (ed.), *Vision and Visual Perception*. New York: John Wiley, 395–413.

Hume, David (1739), *A Treatise of Human Nature*. Ed. L. A. Selby-Bigge and reprinted by Oxford University Press, 1888.

Hungerland, Isabel (1967), 'My pains and yours', in Avrum Stroll (ed.), *Epistemology*. New York: Harper & Row.

Hurvich, Leo M. (1972), 'Color vision deficiencies', in D. Jameson and L. M. Hurvich (eds.), *Handbook of Sensory Physiology*, vii(4). New York: Springer-Verlag, 582–624.

—— (1981), *Color Vision*. Sunderland, Mass.: Sinauer.

—— (1985), 'Opponent-colours theory', in David Ottoson and Semir Zeki (eds.), *Central and Peripheral Mechanisms of Colour Vision*. London: Macmillan.

—— and Jameson, Dorothea (1955), 'Some quantitative aspects of an opponent-colors theory, II: Brightness, saturation and hue in normal and dichromatic vision', *Journal of the Optical Society of America*, 45: 602–16.

—— —— (1957), 'An opponent-process theory of color vision', *Psychological Review*, 64(6): 384–404.

—— —— (1959), 'Perceived color and its dependence on focal, surrounding and preceding stimulus variables', *Journal of the Optical Society of America*, 49: 890–8.

—— —— (1960), 'Perceived color, induction effects, and opponent-response mechanisms', *Journal of General Physiology*, 43(6), Supp: 63ff.

Jackson, Frank (1977*a*), *Perception: A Representative Theory*. Cambridge: Cambridge University Press.

—— (1977*b*), 'Statements about universals', *Mind*, 86: 427–9.

—— (1982), 'Epiphenomenal qualia', *Philosophical Quarterly*, 32: 127–36.

Jacobs, Gerald H. (1981), *Comparative Color Vision*. New York: Academic Press.

James, William (1890), *Principles of Psychology*. New York: Dover, 1950.

Jameson, Dorothea, and Hurvich, Leo M. (1955), 'Some quantitative aspects of an opponent colors theory, I', *Journal of the Optical Society of America*, 45: 546–52.

—— —— (1956), 'Some quantitative aspects of an opponents color theory, III', *Journal of the Optical Society of America*, 46: 405–15.

—— —— (eds.) (1972), *Handbook of Sensory Physiology*, vii(4), *Visual Psychophysics*. New York: Springer-Verlag.

Jenning, Herbert Spencer (1906), *The Behavior of the Lower Organisms*. Bloomington: Indiana University Press, 1976.

Judd, D. B., and Wyszecki, Gunter (1975), *Color in Business, Science and Industry*, 3rd edn. New York: John Wiley.

Julesz, B. (1971), *Foundations of Cyclopean Perception*. Chicago: University of Chicago Press.

Kalke, W. (1969), 'What is wrong with Fodor and Putnam's functionalism?' *Nous*, 3: 83–93.

Kaufman, L. (1974), *Sight and Mind*. New York: Oxford University Press.

Kiang, N. Y. S. (1965), *Discharge Patterns of Single Fibers in the Cat's Auditory Nerve*, Research Monograph no. 35. Cambridge, Mass.: MIT Press.

Kim, Jaegwon (1966), 'On the psycho-physical identity theory', *American Philosophical Quarterly*, 3: 227–35.

—— (1967), 'Psycho-physical correlation laws and theories of mind', *Theoria*, 33: 198–210.

—— (1972), 'Phenomenal properties, psychophysical laws and the identity theory', *The Monist*, 56(2): 177–92.

Kinsbourne, M., and Warington, E. K. (1964), 'Observations on colour agnosia', *Journal of Neurology, Neurosurgery, and Psychiatry*, 27: 296–9.

Kirk, Robert (1974), 'Sentience and behavior', *Mind*, 83: 43–60.

—— (1982), 'Goodbye to transposed qualia', *Proceedings of the Aristotelian Society*, 82: 33–44.

Kitcher, P. (1980), 'Discussion: how to reduce a functional psychology', *Philosophy of Science*, 47: 134–40.

Kohler, I. (1962), 'Experiments with goggles', *Scientific American*, no. 206: 62–86.

—— (1964), 'The formation and transformation of the perceptual world', (tr. H. Fiss.), *Psychological Issues*, 3(4): 1–173. Also published as a monograph by International Universities Press.

Kosslyn, Stephen (1980), *Image and Mind*. Cambridge, Mass.: Harvard University Press.

Kraemar, Eric Russert (1984), 'Consciousness and the exclusivity of function', *Mind*, 93: 271–5.

Krantz, D. H., Luce, R. Duncan, Suppes, Patrick, and Tversky, Amos (1971), *Foundations of Measurement*, i, *Additive and Polynomial Representations*. New York: Academic Press.

Kripke, Saul A. (1971), 'Identity and necessity', in Milton K. Munitz (ed.), *Identity and Individuation*. New York: New York University Press.

—— (1980), *Naming and Necessity*. Cambridge, Mass.: Harvard University Press.

Kruskal, J. B., and Wish, M. (1978), *Multidimensional Scaling*. Beverly Hills: Sage Publications.

Kuehni, Rolf G. (1983), *Color: Essence and Logic*. New York: Van Nostrand Reinhold.

Kuhn, Thomas (1961), 'The function of measurement in modern physical science', *Isis*, 52: 161–90.

Kyburg, H. E. (1984), *Theory and Measurement*. Cambridge: Cambridge University Press.

Lamb, T. D. (1985), 'Properties of cone photoreceptors in relation to colour vision', in David Ottoson and Semir Zeki (eds.), *Central and Peripheral Mechanisms of Colour Vision*. London: Macmillan.

Land, E. H., and McCann, J. J. (1971), 'Lightness and the retinex theory', *Journal of the Optical Society of America*, 61: 1–11.

—— Hubel, D. H., Livingstone, M. S., Perry, S. H., and Burns, M. M. (1983), 'Colour generating interactions across the corpus callosum', *Nature*, no. 303: 616–18.

Landesman, Charles (1989), *Color and Consciousness*. Philadelphia: Temple University Press.

Levine, Joseph (1983), 'Materialism and qualia: the explanatory gap', *Pacific Philosophical Quarterly*, 64: 354–61.

—— (1988), 'Absent and inverted qualia revisited', *Mind and Language*, 3: 271–87

Lewis, Clarence Irving (1929), *Mind and the World Order*. New York: Charles Scribner's Sons.

Lewis, David (1966), 'An argument for the identity theory', *Journal of Philosophy*, 63(1): 17–25.

—— (1970), 'How to define theoretical terms', *Journal of Philosophy*, 67: 427–44.

—— (1972), 'Psychophysical and theoretical identifications', *Australasian Journal of Philosophy*, 50(3): 249–58.

—— (1980), 'Veridical hallucination and prosthetic vision', *Australasian Journal of Philosophy*, 58: 239–49.

—— (1983), *Philosophical Papers*, i. Oxford: Oxford University Press.

—— (1988), 'What experience teaches', in J. Copley-Coltheart (ed.), *Proceedings of the Russellian Society*. Sydney: University of Sydney Press. Reprinted in Lycan (1990), 499–519.

Linsky, Bernard (1984), 'Phenomenal qualities and the identity of indistinguishables', *Synthese*, 59: 363–80.

Loux, Michael J. (ed.) (1979), *The Possible and the Actual*. Ithaca, NY: Cornell University Press.

Luria, A. R. (1973), *The Working Brain*. Harmondsworth, Middx.: Penguin Books.

Lycan, William G. (1973), 'The inverted spectrum', *Ratio*, 15(2): 315–19.

—— (1974), 'Mental states and Putnam's functionalist hypothesis', *Australasian Journal of Philosophy*, 52: 48–62.

—— (1981), 'Form, function and feel', *Journal of Philosophy*, 78: 24–50.

—— (1987), *Consciousness*. Cambridge, Mass.: MIT Press.

—— (ed.) (1990), *Mind and Cognition: A Reader*. Oxford: Basil Blackwell.

MacLeod, D. I. A. (1985), 'Receptoral constraints on colour appearance', in David Ottoson and Semir Zeki (eds.), *Central and Peripheral Mechanisms of Colour Vision*. London: Macmillan.

—— and Lennie, P. (1974), 'A unilateral defect resembling deuteranopia', *Modern Problems in Opthamology*, 13: 130–4.

Marcel, Anthony J. (1983a), 'Conscious and unconscious perception: experiments on visual masking and word recognition', *Cognitive Psychology*, 15(2): 197–237.

—— (1983b), 'Conscious and unconscious perception: an approach to the relations between phenomenal experience and perceptual processes', *Cognitive Psychology*, 15(2): 238–300.

Margolis, Joseph (1966), 'Awareness of sensations and the location of sensations', *Analysis*, 27: 29–32.

—— (1970), 'Indubitability, self-intimating states and logically privileged access', *Journal of Philosophy*, 67: 918–31.

Marr, David (1979), 'Representing and computing visual information', in P. H. Winston and R. H. Brown (eds.), *Artificial Intelligence: An MIT Perspective*, ii. Cambridge, Mass.: MIT Press.

—— (1982), *Vision*. San Francisco: W. H. Freeman.

Maund, J. B. (1981), 'Colour—a case for conceptual fission', *Australasian Journal of Philosophy*, 59: 308–22.

McCann, John H., McKee, S. P., and Taylor, T. H. (1976), 'Quantitative studies in retinex theory', *Vision Research*, 16: 445–58.

McGinn, Colin (1983), *The Subjective View*. Oxford: Oxford University Press.

Michael, Charles R. (1983), 'Color processing in primate striate cortex', in J. D. Mollon and L. T. Sharpe (eds.), *Colour Vision: Physiology and Psychophysics*. New York: Academic Press, 261–89.

Milner, Peter M. (1970), *Physiological Psychology*. London: Holt, Rinehart & Winston.

Mollon, J. D., and Sharpe, L. T. (eds.) (1983), *Colour Vision: Physiology and Psychophysics*. New York: Academic Press.

Murch, Gerald M. (1973), *Visual and Auditory Perception*. New York: Bobbs-Merrill.

Nagel, Ernest (1956), 'A formalization of functionalism', in his *Logic without Metaphysics*. Glencoe, Ill.: Free Press.

Nagel, Thomas (1969), 'Physicalism', in C. V. Borst (ed.), *The Mind–Brain Identity Theory*. London: Macmillan, 214–30.

—— (1979*a*), *Mortal Questions*. Cambridge: Cambridge University Press.

—— (1979*b*), 'What is it like to be a bat?' Originally published in *Philosophical Review*, 83(1974): 435–50. Reprinted with some revisions in Nagel (1979*a*). Also reprinted in Block (1980*b*), 159–68.

—— (1983), 'The objective self', in Carl Ginet and Sydney Shoemaker (eds.), *Knowledge and Mind*. Oxford: Oxford University Press, 211–32.

—— (1986), *The View from Nowhere*. Oxford: Oxford University Press.

Nelson, Jack (1985), 'The diversity of perception', *Synthese*, 64(1): 93–114.

Nelson, R. J. (1975), 'Behaviorism, finite automata and stimulus response theory', *Theory and Decision*, 6: 249–67.

—— (1976), 'Mechanism, functionalism, and the identity theory', *The Journal of Philosophy*, 63(13): 365–85.

Newton-Smith, W. H. (1981), *The Rationality of Science*. London: Routledge & Kegan Paul.

Nickles, T. (1973), 'Two concepts of inter-theoretic reduction', *Journal of Philosophy*, 70(7): 181–201.

Noren, S. J. (1970), 'Smart's materialism: the identity theory and translation', *Australasian Journal of Philosophy*, 48: 54–66.

Parks, Zane (1972), 'Toward a logic of experience', *Philosophia* (Israel), 2: 183–94.

Peacocke, Christopher (1981), 'Are vague predicates incoherent?' *Synthese*, 46: 121–41.

—— (1983), *Sense and Content: Experience, Thought, and their Relations*. Oxford: Clarendon Press.

—— (1984), 'Colour concepts and colour experience', *Synthese*, 58: 365–82.

Perkel, D. H., and Bullock, T. H. (1968), 'Neural coding', *Neurosciences Research Program Bulletin*, 6: 221–348.

Perkins, Moreland (1983), *Sensing the World*. Indianapolis: Hackett.

Pfaff, Donald W. (ed.) (1985), *Taste, Olfaction, and the Central Nervous System: A Festschrift in Honor of Carl Pfaffmann*. New York: Rockefeller University Press.

Piantanida, T. P. (1974), 'A replacement model of x linked recessive colour vision defects', *Annals of Human Genetics* (London), 37: 394–404.

—— (1976), 'Polymorphism of human color vision', *American Journal of Optometry and Physiological Optics*, 53: 647–57.

Pierce, J. R. (1961), *Symbols, Signals, and Noise*. New York: Dover.

Pitcher, George (1970), 'Pain perception', *Philosophical Review*, 79: 368–93.

Pitson, A. E. (1984), 'Basic seeing', *Philosophy and Phenomenological Research*, 45: 121–30.

Popper, K. A., and Eccles, J. C. (1977), *The Self and its Brain*. London: Routledge & Kegan Paul.

Potter, Elizabeth (1980), 'Armstrong and the direct realist theory of perception', *Journal of Critical Analysis*, 8: 75–88.

Potter, Karl H. (1973), 'On a supposed advantage of realistic systems', *Philosophical Studies*, 24: 397–401.

Presley, C. F. (ed.) (1967), *The Identity Theory of Mind*. St Lucia: University of Queensland Press.

Pribram, Karl (1971), *The Languages of the Brain*. Englewood Cliffs, New Jersey: Prentice Hall.

Putnam, Hilary (1970), 'Is semantics possible?' in H. E. Kiefer and M. K. Munitz (eds.), *Language, Belief, and Metaphysics*. Albany: State University of New York Press, 50–63.

—— (1973), 'Meaning and reference', *Journal of Philosophy*, 70: 699–711.

—— (1975*a*), 'Brains and behaviour', in Putnam (1975*b*), 325–41.

—— (1975*b*), *Mind, Language and Reality: Philosophical Papers*, ii. Cambridge: Cambridge University Press.

—— (1978), *Meaning and the Moral Sciences*. Boston: Routledge & Kegan Paul.

—— (1979), *Mathematics, Matter and Method: Philosophical Papers*, i, 2nd edn. Cambridge: Cambridge University Press.

—— (1981), *Reason, Truth and History*. Cambridge: Cambridge University Press.

—— (1987), *The Many Faces of Realism*. La Salle, Ill.: Open Court.

—— (1988), *Representation and Reality*. Cambridge, Mass.: MIT Press.

Quine, W. V. (1960), *Word and Object*. Cambridge, Mass.: MIT Press.

—— (1969), *Ontological Relativity and Other Essays*. New York: Columbia University Press.

—— (1974), *The Roots of Reference*. La Salle, Ill.: Open Court.

Ratliff, Floyd (1965), *Mach Bands: Quantitative Studies on Neural Networks in the Retina*. San Francisco: Holden Day.

Reichenbach, Hans (1938), *Experience and Prediction*. Chicago: University of Chicago Press.

Rhees, Rush (1968), 'Wittgenstein's notes for lectures on private experience and sense data', *Philosophical Review*, 77: 275–320.

Richardson, R. C. (1979), 'Functionalism and reductionism', *Philosophy of Science*, 46: 533–58.

Rock, Irvin (1966), *The Nature of Perceptual Adaptation*. New York: Basic Books.

Rorty, Richard (1982), 'Contemporary philosophy of mind', *Synthese*, 53: 323–48.

Rosenthal, David (1976), 'Mentality and neutrality', *The Journal of Philosophy*, 63(13): 385–415.

Russell, Bertrand (1903), *The Principles of Mathematics*. London: W. W. Norton.

—— (1914), *Our Knowledge of the External World*. London: George Allen and Unwin.

—— (1921), *The Analysis of Mind*. New York: Macmillan.

—— (1940), *An Inquiry into Meaning and Truth*. New York: W. W. Norton.

Sayre, Kenneth (1976), *Cybernetics and the Philosophy of Mind*. London: Routledge & Kegan Paul.

Schiffman, Harvey Richard (1982), *Sensation and Perception: An Integrated Approach*, 2nd edn. New York: John Wiley.

Schiffman, Susan S. (1974*a*), 'Physico-chemical correlates of olfactory quality', *Science*, no. 185: 112–17.

—— (1974*b*), 'Contributions to the physicochemical dimensions of odor: a psychophysical approach', *Annals of the New York Academy of Sciences*, no. 237: 164–83.

—— and Dakis, C. (1976), 'Multidimensional scaling of musks', *Physiology and Behavior*, 17: 823–9.

—— and Erickson, R. P. (1971), 'A theoretical review: a psychophysical model for gustatory quality', *Physiology and Behavior*, 7: 617–33.

—— —— (1980), 'The issue of primary tastes versus a taste continuum', *Neuroscience and Biobehavioral Research*, 4: 109–17.

—— Reynolds, M. Lance, and Young, Forrest W. (1981), *Introduction to Multidimensional Scaling: Theory, Methods, and Applications*. New York: Academic Press.

—— Robinson, D. E., and Erickson, R. P. (1977), 'Multidimensional scaling of odorants: examination of psychological and physicochemical dimensions', *Chemical Senses and Flavor*, 2: 375–90.

Schwartz, Stephen P. (ed.) (1977), *Naming, Necessity, and Natural Kinds*. Ithaca, NY: Cornell University Press.

Seagar, W. (1983), 'Functionalism, qualia, and causation', *Mind*, 92: 174–88.

Searle, John R. (1981), 'Analytic philosophy and mental phenomena', in P. A. French and T. E. Uehling (eds.), *Midwest Studies in Philosophy*, vi. Minneapolis: University of Minnesota Press, 405–24.

Sellars, Wilfrid (1962), 'Empiricism and the philosophy of mind', in Herbert Feigl and Michael Scriven (eds.), *Minnesota Studies in the Philosophy of Science*, i. Minneapolis: University of Minnesota Press.

—— (1963a), *Science, Perception and Reality*. London: Routledge & Kegan Paul.

—— (1963b), 'Empiricism and the philosophy of mind', in Sellars (1963a), 127–96.

—— (1971), 'Science, sense impressions and sensa: a reply to Cornman', *Review of Metaphysics*, 23: 391–447.

—— (1981a), 'Is consciousness physical?', *The Monist*, 64: 66–90.

—— (1981b), 'Mental events', *Philosophical Studies*, 39: 325–45.

Shepard, R. N. (1962), 'The analysis of proximities: multidimensional scaling with an unknown distance function, II', *Psychometrika*, 27, 219–45.

—— Kimball, A. K., and Nerlove, S. B. (eds.) (1972), *Multidimensional Scaling*, i, *Theory*. New York: Seminar Press.

Shoemaker, Sydney (1975a), 'Functionalism and qualia', *Philosophical Studies*, 27: 291–315. Reprinted in Shoemaker (1984).

—— (1975b), 'Phenomenal similarity', *Critica*, 7(20): 2–34. Reprinted in Shoemaker (1984).

—— (1980), 'Causality and properties', in Peter van Inwagen (ed.), *Time and Cause*. Dordrecht: Reidel. Reprinted in Shoemaker (1984).

—— (1981), 'Absent qualia are impossible: a reply to Block', *Philosophical Review*, 90: 581–99. Reprinted in Shoemaker (1984).

—— (1982), 'The inverted spectrum', *Journal of Philosophy*, 79(7): 357–81. Reprinted in Shoemaker (1984).

—— (1984), *Identity, Cause, and Mind: Philosophical Essays*. Cambridge: Cambridge University Press.

Sibley, F. N. (ed.) (1971), *Perception: A Philosophical Symposium*. London: Methuen.

Sklar, Lawrence (1967), 'Types of inter-theoretic reduction', *British Journal for the Philosophy of Science*, 43(2): 109–24.

—— (1977), *Space, Time, and Spacetime*. Berkeley: University of California Press.

Smart, J. J. C. (1959), 'Sensations and brain processes', *Philosophical Review*, 68: 141–56. Reprinted in Borst (1970).

—— (1961), 'Colours', *Philosophy*, 36: 128–42.

—— (1962), 'Brain processes and incorrigibility', *Australasian Journal of Philosophy*, 40: 68–70. Reprinted in Borst (1970).

—— (1963), *Philosophy and Scientific Realism*. London: Routledge & Kegan Paul.

—— (1967), 'Comments on the papers', in C. F. Presley (ed.), *The Identity Theory of Mind*. Brisbane: University of Queensland Press, 84–93.

—— (1970), 'Materialism', in C. V. Borst (ed.), *The Mind–Brain Identity Theory*. London: Macmillan, 159–70.

—— (1971), 'Reports of immediate experience', *Synthese*, 22: 346–59.

—— (1972), 'Further thoughts on the identity theory', *The Monist*, 56(2): 149–62.

—— (1975), 'On some criticisms of a physicalist theory of colors', in Chung-ying Cheng (ed.), *Philosophical Aspects of the Mind–Body Problem*. Honolulu: University of Hawaii Press.

Smith, David (1985), 'Brainstem processing of gustatory information', in Donald W. Pfaff (ed.), *Taste, Olfaction, and the Central Nervous System: A Festschrift in Honor of Carl Pfaffmann*. New York: Rockefeller University Press, 151–77.

Sober, Elliot (1976), 'Mental representation', *Synthese*, 33: 101–48.

—— (1985), 'Panglossian functionalism and the philosophy of mind', *Synthese*, 64: 165–93.

Stalnaker, Robert (1981), 'Indexical belief', *Synthese*, 57: 129–52.

Stevens, S. S. (1975), *Psychophysics: Introduction to its Perceptual, Neural, and Social Prospects*. New York: John Wiley.

—— and Newman, E. B. (1936), 'The localization of actual sources of sound', *American Journal of Psychology*, 48: 297–306.

Stevenson, J. T. (1960), 'Sensations and brain processes: a reply to J. J. C. Smart', *Philosophical Review*, 69: 505–10. Reprinted in Borst (1970).

Stratton, G. M. (1896), 'Some preliminary experiments on vision without inversion of the retinal image', *Psychological Review*, 3: 611–17.

—— (1897a), 'Vision without inversion of the retinal image', *Psychological Review*, 4: 341–60, 463–81.

—— (1897b), 'Upright vision and the retinal image', *Psychological Review*, 4: 182–7.

Strawson, P. F. (1963), *Individuals*. New York: Doubleday.

Sutherland, N. S. (1970), 'Is the brain a physical system?', in Robert Borger and Frank Cioffi (eds.), *Explanation in the Behavioural Sciences*. Cambridge: Cambridge University Press, 97–122.

Teller, Davida Y. (1984), 'Linking propositions', *Vision Research*, 24(10): 1233–46.

Thalberg, Irving (1983), 'Immateriality', *Mind*, 92: 105–13.

Thurstone, L. L. (1927), 'A law of comparative judgment', *Psychological Review*, 34: 273–86.

—— (1959), *The Measurement of Values*. Chicago: University of Chicago Press.

Torgerson, W. S. (1958), *Theory and Methods of Scaling*. New York: John Wiley.

Travis, Charles (1985), 'Vagueness, observation, and sorites', *Mind*, 94: 345–66.

Turvey, M. T. (1977), 'Contrasting orientations to the theory of visual information processing', *Psychological Review*, 84: 67–88.

Tye, Michael (1984*a*), 'Pain and the adverbial theory', *American Philosophical Quarterly*, 21: 319–28.

—— (1984*b*), 'The adverbial approach to visual experience', *Philosophical Review*, 93: 195–226.

—— (1984*c*), 'The debate about mental imagery', *Journal of Philosophy*, 81: 678–90.

Unger, P. (1979), 'Why there are no people', in P. A. French and T. E. Uehling (eds.), *Midwest Studies in Philosophy*, iv. Minneapolis: University of Minnesota Press.

Uttal, William R. (1973), *The Psychobiology of Sensory Coding*. New York: Harper & Row.

Van Cleve, James, and Frederick, Robert E. (eds.) (1991), *The Philosophy of Right and Left: Incongruent Counterparts and the Nature of Space*. Dordrecht: Kluwer Academic Publishers.

Vesey, G. N. A. (1961), 'The location of bodily sensations', *Mind*, 70: 25–35.

—— (1963), 'Knowledge without observation', *Philosophical Review*, 72: 198–212.

—— (1965), *The Embodied Mind*. London: George Allen and Unwin.

Ward, Andrew (1976), 'Direct and indirect realism', *American Philosophical Quarterly*, 13: 287–94.

Warren, Richard M. (1981), 'The measurement of sensory intensity', *Behavioral and Brain Sciences*, 4: 175–223.

—— (1982), *Auditory Perception: A New Synthesis*. New York: Pergamon.

Wasserman, Gerald (1978), *Color Vision: An Historical Introduction*. New York: John Wiley.

—— (1982), 'Materialism and mentality', *Review of Metaphysics*, 35: 715–29.

Welford, A. T. (1968), *Fundamentals of Skill*. London: Methuen.

Westphal, Jonathan (1984), 'The complexity of quality', *Philosophy*, 59: 457–71.

—— (1987), *Colour: Some Philosophical Problems from Wittgenstein*. Oxford: Basil Blackwell.

Wheeler, J. (1975), 'Reference and vagueness', *Synthese*, 30: 367–79.

—— (1979), 'That which is not', *Synthese*, 41: 155–73.

White, B. W., Saunders, F. A., Scadden, L., Bach-y-Rita, P., and Collins, C. C. (1970), 'Seeing with the skin', *Perception and Psychophysics*, 7: 23–7.

Wilcox, Stephen, and Katz, Stuart (1984), 'Can indirect realism be demonstrated in the psychological laboratory?' *Philosophy of Social Science*, 14: 149–58.

Wilkes, Kathleen V. (1984), 'Is consciousness important?' *British Journal of the Philosophy of Science*, 35: 223–43.

Wilson, H. R., and Bergen, D. (1979), 'A four mechanism model for threshold spatial vision', *Vision Research*, 19: 19–32.

—— and Giese, S. C. (1977), 'Threshold visibility of frequency grating patterns', *Vision Research*, 17: 1177–90.

Woodfield, Andrew (ed.) (1982), *Thought and Object*. Oxford: Oxford University Press.

Wright, Crispin (1975), 'On the coherence of vague predicates', *Synthese*, 30: 325–65.

Wright, Edmond (1983), 'Pre-phenomenal adjustments and Sanford's illusion objection', *Pacific Philosophical Quarterly*, 64: 266–72.

—— (1984), 'Recent work in perception', *American Philosophical Quarterly*, 21: 17–30.

Wyszecki, Gunter, and Stiles, W. S. (1967), *Color Science*. New York: John Wiley.

Zaffron, R. (1971), 'Identity, subsumption, and scientific explanation', *Journal of Philosophy*, 67(23): 849–60.

Zeki, Semir (1985), 'Colour pathways and hierarchies in the cerebral cortex', in David Ottoson and Semir Zeki (eds.), *Central and Peripheral Mechanisms of Colour Vision*. London: Macmillan.

Index

Italicized page numbers indicate the location of definitions.